FINANCIAL RISK MANAGEMENT

Financial Risk Management

Keith Redhead and Steward Hughes

Gower

Published by
Gower Publishing Company Limited,
Gower House,
Croft Road,
Aldershot,
Hants GU11 3HR,
England

Gower Publishing Company,
Old Post Road,
Brookfield,
Vermont 05036,
USA

British Library Cataloguing in Publication Data

Redhead, Keith
  Financial risk management.
  1. Business enterprises—Finance
  2. Risk management
  I. Title   II. Hughes, Steward
  658.1'52   HG4026

  ISBN 0-566-02652-X

Printed in Great Britain at the
University Press, Cambridge

Contents

Illustrations

Figures

Tables

Preface

Businesses of all types face risks arising from fluctuations in exchange rates and interest rates. Adverse movements in these rates can seriously threaten the profitability of enterprises. Similarly, portfolio managers face risks arising from volatility in bond and equity markets.

This book is intended as an introduction to the techniques available for managing these various risks. It is primarily aimed at readers with some familiarity with finance but does not presuppose prior knowledge of exposure management. The emphasis throughout is on hedging rather than arbitrage or speculation (speculation is more usually referred to as 'trading' in this context). However, some attention is paid to these areas since they play crucial roles in the markets concerned.

This book will be of use to those operating in a wide variety of organizations including businesses of all types – manufacturing, service, financial – and public sector bodies such as local authorities. There are very few organizations unaffected by financial instability, and the management of that instability is becoming a vital dimension of financial management.

We have tried to write self-contained chapters that allow the reader to understand individual chapters without having studied the previous ones. The need to avoid excessive repetition inevitably inhibits the full achievement of this objective and the reader must therefore be aware that concepts relevant to one chapter may be dealt with elsewhere. This is particularly true of the chapters dealing with futures and swaps.

We would like to thank Victor Levy of Arthur Andersen & Co. and Ralph Newns of Spicer and Pegler for their very valuable assistance in the preparation of the chapters on the accounting and taxation aspects, and Jaguar Cars Limited for permission to reproduce material from their magazine *Topics*. Finally, we want to express our gratitude to Mamie and Marjorie who have shown commendable patience in their typing of the manuscript.

1 Introduction

The 1970s and 1980s have witnessed exchange rate and interest rate volatility greatly in excess of that of earlier periods. The breakdown of the Bretton Woods exchange rate mechanism in the early 1970s, and its replacement by a system of floating exchange rates, has introduced a source of serious uncertainty to business decision-making. There is uncertainty as to the sterling value of future receipts and payments in foreign currency.

Exchange rates have shown increased volatility during the 1980s. Movements in excess of 30 per cent in a year are not unusual. For example, sterling traded at US$2.40 in 1981, fell to just over $1.00 in 1985, before swinging back to $1.50 in 1986. It is arguable that the collapse of one fifth of UK manufacturing industry during the 1979 to 1982 period can largely be ascribed to the loss of markets caused by the strength of sterling. Another severe blow to industry during that period was the upsurge in interest rates. Both the exchange rate and interest rates reached peak levels during the early 1980s subjecting businesses to a destructive pincer movement. The problem of accommodating to exchange rate movements is further exacerbated by the tendency for movements to be abrupt, adjustments to new levels typically occurring within a three-week period.

It is difficult to plan overseas trade and investment when the sterling values of the resulting cash flows cannot be calculated with any confidence. Even otherwise favourable movements may show muted effects if the level of uncertainty is such that businesses cannot rely on the more favourable rates enduring. Exporters may be slow to react to improvements in competitiveness following a depreciation if they need to be convinced that the international value of the currency is going to stay down.

Very large companies may feel that their geographical spread of trade and investments is so large that they need not worry about currency fluctuations, losses in relation to some currencies being offset by gains on others. This attitude ignores the possibility that a currency can change in relation to others taken in aggregate. Changes in sterling's effective rate (that is the exchange rate relative to a basket of currencies weighted according to each country's importance in UK trade) testifies to this.

The establishment of currency blocs, such as that of the European Monetary System, can remove much of the uncertainty for those countries participating in the arrangements to fix rates of exchange between members. However, risks remain in relation to trading partners outside such arrangements, and even within such systems complete stability of exchange rates is not achieved.

The 1970s also saw a switch in economic policy-making sentiment from Keynesianism, with its preference for a stable interest rate at the expense of an unstable money supply, towards monetarism which asserts the need for money supply control. It is not possible for governments to achieve stability of both interest rates and the rate of growth of the money supply, so instability of interest rates is an inevitable consequence of controlling the money supply. Furthermore, the inter-relationships between domestic and international money markets mean that interest rate volatility causes exchange rate volatility, and vice versa.

Hence businesses now face a financial environment fraught with risk and uncertainty. There is a resultant need for instruments that serve to reduce risk and uncertainty. In other words, there is a demand for techniques for hedging. Hedging involves guaranteeing a future exchange rate or interest rate, or ensuring that losses from adverse movements of such rates are compensated by offsetting gains.

The exposures to exchange rate movements can be subdivided into transaction, translation, and economic exposures. There is a lack of universally accepted definitions of these three types of exposure, in particular with regard to economic exposure, so the definitions used here are inevitably somewhat idiosyncratic.

Transaction exposure

This can be defined as the possibility of gains and losses from the direct effects of exchange rate movements on anticipated cash flows. An exporter with foreign currency receivables stands to lose from a depreciation of the foreign currency relative to the domestic currency whilst an importer with foreign currency payables would lose from an appreciation of the foreign currency relative to the base currency.

Uncertainties as to the domestic currency value of exports invoiced in foreign currency can inhibit exports, since there is doubt as to whether the exports will ultimately prove to be profitable. Uncertainties about the domestic currency cost of imports priced in foreign currency adds to the risk of importing, since the eventual domestic currency price might prove to be uncompetitive. Exchange rate uncertainty can deter international trade.

Uncertainty of export profitability where sales are invoiced in foreign currency might seem to be escapable by means of pricing in the company's own base currency. However this merely transfers the currency risk to the importer who may consequently turn to suppliers prepared to invoice in the importer's currency. Besides a depreciation of the foreign currency, which undermines the home currency profitability of the exports, has as its counterpart an appreciation of the home currency which raises the foreign currency price of the exports and thereby undermines their competitiveness. This effect would be particularly damaging where demand is very sensitive to price movements. Exporters of motor vehicles, textiles, and alcoholic spirits would be familiar with this type of problem.

A particular example of sales volume uncertainty is when a company tenders for a contract. The company must be aware that a tender in its own currency might put it at a considerable competitive disadvantage, but that a tender in a foreign currency would incur currency risk, which is contingent on the success of the tender. A successful tender involves a currency risk whereas an unsuccessful one does not. This poses particular problems and it will be demonstrated that currency options are particularly useful for dealing with such contingent risks.

A successful outcome of a tender leads on to further currency exposure. Many civil-engineering contractors operating in the Middle East have found themselves with contract prices denominated in US dollars and costs denominated in other currencies. Such contractors are vulnerable to a weakening of the US dollar and face the particular problem of covering against such an eventuality over a long time span.

Tenders in foreign currency could be looked upon as causing contingent transaction exposures. Often the exposure present with tenders is regarded as a form of economic exposure. That tends to be the case when economic exposure is treated as a residual encompassing all exposures that do not fit easily under the headings of transaction and translation exposure. The definition of economic exposure proposed here does not readily incorporate exposures present with tendering. So use of the description 'contingent transaction exposure' is preferred.

Importers invoiced in foreign currency also face problems of uncertainty as to the home currency cost of the imports. This is particularly problematical if their sales are very sensitive to price movements, as would be the case if they faced competition from domestic producers unaffected by exchange rate changes or from importers invoiced in currencies that show more favourable movements. In the case of high technology goods there is often a choice between the USA and Japan as the source of supply. Differential movements of the US dollar and the yen against sterling affects the relative price competitiveness of the American and Japanese equipment.

The biggest conceptual problem arises in relation to the date on which the transactions exposure begins. One answer might be that it starts on the date of the invoice. What then of orders that have not yet been invoiced? If an exporter has received an order that will be invoiced in foreign currency then there is an exposure from the date of the order, so long as the foreign currency price is settled at the time of the order. What about orders that have not yet been received but are expected? Consider, for example, a British tour operator selling European holidays. He will need to meet hotel expenses in European currencies and is at risk from appreciations of European currencies relative to sterling. Such appreciations would raise his sterling costs whilst the sterling revenue for each holiday is determined when the price list is produced. Prior to the publication of the price list foreign currency appreciations can be reflected in the prices to be charged. Once the price list is published that is not possible and the tour operator is exposed. So transactions exposure can be regarded as dating from the production of the price list.

The task of identifying transaction exposure might involve evaluating the case in which a trade is priced in one currency but payable in another. There may be doubt as to whether the currency of exposure is the one used for pricing or the one used for payment. The answer is that it is the currency in which the price is expressed. An appreciation of that currency relative to the base currency would increase the price in terms of the base currency. An appreciation of the currency, in which payment is to be made, relative to the base currency that is not accompanied by a corresponding appreciation of the currency used for pricing does not raise the price in terms of the base currency. The higher cost of acquiring the currency of payment per unit (e.g. per $1) would be offset by the smaller number of units (e.g. dollars) required to match the value of the good or service traded expressed in terms of the currency of pricing.

Translation exposure

This is alternatively known as accounting or balance sheet exposure. It arises from mismatches between assets and liabilities in foreign currencies. For example, if a UK company has a subsidiary in the US it has an asset, the subsidiary, denominated in US dollars. If the company does not have US dollar liabilities sufficient to offset the value of its asset it has an exposure. A depreciation of the US dollar relative to sterling would reduce the balance sheet valuation of the subsidiary, since the balance sheet of the parent company would be expressed in sterling. Likewise a company with net liabilities in a currency would be at risk from an appreciation of that currency. For example a company may have raised a loan in Swiss francs, attracted by low Swiss interest rates, and then sold the francs for sterling so as to finance a UK based investment. The balance sheet would show an increase in the sterling value of liabilities in the event of the Swiss franc appreciating relative to sterling.

The question arises as to whether translation exposure is important. If it is felt to be of no real significance then the company need not seek to hedge the exposure. It might be argued that the balance sheet variations in the base currency valuations of assets and liabilities are paper adjustments with no real significance. The fact that the sterling value of the subsidiary in the US fluctuates with the gyrations of the US dollar/sterling exchange rate may have no impact on the operation or profitability (in US dollars) of the subsidiary. So the costs involved in hedging the translation exposure might be regarded as pointless since there is no real risk from currency movements. This point of view is valid if exchange rate movements are seen as fluctuations around essentially constant rates. However if there is an underlying trend in an exchange rate the trend may be of real significance even though fluctuations around it may not. A long-run tendency for the US dollar to fall relative to sterling would be of real significance to the parent company. Even if the depreciation of the dollar has no effect upon the operation of the subsidiary the sterling value of the future stream of profits accruing to the parent from the subsidiary would decline and it is appropriate that such a decline should be reflected in the parent company's balance sheet valuation of the subsidiary. Such a decline in the sterling value of the subsidiary is of real significance to the parent company which may feel that some currency hedging may be necessary.

Ignoring exchange rate fluctuations around a basically constant long-run rate might be appropriate in the case of assets such as subsidiary companies since such assets are long lasting, and may even be treated as everlasting. Shorter-lived assets pose the problem that their maturity dates could coincide with particularly unfavourable exchange rates. Foreign currency liabilities are likely to be subject to such risks. Debts may have maturity dates without roll-over facilities. Even if the sterling/US dollar exchange rate merely fluctuated around a constant long-run level it would be unfortunate for the UK borrower of US dollars if repayment fell due when the dollar was particularly strong against sterling. Assets and liabilities that cannot be treated as being perpetual, particularly when they have inflexible maturity dates, do provide exposures with real significance for companies. It would seem appropriate that serious consideration be given to hedging the currency risks arising from such translation exposures.

Economic exposure

Economic exposure will be defined here as exposure to the effects of exchange rate movements on the economic environment of the company such that the volume of turnover is affected or the prices of its domestic inputs or outputs change relative to other prices within the domestic economy. The effects might arise from changes in the degree of competition, both from producers of similar goods and from producers of other goods, to or from which consumers might switch their expenditure. The effects might also arise from other sources, such as government policy reactions to movements in currency values or pressure on wages arising from price inflation caused by currency depreciation.

A company whose costs are entirely in domestic currency, has no alternative sources of inputs that might be affected by exchange rate changes, sells only in the domestic market, and faces no competition from products whose prices could be affected by exchange rate changes is the most immune from economic exposure. However, such a company is not totally immune since exchange rate changes might have effects that no firm could avoid. For example, a declining international value of sterling could lead to a rise in interest rates which reduces the general level of expenditure within the economy and increases the cost of servicing debts.

Exchange rate movements can affect the degree of competition from other producers by affecting their cost structures or their local currency selling prices. A company selling entirely in the domestic market with costs arising only in domestic currency would suffer from an appreciation of the domestic currency since competing imports would be cheaper as would the goods from domestic competitors whose costs are partially in foreign currencies.

Changes in the international value of a country's currency can have additional significance for a company locating a subsidiary in that country with a view to providing a cheap source of supply to either the home market of the parent or to other customer countries. For example, a Japanese car manufacturer establishing a plant in the UK with a view to providing competitively priced cars to European markets would not be pleased to see an appreciation of sterling against the other European currencies.

Some commodities are conventionally priced in particular currencies. The pricing of oil in US dollars is a notable example. Companies with revenues in other currencies can be vulnerable to appreciations of the US dollar against the currency or currencies in which they receive their revenue. Airlines is one example of this type of exposure. If they have also bought aircraft from American manufacturers and have resulting US dollar liabilities there is a further exposure to appreciations of the dollar relative to the currencies in which revenues are received.

It was mentioned earlier that transaction exposure might be regarded as existing from the date of publication of the price list. Suppose that an exporter attempts to avoid the transaction exposure arising from prices in foreign currency by issuing a price list, to foreign buyers, in the seller's home currency. The effects of exchange rate movements would then show up in volume terms. Whilst an appreciation of the domestic currency would not now reduce the domestic currency value of exports receipts, per unit of exports, it would tend to reduce the volume of exports since foreign currency prices would have risen.

Hidden exposures

There may be transaction, translation and economic exposures that are not apparent at first sight. For example, a domestic supplier may use imported inputs so that a company using that supplier has an indirect transaction risk, since a rise in the costs of the supplier, arising from domestic currency depreciation, could cause that supplier to raise the prices that it charges to its customers. Another example might be the case of an importer that is invoiced in domestic currency but finds that the prices are varied by the foreign supplier to reflect exchange rate movements so as to maintain constant prices in terms of the currency of the foreign supplier.

Hidden transaction and/or translation exposure can arise in the case in which a foreign subsidiary faces its own exposures. Suppose that a US subsidiary of a UK parent company exports to Australia. The US subsidiary may face an Australian dollar exposure and could suffer losses arising from adverse movements of the Australian/US dollar exchange rate. Such losses would undermine the profitability of the subsidiary. There is an indirect transaction exposure in that the profit receipts from the subsidiary would be reduced. The parent will also face a translation exposure if the reduced profitability of the subsidiary is reflected in the parent company's balance sheet valuation of the subsidiary.

Interest rate exposure

The subject of interest rate exposure has received far less attention than that of currency exposure. It can be subdivided in a manner that parallels the subdivisions of currency exposure. These subdivisions will be termed cash flow exposure, portfolio exposure, and economic exposure.

Cash flow exposure

A company wishing to borrow a sum of money, or a company which has a debt on which interest is paid on a floating rate basis, stands to suffer from a rise in interest rates. The cash flow required to service the debt would rise. Conversely, a company, or fund manager, with deposits on which interest is payable on a floating rate basis is exposed to the risk that interest rates might fall.

Fluctuations in interest rates provide uncertainty to both borrowers and lenders. Business planning may be inhibited by uncertainty about future interest rates. Increases in interest rates on money already borrowed can severely impinge on cash flow. Techniques for reducing uncertainty as to future interest rates could remove a major obstacle to planning and investment.

The need for instruments to hedge the cash flow exposure to interest rate movements can be illustrated by the following hypothetical example. A company treasurer projects on 1 February that he will receive £1 million from the sale of assets on 1 March. In the light of the company's financial requirements he decides that he will invest the money, when it is received on 1 March, in a 90-day Sterling Certificate of Deposit. The current rate of interest on such assets is 11¼ per cent p.a. which would yield £27 739 over the period of the investment. However, the rate of

interest payable may have fallen by 1 March reducing the receipts
from the proposed investment. The treasurer might seek to avoid
such a possibility by attempting to 'lock in' the 1 February interest
rate, or at least remove the risk of an unexpected fall in the interest
rate.

Portfolio exposure

There is an inverse relationship between interest rates and asset
prices. The relationship is strongest with long-term assets such as
equities and long gilts. A portfolio holder is exposed to the risk
that interest rates might rise which would reduce the value of a
portfolio.

For example, a fund manager may have a portfolio of gilts
worth £10 million. In the event of a rise in interest rates there
would be a decline in the value of the portfolio. For instance, a
rise from 9 to 11 per cent p.a. could wipe as much as £1.8 million
from the value of the portfolio. The fund manager may be anxious
about the possibility of a rise in interest rates. One way to avert
this danger is to sell the portfolio, but that would be an expensive
and inconvenient operation. Such a fund manager would have an
interest in techniques for hedging against the risk of such a fall in
the value of the portfolio that do not entail the costly procedure of
selling, and subsequently repurchasing, the gilts in the portfolio.

Economic exposure

Interest rate changes may have indirect effects on a company
by changing its economic environment. If a company faces competition from highly-geared producers, that competition could be
intensified in the event of a fall in interest rates. A company
involved in the production of capital goods or goods frequently
purchased with credit may face a reduction in demand following
a rise in interest rates. The house-building industry is particularly
likely to find that interest rate changes, via effects on mortgage
rates, affect demand for its products. Interest rate changes can
affect exchange rates, movements in which have impacts on companies. These are just a few examples of the sources of economic
exposure to interest rate changes.

Share price risk

Risks to portfolio holders, and potential buyers, of share price volatility were present long before currency fluctuations and interest rate instability became major problems. However, it was only in the wake of the development of techniques for managing currency and interest rate risks that instruments for hedging against general stock market movements became available.

Before the development of futures and options based on stock indices the only way for a fund manager with a large, well-diversified portfolio to avoid losses from a general fall in the market was to sell the portfolio and repurchase it after the fall. Not only was this administratively inconvenient and expensive in terms of transaction costs but the selling activity itself may have depressed the prices at which the shares could be sold.

Fund managers, in addition to seeking to protect portfolio values against bear markets, might also wish to participate in the gains from a rising market prior to the receipt of the money to be invested. For example, a pension fund manager expects to receive £1 million in three weeks' time and intends to use it to buy a balanced portfolio of equities. He may anticipate that share prices will rise in the interim so that less is bought with the money when it is received. If he finds that borrowing on the strength of the anticipated receipts is difficult or expensive he would have an interest in risk management instruments that allow him to participate in the gains from a bull market prior to making the actual investments.

Risk management strategies

Hedging is the process of reducing exposure. A company may choose to hedge nothing, hedge everything, or hedge selectively. It may also speculate, wittingly or unwittingly.

Hedging nothing can occur for two reasons. Firstly, a firm may be unaware of the risks or of the opportunities for reducing those risks. Secondly, it may take the view that exchange or interest rates will remain unchanged or move in its favour. Effectively the firm is speculating: if its expectations prove correct it will benefit but, if not, it stands to incur losses.

Hedging everything is the only way to avoid all risk. However, many company treasurers opt for selective cover. If they expect currencies or interest rates to move to their disadvantage they hedge but if they expect movement in their favour they leave the exposure uncovered. This is really speculation. It is interesting that whilst professional forecasters persistently fail, on average, to predict accurately, comparative amateurs operating in treasury departments nevertheless continue to believe that they have the gift of foresight that produces accurate forecasts.

One disadvantage of hedging everything is that the total costs involved, in terms of commissions and premiums, may be substantial. Selective cover may be seen as one way of reducing total costs. Another is to cover risks only after exchange or interest rates have moved to a degree. It could be decided that a certain amount of adverse movement can be tolerated but that when the acceptable limit has been reached the position should be fully hedged so as to avoid further loss. This approach avoids paying for cover in situations where the exchange or interest rate remains stable or moves in an advantageous direction.

In the case of portfolio management an attempt to cover only part of the risk has a counterpart in using risk management instruments to increase the risk. A fund manager expecting gilt or share price increases might take futures or options positions to benefit from such increases. If his forecasts turn out to be correct then the gains on the portfolio are added to. This is obviously a form of speculation and could be paralleled by those managing currency or interest rate risks. Even if one chooses to eliminate from the definition of speculation cases in which there is a decision not to hedge all of the exposure one cannot eliminate cases where it is decided to use risk management instruments to increase the extent of the exposure.

2 Accounting for translation exposure

In the previous chapter the difference between transaction and translation exposure was distinguished. Briefly, transaction exposure is concerned with exposure to foreign exchange movements when transactions are undertaken in foreign currencies, for example the business of exporting and importing goods and services denominated in foreign currencies. Translation exposure, on the other hand, is concerned with the translation of the balance sheets of foreign subsidiaries. Thus, whereas transaction exposure is concerned with risk to the cash flow arising from foreign currency movements, translation exposure is concerned with risk to the balance sheet when the assets and liabilities of the subsidiary are translated into the currency of the parent company. It is this problem of balance sheet, or translation exposure, that is now discussed.

Measuring translation exposure

Attempting to identify the extent of translation exposure is a controversial issue, largely because of the different accounting approaches that have been used over the years. In essence, the parent company can be regarded as being exposed in the currency of the subsidiary to the extent of the entire net worth of the subsidiary. Or, to put it another way, balance sheet exposure is said to arise when there is a mismatch between the assets and liabilities denominated in foreign currencies. Thus, the parent company is exposed to the extent that the net worth of the subsidiary is unmatched by liabilities such as foreign currency loans denominated in the same currency.

However, in practice, the accounting treatment of translation exposure has not always taken such a simplistic approach. In particular, the controversy has centred upon the problem of whether the accounting treatment should focus upon the net risk as outlined above or whether it should concentrate upon the component parts of the balance sheet and, in particular, distinguish between the foreign exchange effects upon the monetary and non-monetary items. This controversial issue is now examined.

The accounting treatment of translation exposure

The UK Accounting Standards Committee and its counterparts in other countries have grappled for many years with the thorny problem of accounting for foreign currency translation. The basic issue concerns which method should be used in translating the financial statements of foreign subsidiaries for incorporation in the consolidated financial statements of the parent company. This is of particular importance since all companies which have foreign subsidiaries have an obligation to translate their subsidiaries' balance sheets into the parent company's currency for the purpose of consolidation.

The latest official pronouncement in the UK is SSAP 20, *Foreign Currency Translation*, published in 1983. However, before this latest standard is considered, it is worthwhile examining the two basic methods which have been used over the years, since the problems that have arisen in the use of these methods have had a fundamental influence upon the nature of the standard.

There are two exchange rates which suggest themselves as possible rates at which subsidiaries' balance sheets may be translated. The first is the exchange rate in force at the balance sheet date which is often referred to as the 'closing rate'. The second is the exchange rate at the time of the original transaction and this is often referred to as the 'historic rate' or the 'temporal rate'. Over the years, various combinations of these two exchange rates have been applied to different types of asset and liability, but over the last decade companies have tended to use what have become known as either the 'closing rate' or the 'temporal' method.

The closing rate method

The main principle underlying this method is that the parent company has a net investment in its subsidiary and that the entire net worth of the subsidiary is at risk in the event of exchange rate fluctuation. This 'net investment concept', as it is called, is based upon the approach that the subsidiary is, in general, an independently operating business, whose day-to-day business operations are not usually dependent upon the holding company's reporting currency. Indeed, it envisages that the foreign subsidiary may be wholly or partly financed by local currency borrowings. Given these assumptions, the net investment concept takes the view that the parent company's investment is in the business operation as a whole and not in the individual assets and liabilities of the subsidiary.

The net investment concept takes the approach that all the items in the balance sheet of the subsidiary company should be translated at the closing rate of exchange and incorporated into the holding company's consolidated balance sheet. Thus, as the exchange rate changes, from one balance sheet date to the next, a gain or loss will result for the parent company as the net worth of the subsidiary changes in terms of the parent company's currency. These gains or losses do not give rise to cash flows since they are the result of translations of the net worth of the subsidiary into the consolidated balance sheet, where they are treated as capital items and reported as being a movement in capital reserves.

It follows from the above that where the gains and losses from exchange differences do give rise to cash flows, these are part of the ordinary business transactions of the subsidiary and will be recorded in its profit and loss account. This approach takes the view that the best indication of the performance of a foreign subsidiary is the net profit shown in its local currency financial statements. These local currency results of foreign subsidiaries are then translated at an average rate for the year for incorporation in the consolidated profit and loss account.

The temporal method

Unlike the closing rate method, the temporal method does not assume that foreign operations are normally carried out through foreign subsidiaries which operate as separate or semi-independent business entities. Rather, its underlying assumption is that the affairs of a foreign subsidiary are so closely interlinked with the parent company that the business of the foreign subsidiary should be regarded as a direct extension of the business of the parent company. In such a case, it is argued that the cash flows of the subsidiary will have a direct impact upon the cash flows of the parent company. The parent company will also provide the principal source of finance for the subsidiary. In such circumstances, it is argued that the temporal method is most appropriate.

Under the temporal method a distinction is made between assets and liabilities recorded in the balance sheet at historical cost and those items recorded at current values. Non-monetary assets which are recorded at historical cost are translated at historical rates of exchange or at the rates ruling when the items were first recorded in the accounts. On the other hand, monetary assets and liabilities together with any assets carried at current values are translated at the rate of exchange in force at the balance sheet date. Exchange differences on these items carried at current values will arise in so far as the rate of exchange used to translate these items has changed between the balance sheet dates. Thus, unlike the closing rate method, only some of the items in the balance sheet will vary with exchange rate changes.

Moreover, there is also a difference in the treatment of these currency gains and losses. Whereas, under the closing rate method such translation gains and losses were treated as movements in reserves in the consolidated balance sheet, the temporal method takes the approach that such gains and losses should be reported as part of the profit or loss for the year from business operations because of the close relationship between the cash flows of the subsidiary and those of the parent. Thus, under the temporal approach, all currency gains and losses are taken direct to the consolidated profit and loss account.

Comparison of the two methods

From the above it is clear that the controversy over which method to apply in accounting for translation exposure is likely to be coloured by the view taken of the relationship between the parent company and the subsidiary. In so far as the subsidiary is operated as a semi-autonomous entity, the closing rate method is likely to be favoured. Conversely, where the subsidiary is simply an extension of the business of the parent company, the temporal method may be preferred. In addition to the parent/subsidiary relationship, the two methods can be compared in relation to the efficiency with which they deal with the following issues.

Measurement of exposure

Compared to the net investment approach of the closing rate method, the temporal method provides a poor measure of the net assets exposed to risk. This is because the temporal method translates fixed assets at historical cost so that they are not regarded as being exposed to foreign exchange risk. This contrasts with the closing rate method which takes the view that all assets are exposed to risk. Indeed, because it ignores fixed assets carried at historical cost, the temporal method will frequently give the impression that there is a negative exposed net worth. This can be seen in the example given in Table 2.1 which demonstrates that by ignoring the fixed assets the temporal method suggests that the subsidiary is a net liability rather than a net asset to the parent company. Thus the closing method suggests a net asset exposure of £70 000 whereas the temporal method suggests a figure of −£30 000!

Although the closing rate method is superior to the temporal method in estimating the amount of assets exposed to foreign currency movements, it still falls short of giving an estimate of true exposure. This is because the current value of the fixed assets is unlikely to change directly proportional to the exchange rates. If, in Table 2.1, the fixed assets were now worth £200 000, then the true economic exposure would have been £170 000.

The instability of reported profits

One problem with the temporal method is its effects upon the

instability of reported profits when exchange rates change. Under
the temporal method, it must be recalled, the effect of exchange
rate changes on the net exposed assets will be carried through to
the consolidated profit and loss account. Thus, in the previous
example a 10 per cent depreciation of sterling would be recorded
in the consolidated profit and loss account as a £3000 loss (i.e. 10
per cent of £30 000). This contrasts with the closing rate method
whereby the effect of the exchange rate on the net assets exposed
would have been to bring about a movement on reserves in the balance sheet reflecting a change in the net worth of the investment,
rather than as a change in the profitability of the subsidiary.

Table 2.1
Accounting exposure – subsidiary's balance sheet

		Temporal method	Closing rate method
Assets:	£	£	£
Fixed assets	100 000		100 000
Debtors	25 000	25 000	25 000
Cash	35 000	35 000	35 000
	160 000		
Liabilities:			
Share capital			
and reserves	70 000		
Creditors	45 000	45 000	45 000
Local debt	45 000	45 000	45 000
	160 000		
Net accounting exposure		(30 000)	70 000

The financing decision

American companies, in particular, which made use of the
temporal method in order to comply with the American Financial
Accounting Standard FAS 8 frequently found that the fluctuations
in reported earnings that resulted caused them to take financing
decisions which were dictated by accounting criteria rather than

economic criteria. For example, it would be reasonable to assume that an American company with a German subsidiary would fund its German mark denominated asset by some form of German mark denominated debt, in order to reduce currency exposure. However, under the temporal method, the fixed assets in the German subsidiary would have been translated at a historical rate of exchange whereas the debt finance in the parent company would have been translated at current rates. Hence, a depreciation of the dollar against the German mark would be reported as a reduction of profit since the debt is now more expensive to repay and has not been offset by a revaluation of fixed assets. Thus, a correct financing decision from a hedging point of view will have led to a reduction of reported profits. The consequence was that some companies did not hedge their foreign assets with foreign borrowings, in order to get around this accounting problem.

This again is in contrast to the closing rate method which, as shown above, does not produce such fluctuations in reported profits, and allows financing decisions to take place which attempt to genuinely hedge the risk of currency exposure.

Ratio analysis

Since the closing rate revalues all assets and liabilities at the same exchange rate, it has the advantage that the translation process does not distort the existing balance sheet ratios of the subsidiary. This, again, contrasts with the temporal method, under which different assets are translated at different exchange rates, so that the existing balance sheet ratios of the subsidiary will not be accurately translated across to the parent.

The conflict with prudence

One main criticism of the closing rate method is that it is in conflict with the prudence concept which does not allow any gains to be recognized until they are realized. The closing rate method by revaluing the fixed assets of the subsidiary at the closing exchange rate clearly has the effect of recognizing a gain in the books of the parent company even though the gain has not been realized by the sale of the asset. The temporal method avoids this problem by valuing such assets at the original historic exchange rate.

Thus it would appear that each method has its advantages and disadvantages. However, the balance of opinion, as will be seen in the concluding section, has come down in favour of the closing rate method.

Statement of Standard Accounting Practice 20

SSAP 20, published by the Accounting Standards Committee in April 1983, has been, like many other accounting standards, the product of considerable debate which took place upon the various exposure drafts that preceded it. Exposure Draft 16, published in September 1975, did not require any particular method of translation to be adopted but merely suggested how exchange differences could be treated. This was followed by ED 21, published in September 1977, requiring that companies be obliged to use either the temporal method or the closing rate method and that no other treatment was acceptable. Although this narrowed down the scope open to companies, it still left them free to choose either of these methods. ED 21 was superseded in October 1980 by ED 27 which was based on the net investment concept. It urged that the closing rate method should normally be used, but that the temporal method may be used where the directors consider that it will more fairly reflect the manner in which the business is conducted. Although there were some minor changes of detail, SSAP 20 published in April 1983 essentially adopted the same approach as ED 27. It included the following issues.

The method to be adopted

On the issue of which method to use in the preparation of consolidated financial statements, paragraph 52 of SSAP 20 states that: 'the closing rate/net investment method of translating the local currency financial statements should normally be used'. However, paragraph 55 also notes that 'in those circumstances where the trade of the foreign enterprise is more dependent on the economic environment of the investing company's currency than that of its own reporting currency, the temporal method should be used'.

What SSAP 20 clearly lays down is that companies are no longer free to choose which method of translation they will adopt. Companies will normally be expected to adopt the closing rate method and it is only in specific circumstances that the temporal method may be used.

How to apply the closing rate

SSAP 20 also lays down the way in which the closing rate should be applied. It states that the opening net investment in a foreign enterprise should be retranslated at the closing rate and recorded as a movement on reserves. It allows the profit and loss account of the foreign subsidiary to be translated at the closing rate or at an average rate for the period but emphasizes that, where an average rate is used, the difference between the profit and loss account translated at an average rate and at the closing rate should be recorded as a movement on reserves. These procedures are illustrated in the following example of the closing rate method advocated by SSAP 20.

A UK company owns the entire share capital of an American subsidiary. At the original balance sheet date this net investment amounted to $1 million when the exchange rate was £1 = $1.25. By the following balance sheet date the exchange rate was £1 = $1.50. During the year the American subsidiary had made a profit of $150 000 which the UK company translates for consolidation purposes at an average rate for the year of £1 = $1.35. These exchange rate movements are then translated into the consolidated accounts as follows.

(a)   First, the net investment at the start of the year should be translated at the closing exchange rate and the difference taken as a movement on reserve.

Net investment at closing exchange rate = $1 million	1.50 =	666 667
Net investment at original exchange rate = $1 million	1.25 =	800 000
Reduction in net investment		(£133 333)

This reduction in net investment of £133 333 is then shown in the consolidated balance sheet as a reduction from reserves.

(b)   The difference between the profit for the year translated
       at an average rate and the profit translated at the closing
       rate would also be shown as a movement on reserves.
       Thus:

Profit of $150 000 at average rate = $150 000	1.35 = 111 111
Profit of $150 000 at closing rate = $150 000	1.50 = 100 000
Additional movement on reserves	£11 111

Thus, there is an additional movement on reserves of £11
111.

(c)   It is interesting to note how this consolidation procedure
       has changed the net investment. The new net investment
       to be used as the basis for the following year is calculated
       as follows:

Net investment at original exchange rate	800 000
Reduction in net investment	(133 333)
Profit for year at average rate	111 111
Additional movement on reserves	(11 111)
Net investment at end of year	£766 667

The use of foreign currency borrowing as a hedge against group equity investments in foreign enterprises

As discussed earlier, the temporal method tends to distort the
true profit position in cases where foreign currency borrowings
have been used to finance an equity investment in the same
currency. SSAP 20 recognizes this financing procedure as being
a legitimate hedge and allows exchange gains and losses on the
foreign currency borrowings to be offset as reserve movements
against exchange differences arising on the retranslation of the net
investments, rather than taking them direct to the profit and loss
account.

However, SSAP 20 only allows such offset if certain conditions
are fulfilled, these criteria being laid down under paragraph 51 for
individual companies and paragraph 57 for consolidated financial
statements. As consolidated financial statements are the prime
concern here, the criteria for offset laid down in paragraph 57 are
shown below:

(a) the relationships between the investing company and the foreign enterprises concerned justify the use of the closing rate method for consolidation purposes;

(b) in any accounting period, the exchange gains and losses arising on foreign currency borrowings are offset only to the extent of the exchange differences arising on the net investments in foreign enterprises;

(c) the foreign currency borrowings, whose exchange gains or losses are used in the offset process, should not exceed, in the aggregate, the total amount of cash that the net investments are expected to be able to generate, whether from profits or otherwise; and

(d) the accounting treatment is applied consistently from period to period.

In so far as the true exposure is different from the accounting exposure as identified in SSAP 20, then the constraints imposed in paragraph 57 will not permit a complete hedge.

Conclusion

The application of SSAP 20 will go a long way towards removing the variability of accounting treatment of translations exposure. This process has also been considerably assisted by the withdrawal in the US of FAS 8, which advocated the adoption of the temporal method, and its replacement with the Statement of Accounting Standards No. 52 published in December 1981 with its emphasis upon the closing rate method. In a world of multinational companies it is pleasing to note that, at least on the issue of translations exposure, countries are adopting broadly similar standards.

3 Pricing, and timing cash flows

The risks arising from transactions involving foreign exchange might be managed by pricing policies relating to the level of prices or the currencies in which they are denominated. Alterations to the dates upon which money changes hands can also have significant impacts on exposure.

Currency of invoice

Transactions risk can be reduced if the currency, or currencies, received corresponds to the currency, or currencies, of cost. The simplest example is that of an exporter whose costs are in his home currency and who seeks to avoid transactions risk by invoicing in his own currency. The difficulty with this approach is that the customer may want to be invoiced in his base currency and the exporter's refusal to invoice in the importer's currency could cause the sale to be lost.

The exporter may incur costs in currencies other than his home currency, for example for imported components or raw materials. In such a situation he may wish to invoice his exports in the currencies in which he pays for his imports. Such matching would reduce currency risk. Indeed, an exporter who, for marketing reasons, is obliged to invoice in the currency of the importer's choosing may try to get his foreign suppliers to invoice in that currency.

It is dangerous to invoice in, or be invoiced in, currencies for which there are poor hedging facilities. In particular, if it is not possible, or excessively expensive, to obtain forward cover then (in the absence of the matching mentioned above) the company should avoid invoices in that currency. If the currency of invoice is prone to adverse changes in value the importance of this point is enhanced.

It may be that neither the exporter nor the importer is prepared to accept the invoice being in terms of the other's currency. For example, an export by a British company to a Central American country may face the problem that there is no market in forward contracts to cover the exchange risk between the two currencies. In such a situation they may decide to denominate the invoice in US dollars. There is no problem in obtaining cover between sterling and the US dollar (by way of forwards, futures, or options). In its turn the currency of the Central American country may be readily covered against the US dollar or may simply have a reasonably stable relationship with the dollar (in fact, a number of small countries fix their exchange rates against the US dollar).

Cushions

An exporter invoicing in foreign currency can add a margin to the price so as to allow for the possibility of a depreciation of the currency concerned. The size of this cushion would be dependent upon the level of volatility experienced in the relevant exchange rate. Similarly, an importer who is invoiced in foreign currency might build a margin into the selling prices in the domestic market in order to cover the possibility of an appreciation of the foreign currency against the home currency.

The obvious problem with using pricing to cover for exchange rate risk is that sales may be lost as a result. More generally prices would be pulled away from the optimal level determined in the light of the objectives of the firm.

Currency cocktails

It is possible to denominate transactions or assets/liabilities in terms of baskets of currencies. Two of the best known of these currency cocktails are the Special Drawing Right (SDR) issued by the International Monetary Fund and the European Currency Unit (ECU). The ECU is the unit of account of the European Monetary System and is composed of the currencies of the member countries. On 17 September 1984 the value of each ECU was determined as:

	0.719	Deutschmarks
plus	0.0878	pounds sterling
plus	1.31	French francs
plus	140.00	lire
plus	0.356	guilder
plus	3.71	Belgian francs
plus	0.219	krone
plus	0.00871	Irish pounds
plus	1.15	drachma
plus	0.14	Luxembourg francs

The advantage of using a currency cocktail from the point of view of reducing exchange rate risk arises from the fact that fluctuations between a currency and a basket of currencies are likely to be less than those between individual currencies. Movements of an exchange rate are caused by changes, in both of the currencies concerned, in relation to the world's currencies as a whole. A basket of currencies is going to show little or no movement against currencies in general. A composite currency which is derived from all the currencies in a trading bloc (as the ECU nearly is) will, by definition, not fluctuate against currencies in general within that trading bloc. So the only major source of volatility is the home currency and, in consequence, exchange rates between individual currencies and baskets tend to be more stable than those between individual currencies.

The timing of cash flows

Conceptually, the simplest way to deal with exposure is to avoid it. Denominating invoices in a company's home currency may be one form of avoidance, another is the control of the timing of payments and receipts.

In the case of transactions risk an importer invoiced in foreign currency might seek prepayment. This approach would be particularly appropriate if the company expects an appreciation of the currency of invoice. Prepayment so as to avoid the necessity of paying more of the home currency for the requisite foreign currency appears to make sense. There are, however, liquidity considerations. There is a cost, in the form of interest paid on money borrowed to finance the prepayment or interest receipts forgone on funds used for the purpose.

If the decision to prepay is influenced by expectations of exchange rate movements there is an element of trading (that is, speculating) involved. If a company merely wished to avoid the possibility of an adverse exchange rate movement and carried out the avoidance measure without regard to any expectations of exchange rate changes then it would be purely hedging. As soon as it takes account of expectations it is also (and perhaps wholly) involved in trading. A company that prepays if it expects the currency of an invoice to appreciate and attempts to delay payment if a depreciation is expected is really involved in speculation rather than hedging. It is seeking to retain liabilities in currencies that are expected to depreciate and to reduce liabilities in those expected to appreciate. Speeding up payments is often referred to as 'leading' and delaying them as 'lagging'.

Lagging of payments or receipts cannot be for hedging purposes (unless the exposures are created in order to offset other exposures). When a company lags it is increasing its exposure to exchange rate changes and hence is adding to, rather than reducing, its exchange rate risks. An importer expecting a depreciation of the currency of invoice might delay payment so that it can acquire the foreign currency when it has fallen in price. A short position in foreign currency is being taken in order to benefit from an expected exchange rate movement. Such behaviour is speculation rather than hedging.

Leading and lagging can be carried out in a number of ways. The timing of purchases and sales may be changed. Making purchases as early as possible is one means of reducing exposure to future exchange rate movements. The timing of payments and receipts may be adjusted independently of the timing of purchases and sales. Also the timing of the acquisition or disposal of the foreign currency can differ from that of the payments or receipts. If a foreign currency is expected to appreciate, the recipient may hold it for some time prior to selling it for home currency.

Offsetting

Offsetting is a technique of currency management that is best suited to multinational companies. Offsetting becomes possible when there are two-way flows in a currency. If a company has both payments and receivables in US dollars its transactions exposure might be limited to the difference between the payments and receipts. In the case of multinational companies the payments and receipts do not even need to be in the same currency. A British parent company may trade with a subsidiary in Germany and invoice its exports to the German subsidiary in sterling whilst the German subsidiary invoices its exports to the parent company in Deutschmarks. By using a shadow exchange rate the two payments can be deemed to cancel each other with the cash flow between the countries being limited to the difference between the payments. This difference is the only exposure faced by the multinational. However, offsetting, whilst straightforward in principle, provides considerable administrative difficulties.

Timing is a particular problem. Although annual cash movements may appear to be amenable to offsetting it may be the case that flows in one direction are separated in time from flows in the other direction. Offsetting would then depend upon the company's ability to manipulate the timing of receipts and payments. Without such matching in terms of timing there could be liquidity problems for some parts of the multinational. If the German subsidiary's exports to the British parent company occur several months before the parent's exports to the subsidiary, the subsidiary will have to wait longer for its receipts. Instead of receiving money when it exports it may have to wait until it has the money that would otherwise have been used to finance its imports from the parent. The difference in timing could also produce difficulties as to the determination of the shadow exchange rate. For example, if the shadow exchange rate is the one prevailing when the German subsidiary exports and sterling then weakens against the Deutschmark prior to the subsidiary's importing from the parent, the subsidiary will be paying more Deutschmarks for its imports than would be the case if offsetting was not operating. The management of the German subsidiary would feel that its profits, on which it is judged, had been creamed off to the benefit of the parent. This could undermine enthusiasm for, and cooperation with, the practice of offsetting.

The problem of timing concerns both the typical pattern of payment flows and the reliability of that pattern. If payments in one direction are normally separated by a considerable period of time from payments in the other direction, the scope for offsetting will be limited. Even if, on average, the flows are well matched the ability to offset will be reduced if the flows cannot reliably be predicted. There could be delays in delivery; there may be capricious variations in the quantities traded, or the prices at which they are traded. The company treasurer has to decide whether the degree of synchronization and its reliability are sufficient for offsetting to be used.

4 Forward currency: some principles

The most popular technique for covering foreign exchange risk is forward buying or selling of currencies. A forward purchase is an agreement to buy foreign currency at a rate of exchange determined in the present on a specified future date, or during a future period. Likewise a forward sale. This technique removes all uncertainty as to how much future payables or receivables are worth in terms of domestic currency.

A particular type of money market transaction that involves a forward operation is the swap. A swap consists of the spot purchase of a currency and the simultaneous forward sale of the same currency (or spot sale and forward purchase). When a forward transaction is not part of a swap operation it is referred to as an 'outright' deal. Outright forward transactions can be for the purposes of either hedging or trading (speculating). The facility of knowing the rate of exchange for a transaction in advance eliminates the risk of adverse movements of the exchange rate and hence provides a means of hedging foreign exchange risk. Traders may undertake forward positions in the expectation that the spot rate that will prevail on the day the forward contract matures will differ from the forward rate obtained. If a trader expects the spot rate on a day to be lower than the forward rate relating to that day he will sell forward in the anticipation that he will, when that day arrives, be able to buy spot at a cheaper price than that for which he contracted to sell. He thus makes a profit in the process of meeting his forward commitment. Likewise a trader expecting the spot rate to be higher than the forward rate will buy forward in the anticipation of being able to sell the currency bought at a higher price on the spot market.

Premiums and discounts

If the forward rate for a currency exceeds the spot rate, that currency is said to be at a premium. For example, if the spot rate of sterling in terms of US dollars is £1 = $1.40 whilst the six-month forward rate is £1 = $1.45 then sterling is said to be at a premium against the dollar. Conversely, if the forward rate is less than the spot rate the currency is said to be at a discount. With a spot exchange rate of £1 = $1.40, a forward rate of £1 = $1.35 means that sterling is at a discount against the US dollar (correspondingly the dollar is at a premium against sterling).

Table 4.1
Pound spot – forward against pound

9 October	Day's spread	Close	One month	% p.a.	Three months	% p.a.
US	1.4100–1.4180	1.4150–1.4160	0.47–0.44c pm	3.86	1.19–1.15pm	3.31
Canada	1.9274–1.9370	1.9300–1.9330	0.56–0.47c pm	3.20	1.37–1.24pm	2.70
Netherlands	4.20¼–4.22¼	4.21–4.22	2¼–2c pm	6.06	6–5¾pm	5.58
Belgium	75.77–76.00	75.90–76.00	24–18c pm	3.32	51–43pm	2.48
Denmark	13.54½–13.58¾	13.57–13.58	4–3ore pm	3.10	9⅝–8½pm	2.68
Ireland	1.2070–1.2114	1.2085–1.2095	0.30–0.16p pm	2.28	0.71–0.41pm	1.85
W. Germany	3.73–3.75¼	3.74–3.75	2⅜–2¼pf pm	7.43	6½–6¼pm	6.83
Portugal	231.32–236.26	232.02–235.76	10c pm–280 dis	–6.95	340–1295dis	–14.03
Spain	228.43–229.44	228.66–228.97	10c pm–40 dis	–0.79	30–150dis	–1.57
Italy	2,520½–2,528	2,524¾–2,525¾	3–7 lire dis	–2.38	13–17dis	–2.38
Norway	11.40¼–11.18¼	11.16¾–11.17¾	⅛–1⅛ore dis	–0.67	2¼–3¼dis	–0.99
France	11.40–11.42¾	11.41–11.42	2¼–1½c pm	1.97	3⅜–1⅝pm	0.88
Sweden	11.26¼–11.30¾	11.28¾–11.29¾	2¼–3¼ore dis	–2.93	7⅜–8⅜dis	–2.80
Japan	303¼–307	303½–304½	1.45–1.34y pm	5.51	3.83–3.71pm	4.97
Austria	26.23–26.34	26.31–26.34	16⅞–15¼gro pm	7.32	40⅜–36⅛pm	5.81
Switzerland	3.06½–3.08¼	3.07¼–3.08¼	2⅛–2c pm	8.06	5½–5¼pm	7.00

Belgian rate is for convertible francs. Financial franc 76.50–76.60.
Six-month forward dollar 1.95–1.90c pm. 12-month 3.05–2.90c pm.

Source: *Financial Times*, 10 October 1985.

Table 4.1 shows how forward rates are reported in the *Financial Times*. The letters 'pm' indicate that the currency is at a premium against sterling and 'dis' indicates a discount. The forward rates are obtained by subtracting the premium from, or adding the discount to, the quoted spot price of sterling. For example, the spot price for sterling at the close of business is quoted as US$1.4150 –1.4160 (sterling can be sold for $1.4150 per £1 and bought for $1.4160) and the dollar is at a three-month premium of 1.19–1.15 cents. This implies a forward rate of $1.4031–1.4045.

The premiums and discounts are also reported in terms of per cent per annum. In Table 4.1 the dollar premium is quoted as 3.31 per cent p.a. This percentage is ascertained from the following formula:

$$\frac{(\text{Premium} \times 365 \times 100)}{\text{Spot rate} \times \text{Number of days to maturity}}$$

This formula can be more readily understood by rewriting it as:

$$\text{Percentage} = \frac{\text{Premium}}{\text{Spot rate}} \times \frac{365}{\text{Number of days to maturity}} \times 100$$

The first component, Premium/Spot rate, expresses the premium as a proportion of the spot rate. The second component, 365/Number of days to maturity, annualizes the figure. It alters the first ratio to produce the number that would be found for the 12-month premium if the 12-month forward premium was proportional to the three-month (or whatever) premium. So in the case of three-month forwards this adjustment would multiply the first ratio by four whilst in the case of one-month forwards the multiplication would be by about 12. Finally, the resulting figure is multiplied by 100 in order to convert the decimal into a percentage.

The bid-offer spread (the difference between the buying and selling prices) is always larger for forward foreign exchange than for spot. From Table 4.1 it can be seen that, in the case of the US dollar, the spot spread is 0.1 cent ($1.4150–$1.4160) whilst the forward spread is 0.13 cent. It is thus possible to see whether there is a premium or a discount even in the absence of a direct indication (in the case of the Reuters board there is no indication such as 'pm' and 'dis'). The quoted numbers should be added to, or subtracted from, the spot numbers according to whichever increases the bid-offer spread. So in the case of the three-month forward rate against the dollar the spread is increased by subtracting 1.19–1.15 from the spot prices. It follows that the US dollar is at a premium against the pound (the pound is at a discount against the dollar). In the case of the Italian lira the numbers for the three-month forward rate are 13–17. The bid offer spread is increased by adding these to the spot rates to yield 2537¾–2542¾. The lira is thus at a discount against sterling.

Determination of forward rates

To build up the picture of how forward exchange rates are determined it is useful to begin with considering how a bank might deal with a customer's request to buy or sell foreign currency forward. For example, a customer wishes to sell US$1 million for sterling six months forward. To avoid exchange risk the bank could sell dollars at the time that the forward deal is agreed. The dollars would be obtained by borrowing them at the current Eurodollar rate and the sterling obtained would be invested. Suppose that Eurodollar six-month interest rates are 15 per cent p.a. and sterling six-month rates are 10 per cent p.a. The position of the bank immediately after the forward deal is agreed is:

10 March

£	$
Buys £800 000 at £1 = $1.25	Sells $1 000 000 at £1 = $1.25
Lends £800 000 at 10% p.a.	Borrows $1 000 000 at 15% p.a.

The position of the bank when the forward contract matures is:

10 September

£	$
Is repaid £800 000 principal	Repays $1 000 000 principal
plus £40 000 interest	plus $75 000 interest
Pays customer a sum of sterling	Receives $1 000 000 from customer

The sum of sterling paid to the customer is not the £800 000 that was purchased for $1 million on 10 March – the interest payments

must be taken into account. In particular, the excess of the interest on the dollar borrowing over that received from the sterling
lending must be deducted from the £800 000 in order to ascertain
the sum of sterling to be paid to the customer. It is necessary to
obtain a forward exchange rate in order to express $75 000 in
terms of sterling. For this purpose an approximate forward rate is
generated, and this is ascertained by the following formula:

$$\text{Approximate forward rate} = \text{spot rate} + \frac{\left(\begin{array}{c}\text{Interest rate for dollars} - \text{Interest rate for sterling}\end{array}\right) \times \text{Spot rate} \times \text{Number of days to maturity}}{100 \times 365}$$

In the present example, this formula produces a rate of £1
= $1.2812½. The rationale underlying this formula will be
explained below.

The $75 000 interest payment when converted to sterling using
the approximate forward rate becomes £58 536. The interest payable by the bank, net of interest receivable, is thus £18 536. The
bank thus undertakes to exchange £781 464 for $1 million in six
months time. In other words, the six-month forward exchange rate
offered by the bank on 10 March is £1 = $1.2796½ (1 000 000 ÷
781 464 = 1.2796½). Sterling is at a premium of 296½ points,
that is 2.96½ cents per £1:

Forward price	$1.2796½
Spot price	$1.2500
Premium	$0.0296½

As a percentage per annum the premium works out to be 4.74 per
cent p.a.

When this rate of premium is compounded with the rate of
interest on sterling deposits the net result is 14.98 per cent p.a.
(for six months 1.0237 × 1.05 = 1.0749 which implies 7.49 per cent
for six months or 14.98 per cent on an annualized basis).

Thus there is no significant difference in terms of return
between investing in a dollar deposit (in this case at 15 per
cent p.a.) and buying sterling spot whilst selling it forward and

investing that sterling between purchase and sale. The forward premium on sterling offsets the interest differential between dollar and sterling deposits. This is the interest rate parity relationship.

It is this relationship which underlies the formula for ascertaining the approximate forward rate. The formula estimated the forward premium by applying the interest rate differential to the spot rate and adjusting for the period to maturity.

The 'rule of thumb' is that if interest rates on foreign currency deposits are higher than those on sterling deposits then sterling will be at a premium against foreign currency, whereas if the sterling interest rates are the higher then sterling will be at a discount. The premium or discount compensates for the interest rate differential between deposits in the two currencies (note that the relevant interest rates are those on Eurocurrency deposits).

Case Studies: Using forwards to restructure debts

1   A company has purchased a mainframe computer from an American firm for $6 000 000, payable in four annual instalments. The first instalment is payable immediately. The US company allows credit at 6 per cent p.a. The purchaser, whose revenues are in sterling, is at risk from an appreciation of the US dollar against sterling. The purchaser shops around for forward contracts and finds that the UK subsidiary of an American bank is prepared to offer one, two and three-year forward contracts at £1 = $1.47, £1 = $1.44, and £1 = $1.41, respectively. The spot rate is £1 = $1.50. The purchaser agrees to buy forward dollars as follows:

1 year hence	$1 590 000 for £1 081 632
2 years hence	$1 685 400 for £1 170 416
3 years hence	$1 786 524 for £1 267 038

The future sterling cash flows are thus predetermined and exchange rate risk is eliminated. Effectively the 6 per cent p.a. dollar liability is converted to a sterling liability of about 8 per cent p.a.

2   A company wishes to borrow 10 million Finnish markka for two years but can only borrow on a six-month floating rate basis.

Forward contracts can be used to create a liability on a fixed rate basis.

The company borrows 2 million Eurodollars for two years at 6 per cent p.a. The spot exchange rate is $1 = 5 markka and the two-year forward rate is $1 = 5.10 markka. The company buys 10 million markka spot and agrees to forward sales of markka as follows:

    2 years hence   11 460 720 markka for $2 247 200

To repay the 2 million Eurodollar loan US $2 247 200 is required. The company has guaranteed that 11 460 720 markka will be required at the end of the two years. This sum is equivalent to a fixed annual rate of about 7 per cent on the initial 10 million markka.

Maintaining interest rate parity

The interest rate parity relationship is maintained by the mechanism of covered interest arbitrage. This arbitrage involves making profits from divergences between the interest rate differential, on the one hand, and the premium/discount expressed as a percentage change from the spot exchange rate on the other.

Suppose that the sterling short term interest rate is 10 per cent p.a. whilst the corresponding dollar rate is 8 per cent p.a. The dollar stands at a premium against sterling and this premium implies an appreciation of the dollar at a rate of 2 per cent p.a. Suppose further that this interest rate parity relationship is disturbed by an increase in the dollar interest rate to 9 per cent p.a. An opportunity for arbitrage profits emerges. A bank in the UK could borrow sterling at 10 per cent p.a., exchange it for dollars, deposit those dollars at 9 per cent p.a. and simultaneously sell the principal plus interest forward. Inclusive of the 2 per cent p.a. guaranteed appreciation of the dollar, the dollar deposit yields 11 per cent p.a. in terms of sterling. There is a net gain of 1 per cent p.a., and there is no risk involved. This arbitrage is illustrated by Figure 4.1.

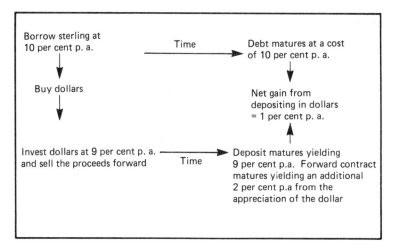

Figure 4.1 Covered interest arbitrage

The process of taking advantage of the arbitrage opportunities tends to restore interest rate parity. In particular, the spot purchase of dollars tends to raise the spot price of dollars and the forward sale of dollars tends to depress the forward price. The rising spot price and falling forward price reduces the dollar's premium. The premium will decline so long as the arbitrage is pursued and the arbitrage will be pursued so long as the premium exceeds the interest rate differential. In Figure 4.1 there is scope for arbitrage profits so long as the dollar's premium against sterling exceeds 1 per cent p.a. (In addition, borrowing sterling and lending dollars tends to raise sterling interest rates relative to dollar rates so that a widening interest rate differential may contribute to the restoration of interest rate parity.)

Cause and effect

Interest rate parity establishes a close relationship between the spot exchange rate and the forward exchange rate. The question arises, however, as to whether the spot rate is determined by market forces and the forward rate follows it or whether the forward rate takes the lead and the spot rate follows. There are advocates of both views although probably most would take the view that the spot rate determines the forward rate rather than vice versa. This view has the greatest intuitive appeal since to postulate that the forward rate determines the spot rate seems to suggest that the tail wags the dog.

Nevertheless, the alternative view should not be rejected out of hand, and there are sound reasons for taking it seriously. Firstly, changes in underlying economic and political circumstances seem likely to lead to a greater volume of forward deals than spot deals. Bodies deciding to hedge previously unhedged positions because of the changes would do so in the forward market. Speculators seeking to profit from their anticipations of exchange rate movements are likely to do so using forward rather than spot exchange because of the higher leverage involved in forward positions. The forward market thus establishes an exchange rate and the spot market adjusts to it.

Secondly, there is reason to believe that the forward rate corresponds to the expected rate and is therefore not determined by the spot rate. Speculators have expectations about the level of future exchange rates and if forward rates differ from these expectations there is a perceived scope for speculative gains. Furthermore, the pursuit of these speculative gains would tend to move the forward rate towards the expected rate. Suppose, for example, that the three-month forward rate was above the rate that was generally expected. It would be worthwhile to sell forward exchange with a view to honouring the contract by means of buying spot when the contract matures. If the expectation is correct the currency is bought at a lower price than that at which it is sold. Conversely, a forward rate lower than the expected rate would lead speculators to buy forward in anticipation of selling at a higher price when the contract matures. In the former case the forward sales by speculators would depress the forward rate towards the expected rate whereas in the latter case their forward purchases would raise the forward rate towards the expected rate. So there is reason to believe that the forward rate would tend to represent the expected rate. Since the expected rate is unlikely to be mechanistically determined by the spot rate it seems plausible that the line of causation goes from the forward rate to the spot rate.

For example, if sterling looks as though it might weaken because oil prices have fallen, previously unhedged positions might become hedged. Potential hedgers may be prepared to leave positions exposed until the fear of a sterling depreciation emerges. The emergence of such a fear leads to forward sales in order to avert the risk of loss from a considerable depreciation. Traders may also enter the forward market in the anticipation of making profits. If a trader expects the future spot rate to be below the forward rate he sells forward with a view to meeting the forward contract when it matures by buying spot at a lower price. The total effect is to drive down the forward price of sterling.

An increasing forward discount (or decreasing premium) for sterling would render sterling investments less attractive relative to investments in other currencies. The rate of depreciation of sterling would exceed the interest differential in favour of sterling. Arbitrageurs would sell sterling spot in order to switch their investments from sterling to other currencies. This puts downward pressure on spot sterling which declines in value thereby maintaining interest rate parity. Thus the forward sales of sterling bring about matching depreciations of forward and spot sterling leaving the premium/discount unaffected (unless there has been some impact on the interest rate differential).

Finally, in this context, it is interesting to note that futures rates are frequently used as a source of information by operators in the spot market. This use of futures rates suggests that they are seen as being determined independently of spot rates. Since forward rates are unlikely to diverge significantly from futures rates it follows that forward rates are also seen as being determined independently of spot exchange rates.

Abstract

The following is from an article that appeared in the December 1986 issue of *Topics*, a magazine published by Jaguar PLC for its employees. This illustrates the use of forward foreign exchange by a manufacturing company.

Selling forward – how does it work?

Over the past two years Jaguar has been 'selling forward' or 'hedging' some of the foreign currencies it receives from export sales.

Exactly what does 'selling forward' mean? Why do Jaguar do it? How does it work?

The intricacies of selling forward are complex, although the basic principle is fairly simple. This article is intended to answer the most frequently asked questions expressed by employees wanting to understand hedging.

Dollar receipts

Jaguar is paid in dollars for each of the cars it sells in the USA. The foreign currency is transferred through the banking system from America to Jaguar's bank in England. Unless these dollars are 'sold forward', i.e. sold in advance, Jaguar would exchange them for sterling at whatever rate of exchange existed on that day. The exchange rate is, therefore, very important. The link between profits and exchange rates is quite easy to show.

A car selling in the USA at $35 000 with the pound at $1.30 would, once the dollars were converted into sterling, produce £26 923. With the pound at $1.45, for the same car, Jaguar would receive only £24 138. That's a drop of nearly £3 000.

Exchange rate fluctuations

Over the past six years the dollar has dropped from a high of 2.45 to the pound to a low of 1.05 to the pound.

In 1984, at the time of Jaguar's privatization, the dollar stood at 1.33 to the pound. Recently, it has steadied at around 1.45.

Minimizing the risks

Jaguar's fortunes are linked directly to exchange rates and it therefore has to try to minimize the effect of the fluctuations over which it has no control. It does this by selling forward.

How hedging works

The company sells some of the dollars it expects to receive in the future – generally 12 months hence – to major banks who quote a 'future' price. This future price is based upon the difference between interest rates in the USA and the UK.

It works like this. Say in December 1986 Jaguar decide to sell forward one million dollars on a 12-month contract. That is, it is selling in advance one million dollars it expects to receive in December 1987. On the day it sells forward the exchange rate is $1.47/£. The bank contracting to buy $1 million would calculate what it can make from the variance in the UK and USA interest rates and quote a 'future' exchange rate, for example:

Say the USA interest rate is 6 per cent and the UK interest rate is 10 per cent.

$1 million borrowed in the USA at 6 per cent	= $1 060 000
$1 million exchanged for sterling at $1.47/£	= £ 680 272
£680 272 invested in the UK at 10 per cent	= £ 748 299 after one year
$1 060 000 divided by £748 299	= 1.4165
Therefore 'future exchange rate'	= $1.4165 to the pound

Using this example, by selling forward at a rate of $1.4165 to the pound rather than exchanging the dollars on the day of receipt for $1.47 to the pound, Jaguar would receive far more – equating to an extra £899 on a $35 000 car.

Please note, Jaguar actually exchanges the money on the day the contract matures. It is the promise of a future exchange rate which it receives on the day it sells forward.

Currency options

The future rate is agreed at the time the contract is taken out, and no one can 'crystal ball gaze' or know what actually will happen to the rate. Therefore, the method of hedging described above can result in selling forward for rates less advantageous than they actually turn out to be.

Dealing in currency options – a prudent practice which Jaguar carries out – can minimize this risk.

When Jaguar buys a currency option it buys the right to exchange foreign money for sterling at a fixed rate at a given time in the future. However, it doesn't have to exercise that right when the option matures.

For example, say in December 1986 Jaguar buys an option to exchange dollars 12 months later at $1.45/£. If in December 1987 the actual rate was $1.50/£ the company would take up the option and benefit. If, however, the actual rate in December 1987 was $1.35/£ there would be no point in taking up the option. In such a case only the cost of buying the option (a comparatively small sum) would be forfeited.

The results

As can be seen from Jaguar's financial results, the prudent policy of selling forward has been very successful over the past two years. Indeed, if today's currency exchange rates had existed in 1985 and if Jaguar had not sold forward, the decline of the dollar would have reduced Jaguar's profits after tax in 1985 by around one-third.

Most importantly, through selling forward, Jaguar has been able to know in advance how much it will get for the foreign currency it receives from export sales. This means the company can plan accordingly because, once hedging has taken place, it is immaterial whether the pound then rises or falls against the dollar. Jaguar cannot afford to gamble on exchange rates rising or falling – there is too much at stake.

By providing a 'cushion' when exchange rates are moving adversely, hedging has allowed Jaguar the time to react and plan accordingly. This, in turn, has promoted City confidence as shareholders don't want to see vast swings in income and profits.

Most major companies who export their products – including Mercedes – sell forward some of their foreign currencies.

Jaguar has not only hedged dollars but has also sold forward other currencies received from sales in such countries as Canada, Australia, Germany and Japan.

The future

Whether Jaguar can continue to receive benefits from currency hedging will depend upon the actual rates of exchange and the differentials in interest rates.

For example, in the first half of 1985 when the actual dollar/pound rate ranged from 1.05 to 1.32 it was quite easy to hedge on a 12-month contract for a rate of 1.27. This benefited Jaguar because in the first half of 1986 the actual rate turned out to be around 1.48.

However, now that the dollar/pound exchange rate is around 1.45 and interest rates have altered, the opportunities for selling forward at such advantageous rates have all but disappeared – some have said that 'the goose which laid our golden eggs has died'.

5 Forward currency: some practical considerations

Having considered the basic concepts underlying currency forwards, techniques are now examined for dealing with problems arising in the use of forwards – such as extending forwards, dealing with uncertain cash flow dates, hedging when no direct forwards exist between two currencies, ascertaining forward rates for irregular dates, and hedging the contingent risks that accompany tenders.

Extending a forward contract

It may be that the date on which a cash flow is due is postponed. A hedger with a forward contract might then need to extend the contract. The extension is likely to involve the first contract being settled by means of an opposite contract and a new contract being agreed.

For example, on 1 May a hedger buys sterling three months forward against US dollars at a forward rate of £1 = $1.50. By 1 July it is clear that the exchange of currencies will be delayed by a month. The hedger needs a forward contract for 1 September. The 1 August contract is settled and a 1 September contract agreed. The settlement of the first contract will involve a payment or receipt if the 1 August forward rate has changed since 1 May. Consider the following rates:

1 May	Three-month forward rate	£1 = $1.50
1 July	One-month forward rate	£1 = $1.48
	Two-month forward rate	£1 = $1.47

The contract taken out on 1 May to buy sterling at £1 = $1.50 on 1 August is settled on 1 July by taking out a contract to sell the same amount of sterling at £1 = $1.48 on 1 August. There is a loss of 2 cents per £1.

On 1 July a contract to buy sterling at £1 = $1.47 on 1 September is taken out. Taking the 2 cents per £1 loss into account the effective forward price of sterling is £1 = $1.49.

An alternative approach would be to take the difference between the August and September rates on 1 July and apply it to the original forward rate. In the preceding example, sterling is at a 1 cent discount between 1 August and 1 September. Extending the forward contract from 1 August to 1 September could take the form of applying the August to September discount to the original forward rate. The forward rate thereby obtained would be $1.50 − $0.01 = $1.49. (Although this is the same as the effective forward rate obtained by means of the previous technique the two rates may not turn out to be precisely the same.)

Option date forward contracts

Normally, forward contracts relate to a single future maturity date. However, such fixed date contracts may not be ideal for a customer who is uncertain as to when he will receive, or need to provide, foreign currency. In such a case it is possible to obtain a forward option contract whose maturity date lies within a range of dates, the customer having the right to choose the specific date.

The customer pays a price for this degree of flexibility since the forward rate will be the least favourable fixed date contract rate for the period. Suppose, for example, that the two-month forward rate for sterling against the US dollar is £1 = $1.40 whilst the three-month forward rate is £1 = $1.39. A customer wanting to buy sterling sometime between two and three months would pay the highest price, which is $1.40 (assuming that the price does not reach a higher level during the period). The bank providing the contract assumes that the chosen maturity date will be the least favourable from the point of view of the bank. Likewise someone selling sterling forward would receive the rate of £1 = $1.39. The bank assumes that the chosen maturity date will fall at the end of the period.

The bank determines the forward rates in this way in order to avoid losses. The consequence is that the customer may be quoted a rate that is very unfavourable compared with fixed date forward contracts.

Currency hold accounts

A less expensive means of adding flexibility to forward exchange contracts is the use of currency hold accounts. These are suitable for companies faced with continuous flows of business in a foreign currency. They are bank accounts in the relevant foreign currencies. If the holder of a forward contract to buy a currency finds that the currency is needed later than expected the currency purchased under the forward contract is deposited in the hold account until it is required. Conversely, if the currency is needed before the maturity date of the forward contract the company goes into overdraft in order to meet its foreign currency payment and subsequently pays off the overdraft with the currency purchased when the forward contract matures.

Overlapping option date forwards

Option date forwards normally allow the customer to spread out the currency transactions rather than requiring the total purchase or sale to be conducted on one day. This is particularly convenient for a company anticipating a stream of payments or receipts, as opposed to occasional isolated payments/receipts.

The tendency to be quoted the most disadvantageous fixed date price available over the relevant period leads customers to use the shortest possible option date period, since this may eliminate the most unfavourable rates. Shortening the option period increases the uncertainty as to whether the relevant payments/receipts will fall within that period. These conflicting influences on the choice of option period can be reconciled by means of overlapping option date forwards.

This procedure involves covering part of the currency flow with short period options and the remainder with longer period options. For example, currency receipts may be expected in each of three future months but only two-thirds of the anticipated monthly receipts is expected with certainty to accrue during the relevant month. Two-thirds of the total receipts would be covered by one-month options and the remainder might be covered by an option date forward extending over the full three months. As currency is received during a month the forward sale facility specific to that month is used first, and when it is used up the remaining receipts in that month are sold using the three-month option facility.

Forward cross rates

It may be the case that the forward market between two currencies is illiquid, or even non-existent. In such a situation, forward cover might be generated by using two separate forward transactions using a third currency. For example, a Spanish importer may wish to buy Canadian dollars forward. If the forward market between Spanish pesetas and Canadian dollars was inadequate the Spanish importer could choose to buy US dollars forward, against Spanish pesetas, and simultaneously sell the US dollars forward, against Canadian dollars. The forward rate effectively obtained for Canadian dollars against Spanish pesetas is a cross rate.

Suppose that the market rates for three-month forwards are as follows:

US$/peseta spot	160.00	160.10
3-month premium	0.20	0.27
		160.37
US$/Canadian $ spot	1.4000	1.4010
3-month premium	0.0015	0.0020
	1.4015	

The importer buys US dollars with pesetas paying 160.37 pesetas per US dollar. He then buys Canadian dollars with the US dollars received obtaining 1.4015 Canadian dollars per US dollar. The importer pays 160.37 pesetas and receives 1.4015 Canadian dollars. He thus pays: 160.37 / 1.4015 = 114.43 pesetas per Canadian dollar. This is the three-month forward buying cross price of Canadian dollars against Spanish pesetas.

Foreign exchange transactions that use a vehicle currency, which is most often the US dollar, involve suffering the bid-offer spread twice. In the example above the US dollar is purchased for the higher of two prices and sold for the lower of two prices.

The premium or discount between the two currencies can be ascertained by reference to the spot cross rate. In the present example the spot cross rate is 160.10 / 1.4000 = 114.36 pesetas per Canadian dollar. The peseta is at a discount against the Canadian dollar (of 0.24 per cent p.a.).

Indirect forwards

If the currency for which the company wishes to obtain cover is part of a currency bloc, or has a fairly stable relationship with a major currency, there is scope for indirect cover. For example, if an American firm wanted to cover foreign exchange risk arising from invoicing in Danish kroner and found that forward cover against the kroner for the relevant period was not available it could look to the Deutschmark instead. Denmark and West Germany are both participants in the exchange rate arrangements of the European Monetary System. The resulting stability between the kroner and the Deutschmark means that the American firm can operate by means of cover against the Deutschmark. If the American firm needs to pay in kroner at a future date it can buy Deutschmarks forward and then, upon receipt of the Deutschmarks, sell them spot for kroner.

Broken dates

There are standard contract periods for forward transactions. These standard periods are one, two, three, six and 12 months. A forward deal with a 'broken date' is one whose period falls between two standard periods, for example nine months.

The exchange rate for a broken date forward contract is obtained by extrapolation. The difference between the rates for the two closest standard period dates is divided by the number of intervening days. The result is multiplied by the number of days between the broken date and the later standard period date. The figure obtained is subtracted from, or added to, the forward rate relevant to the later date to obtain the forward rate for the broken date.

Suppose that the three-month forward rate for sterling against the US dollar is $1.40 whilst the six-month forward rate is $1.37. The four-month forward rate is calculated as follows:

$$\text{3-month rate} - \text{6-month rate} = \$1.40 - \$1.37 = \$0.03$$

$$\$0.03 \times {}^{60}\!/_{90} = \$0.02$$

(assuming that 90 days elapse between the two standard maturity dates and 60 days separate the four-month broken date from the six-month standard date). The 2 cents is added to the six-month rate in order to obtain the four-month rate:

$$\$1.37 + \$0.02 = \$1.39$$

Forwards against forwards

By entering two opposing forward contracts, with different maturities, it is possible to take a position on future interest rate differentials whilst avoiding exchange rate risk. Suppose, for example, a bank sells sterling 12 months forward against US dollars, and simultaneously buys sterling six months forward. The premium/discount for the 12-month forward together with that of the six-month forward implies a premium/discount, and hence interest rate differential, for the six months remaining after the shorter contract matures. If the dealer expects the interest rate differential to be different from the implied differential he could take the forward against forward position in anticipation of profiting from it. Meanwhile he is protected from exchange rate risk. Any movements of exchange rates, and the corresponding movements in forward rates, would involve losses on one contract offset by gains on the other. In practice, forward against forward positions are created not by means of two outright forward transactions but through two swaps in which the spot elements cancel each other out.

Suppose that for the future period the US dollar stands at an implied discount against sterling and that a dealer expects the differential in favour of Eurodollar interest rates to be greater than that currently implied. He would therefore be expecting an increase in the discount. In order to profit he sells dollars forward for the longer maturity and buys for the shorter. If the discount increases as expected he will, when the shorter contract matures, be able to take out a contract to buy forward with a maturity date identical to that of the remaining contract and profit from it. The larger discount implies that he will, upon maturity of the contracts, buy at a lower price than that at which he sells. There is no risk that a rise in the value of the dollar prior to the maturity of the shorter contract will undermine the profitability of the operation because the increase in the forward buying price of dollars would be matched by a higher spot price at the time that the shorter contract matures. There would be a profit from buying at the price agreed for the shorter contract and selling at the spot price and this gain would cancel the loss arising from the higher price on the new contract.

Offsetting

A bank agreeing to a forward purchase or sale by a customer will want to lay off the risk that arises. For example, if a customer takes out a contract to buy US dollars against sterling on a future date the bank acquires a risk that the dollar will have risen above the agreed forward price by that date. The bank risks having to sell dollars at a price lower than that at which it buys. So the bank will want to hedge.

One way in which the bank could reduce its risks would be to buy the dollars spot and invest them pending maturity of the forward contract. There are other approaches that the bank may choose. It may buy forward itself from another bank or it could use financial futures. To the extent that customers have offsetting requirements, the need to use external hedging instruments is reduced. If there were customers wishing to sell dollars forward on the same maturity date that the forward buyer seeks, the bank would find that risks offset each other. To the extent that forward deals offset each other, the bank will be able to transfer currencies between customers without being exposed itself. The bank's exposure would be limited to the discrepancy between forward sales and forward purchases. It is this net exposure that needs to be hedged.

Tendering

Tendering for contracts poses a particular problem from the point of view of covering foreign exchange risk. The exporter faces an exchange rate risk from the date that the tender is decided upon. However, with some types of hedging the exporter would find himself exposed to risk in the event of the tender proving to be unsuccessful. For example, if the hoped-for currency receipts were sold on the forward market and the tender then turned out to be unsuccessful the tendering company would be committed to a forward sale with no corresponding long position in that currency. It would be exposed to the risk of an increase in the price of the currency. Such an appreciation could produce a situation in which in order to meet the forward sale the company must purchase (spot or forward) at a higher price. So companies that tender are interested in hedging techniques that do not leave them exposed in the event of the tender being unsuccessful.

One approach would be to introduce a currency clause into the tender. The price would be fixed in terms of the home currency but quoted in terms of the foreign currency. The foreign currency quote would depend upon the exchange rate. Should the home currency appreciate, the quote would rise, and vice versa for a home currency depreciation. The uncertainty that the potential purchaser faces in regard to price must handicap the tendering exporter's chances of obtaining the contract.

An alternative approach would be to use currency options. A currency option gives its holder the right, but not the obligation, to sell (or buy) foreign currency in the future at an exchange rate agreed in the present. An exporter could tender in the buyer's currency, which would normally be the best strategy from a marketing point of view, and exercise the option to sell the currency should the tender prove to be successful. In the event of the tender being unsuccessful the would-be exporter could allow the option to expire unexercised, or in the case of traded options might sell it. Thus options are instruments that provide forward cover without leaving the hedger exposed if the tender is unsuccessful.

A buyer of an option pays a premium to the seller for the guarantee provided. The premium will be calculated on the assumption that should it be profitable to exercise the option then it will be exercised. In the case of an option to sell, if the price of foreign currency turns out to be lower than the guaranteed selling price then it is profitable to exercise the option. The tenderer, however, may be interested solely in hedging. Although he would presumably take any available profit from his options in the event of the tender being unsuccessful he might prefer to forego this opportunity in order to pay a smaller premium. One of the United Kingdom clearing banks has offered a 'Tender to Contract' scheme that meets such a preference.

The Tender to Contract scheme offers forward contracts that become operative only in the event of the tender being successful. The unsuccessful tenderer is not left with an uncovered forward position, as would be the case with normal forward currency transactions. The cover is also cheaper than that provided by options. Option premiums are charged in the light of the potential gain to the option holder in the event of the spot price of the currency being sold turning out to be lower than the selling price guaranteed by the contract and the absence of any possibility of loss arising through the spot price being higher than the agreed exercise price (since the option holder retains the right to sell spot). Under the Tender to Contract scheme if the tender is successful the exporter has no choice but to sell at the agreed forward price. So there is not the possibility, offered by options, of ignoring the hedging contract and selling spot if the spot price turns out to be higher than the agreed exercise price. The hedger must endure the loss of selling at the agreed forward price when the spot price of the currency is higher, and correspondingly the bank benefits from the gains involved. Hence the fee to be paid for cover under the Tender to

Contract scheme would be less than the costs involved when using options.

Forfaiting

By forfaiting, an exporter is able to transfer his exchange rate risk on to a bank. The process involves the exporter receiving a cash payment from the forfaiter who in turn obtains the claim on the payment for the exports. Bills of exchange and promissory notes are the types of trade debt most commonly forfaited.

Trades invoiced in US dollars, Swiss francs, and Deutschmarks are the most usual ones to be forfaited. This is because these are the most common Eurocurrencies. The money received by the exporter is equal to the anticipated payment for the exports minus a discount. The discount rate is based upon the Eurocurrency interest rate for the currency involved.

The exchange of foreign currency for the home currency takes place when the goods are delivered, or when the trade paper is received, and so there is no need to hedge foreign exchange risk from that date. Nevertheless, there is hedging implicit in the rate of discount. This is because of the interest rate parity relationship. If the currency of invoice is at a discount in the forward exchange market its Eurocurrency interest rate will be correspondingly at a relatively high level. So the rate of interest at which receivables are discounted is relatively high when the currency of invoice is at a discount against the home currency (vice versa for a premium). So for the period between delivery of the goods and receipt of money in payment from the importer, hedging exchange rate risk by forfaiting is equivalent in cost to hedging by means of forward selling.

An exporter can approach a forfaiter prior to agreeing, or tendering for, a contract. He would be informed of the approximate rate of discount to be used in the forfaiting process so that a price can be decided upon. The exporter can subsequently take up an option for finance to be exercised when the export contract is confirmed. When the order is confirmed the forfaiter will commit funds for the purchase of the trade paper in advance of its delivery.

There are some additional costs for the exporter. The forfaiter charges a commitment fee for the period between the agreement to forfait and the actual delivery of the trade paper. There would also be a charge for the option for finance, unless the latter is very short (just a day or two). The commitment fee takes account of the forfaiter's funding requirements and both fees seek compensation for the forfaiter in relation to the risk of interest rate and exchange rate changes that might occur after the forfaiting terms have been agreed.

6 Forward interest rates

Forward rate agreements (FRAs), sometimes referred to as future rate agreements, provide a technique for locking-in future short-term interest rates. They are analogous to forward foreign exchange contracts.

BBA interest settlement rate

A panel of 12 banks is established by the British Bankers' Association for the purpose of ascertaining the BBA interest settlement rates. The rates are fixed by reference to market rates for deposits in the London interbank market. The fixings are made at 11.00 a.m. each day and are obtained by taking quotations from eight banks in the panel and averaging the middle four quotations. The BBA interest settlement rates differ from LIBOR (the inter-bank rate) in being expressed in decimals rather than fractions.

Hedging with FRAs

Risk is reduced by entering a notional agreement to lend or borrow in the future at a rate of interest determined in the present. A set of bid-offer spreads is published showing rates of interest for different future time periods, for example the published spreads for sterling might indicate a bid-offer spread of 10.75000–10.62500 for sterling lent for a two-month period starting one month from the present and 10.87500–10.75000 for a three-month period commencing nine months from the present. The customer and the bank agree that compensation will pass between them in respect of any deviation of interest rates, on the date that the loan was due to be made, from the rates published at the time of the agreement.

For example, a corporation has a floating rate loan of £1 million and would like to be certain as to what rate of interest it will be charged on the loan for the three-month period commencing three months from the present. It might ascertain from the published bid-offer spreads that for sterling three-month loans, taken out three months from the present, the spread is 10.62500–10.50000. The corporation could attempt to guarantee what its interest rate will be by entering a FRA, thereby notionally committing itself to borrow £1 million at 10.625 per cent p.a. in three months' time. The BBA interest settlement rate is used for calculation of the compensation payment to pass between the counterparties. Suppose that the spread for this rate stood at 11.62500–11.50000 when the contract period was reached. The 1 per cent p.a. increase in rates would require the bank to pay the customer a sum equivalent to 1 per cent p.a. for three months on a £1 million loan – totalling about £2500. The money received would compensate the corporation for a rise in the rate of interest on its floating rate loan over the three-month period.

The change in the interest rate payable on a floating rate loan is likely to be equal to, or close to, the change in the BBA interest settlement rate. Had interest rates fallen, the compensation payment would have been made in the opposite direction so that the corporation would have lost on its FRA but gained from the lower rate on its floating rate loan. In either case an interest rate variation on the loan would have been offset by a gain or loss on the FRA. The corporation would have achieved its aim of removing uncertainty as to the interest payable.

The actual compensation is slightly less than £2500. This gross sum is discounted at the appropriate BBA interest settlement rate since compensation is paid at the beginning of the interest period whereas the higher interest on the floating rate loan is paid at the end of the interest period. The compensation, plus interest obtainable on it during the interest period, would equal the £25000.

The interest rate that the parties attempt to lock-in is not necessarily the current rate at the time of entering the FRA. The market may expect a change in interest rates between the present and the commencement of the interest period. That change cannot be offset by the use of FRAs. The attempt to hedge tends to guarantee that the interest rate change actually experienced is that which the market anticipated.

Example

These points may be clarified with the help of a numerical example. The example illustrates the case of a corporate borrower with a floating rate loan of £1 million on which the interest rate is reassessed on a six-monthly basis. The latest reassessment has set the interest rate at 12 per cent p.a. whilst the BBA interest settlement rate is currently 11.00000–10.87500. The treasurer wishes to hedge the risk of a rise in interest rates by the date of the next interest rate reassessment. The FRA market is currently quoting 11.50000–11.37500 for six months against twelve months (interest rates for six-month deposits made six months from the present). The company decides to hedge by buying FRAs, thereby notionally committing itself to borrow £1 million six months hence. By the beginning of the interest period the spread stands at 12.50000–12.37500 and the interest on the floating rate loan is 13½ per cent p.a.

1 February

Interest rate for February–July is set at 12 per cent p.a. and the FRA spread stands at 11.00000–10.87500. The company seeks to hedge against an interest rate increase occurring by 1 August.

Buys FRAs for six-month interest period commencing 1 August. FRA interest spread is 11.50000–11.37500.

1 August

Interest rate for August–January is set at 13½ per cent p.a.
An extra 1½ per cent must be paid, amounting to £7500 (1½ per cent on £1 million for six months).

The FRA spread stands at 12.50000–12.37500.
Compensation is receivable in respect of 1 per cent on £1 million for six months, amounting to £5000.

The borrower suffers a loss of £7500 which is offset by a £5000 FRA gain. On 1 February the FRA spread was 11.50000–11.37500 indicating that the market expected a ½ per cent rise in interest rates. The hedging operation did not protect the borrower from that ½ per cent increase but provided protection against the further 1 per cent increase that occurred. Hedging with FRAs thus provides a means of attempting to keep interest rate changes to those predicted by the market. Simultaneously, the customer insures against a rise of less than ½ per cent, since in such a situation the customer pays compensation to the bank. FRA gains and losses offset realized deviations from 12½ per cent p.a. so that the effective interest payable, net of compensation, is 12½ per cent p.a. The corporation has eliminated uncertainty about the future interest rate payable on its floating rate debt.

The removal of uncertainty would be incomplete if the interest rate charged on the loan could change by an extent different from the change in the BBA interest settlement rate. For instance, if the interest on the loan in the example had risen to 13⅝ per cent p.a. then the interest rate increase, net of compensation, would have been ⅝ per cent. The borrower would have failed to guarantee a net increase of ½ per cent. However, changes in borrowing rates are likely to be similar to BBA interest settlement rate changes so that most of the uncertainty is removed.

Closing out

An FRA need not be held until maturity, it can be closed out at any time by entering into a second FRA which is opposite to the original one. The success of hedging operations does not depend upon holding FRAs to maturity. To completely close out an FRA position the second FRA must involve the same principal amount as the first. The interest period would also be the same but the interest rate would probably be different. The published interest rate spread for the relevant future period may have changed between the date of entering into the first FRA and the date of starting the opposing one. Such a difference would lead to a compensation payment. A hedger originally buys, notionally committing himself to borrow, and closes out by selling, notionally committing himself to lend. If, for example, his notional obligation to borrow is at a lower interest rate than that at which he is notionally obliged to lend, he makes a net gain which is received in the form of a compensation payment. The compensation received upon closing out would offset the higher interest payable on the floating rate loan.

Compensation formula

The amount of money that changes hands is given by the following formula:

$$\frac{(L - R) \times D \times A}{(B \times 100) + (L \times D)} \tag{1}$$

where L = the BBA interest settlement rate, R = rate contracted, D = days in contract period, A = contract amount, B = 365 (360 in the case of currencies other than sterling). This formula can be understood by dividing it into two components:

$$\frac{(L - R)}{100} \times \frac{D}{B} \times A = \frac{(L - R) \times D \times A}{(B \times 100)} \tag{2}$$

This expression multiplies the contract amount by the difference between the two interest rates and adjusts this result to take account of the fraction of the year in the contract period.

Since compensation changes hands at the beginning of the contract period, whilst the interest difference has its impact at the end, the appropriate sum for compensation is that given by formula (2) discounted to the beginning of the period. Formula (2) is therefore multiplied by:

$$\frac{1}{1 + \dfrac{(L \times D)}{(B \times 100)}} \tag{3}$$

Formula (2) multiplied by formula (3) yields formula (1).

Case study: seasonal borrowing

A toy company has a seasonal borrowing requirement for the period July–October for the purpose of financing the stocks required to meet the pre-Christmas sales. On 15 January it uses an FRA to guarantee the interest payable on a £2 million three-month loan to be taken out on 15 July. On 15 January the rate for three-month LIBOR six-months forward is 10 per cent p.a. Anticipating a borrowing at LIBOR + 1¼ per cent the toy company thus locks-in an interest rate of 11¼ per cent p.a.

On 15 July LIBOR stands at 12 per cent p.a. The company could borrow £2 million at 13¼ per cent p.a. which involves a repayment of £2 063 191 on 15 October. However, the bank providing the FRA compensates for the deviation of LIBOR on 15 July from 10 per cent p.a. The compensation payment is 2 per cent p.a. for three months on £2 million discounted at LIBOR to reflect the fact that the compensation is paid at the beginning of the period whereas interest is payable at the end of the period. The sum paid by the bank to the toy company on 15 July is £8990. The company thus borrows £1 991 010 instead of £2 000 000. At 13¼ per cent p.a. the sum to be repaid on 15 October is £2 053 918. This is equivalent to paying 11.2275 per cent p.a. on £2 million for the three-month period. By using the FRA the toy company has locked-in an interest rate of about 11¼ per cent p.a. and has thus avoided the 2 per cent p.a. rise in interest rates.

The bank providing the FRA need not be the bank providing the loan. Indeed the FRA might be provided through a money broker rather than a bank. The cash flows under the FRA are limited to the money value of the deviation of LIBOR from the agreed future interest rate.

Interest rate forward-forward positions

It is possible to construct forward positions artificially by borrowing and lending for different maturities. For example, an organization wishing to borrow for three months with the loan being taken out three months from the present could determine the effective interest to be paid by means of a forward-forward operation. It would borrow for six months and lend for three. The net position is a three-month borrowing commencing three months hence.

The interest rate payable can be derived from the three- and six-month rates involved. Suppose that the six-month borrowing were at an annualized interest rate of 11 per cent p.a. whilst the three-month lending was at 10 per cent p.a. The six-month loan could be regarded as being comprised of a three-month loan at 10 per cent p.a. followed by another three-month loan, this time at 11.7 per cent p.a. The first three months' borrowing, at an assumed 10 per cent p.a., is offset by the three-month lending at 10 per cent p.a. The net position is a three-month borrowing at 11.7 per cent p.a., effectively commencing in three months' time.

The borrower has simulated a future loan at an interest rate which is known in the present (three months before the borrowing effectively occurs). This is equivalent to a forward loan. It has two significant drawbacks. First, high margins between interest rates paid to depositors and rates charged to borrowers could render the effective forward interest rate very high. Second, both the borrowing and the lending would appear on company balance sheets. For these reasons, it is likely that forward rate agreements or futures contracts would be more attractive means of managing short-term interest rate risk than forward-forward positions.

7 Forecasting

If foreign exchange and interest rate movements could be accurately forecast, uncertainty would be eliminated. It is therefore important for those concerned with managing risk to consider how forecasting might be attempted and its likely degree of success.

Forecasting exchange rates

Purchasing power parity

This theory is a source of longer-run predictions of exchange rate movements. It has two variants: absolute and relative. Absolute purchasing power parity suggests that the prices of tradeable goods are the same in each country when prices are adjusted by exchange rates (although factors such as transport costs would render the equality less than perfect). Relative purchasing power parity predicts that exchange rate changes are determined by differences between national inflation rates such that countries with relatively high rates of inflation experience exchange rate depreciation.

Thus, observations of relative rates of inflation, or of the underlying causes such as differences in rates of money supply growth, can be used to ascertain the direction of movement of exchange rates. However, this approach is not suitable for short-run forecasts of exchange rates. Rates can differ from those implied by purchasing power parity for several years and at any one time the actual rates are strongly influenced by short-run factors. Not surprisingly the proportion of exchange rate variability explained by purchasing power parity is greater when there are large differences between countries in the extent to which prices change between two points in time. So the usefulness of the theory is greater when inflation rates differ substantially and when longer time periods are considered since longer time periods would be associated with larger price level movements.

Numerous studies, the earliest being soon after the First World War, have tested the relative version of purchasing power parity. On the whole, the studies have shown that over long periods exchange rate variations are well explained by price level changes.

Exchange rates fluctuate around the rates suggested by purchasing power parity. At any time a currency is likely to be overvalued (relative to the rate implied by purchasing power parity) against some currencies and undervalued against others. Table 7.1 shows some calculations of the average absolute percentage deviations from purchasing power parity based upon effective exchange rates (rates that show a currency's value against a weighted basket of currencies).

Table 7.1

Average absolute percentage deviations from purchasing power parity based upon effective exchange rates

	1957–66	1957–72	1957–76
US	1.2	1.7	3.8
UK	0.5	3.1	3.8
France	2.5	3.0	3.0
W. Germany	1.3	2.1	2.7
Italy	1.2	2.3	5.8
Switzerland	0.7	1.4	5.8
Japan	1.9	2.2	3.8

Source: H. Genberg, 'Purchasing Power Parity Under Fixed and Flexible Exchange Rates', *Journal of International Economics*, Vol. 8, pp. 247–76, 1978.

Variability around the rates implied by purchasing power parity appears to have increased over time. The switch from fixed to floating exchange rates and the substantial increase in oil prices are two factors occurring in the early 1970s that would help to explain the increased variability.

The movement towards purchasing power parity may occur through exchange rate adjustments, price level changes, or both, and can take a long time. Studies have suggested that the full adjustment to purchasing power parity can take more than five years although most of the adjustment is typically achieved within two years.

Forward rates as forecasts

There is reason to believe that the forward rate corresponds to the expected rate. Speculators have expectations about the levels of future exchange rates and if forward rates differ from these expectations there is a perceived scope for speculative gains. Furthermore, the pursuit of these speculative gains would tend to move the forward rate towards the expected rate.

For example, suppose that the three-month forward rate was above the rate that was generally expected. It would be worthwhile to sell forward exchange with a view to honouring the contract by means of buying spot when the contract matures. If the expectation is correct, the currency is bought at a lower price than that at which it is sold. Conversely, a forward rate lower than the expected rate would lead speculators to buy forward in anticipation of selling at a higher price when the contract matures. In the former case the forward sales by speculators would depress the forward rate towards the expected rate whereas in the latter case their forward purchases would raise the forward rate towards the expected rate.

There is therefore reason to believe that the forward rate would tend to represent the expected rate. Forward and futures prices are frequently used as sources of price information by operators in the spot market. This use of forward and futures prices suggests that the expected rate is reflected in forward and futures rates.

It appears that forward rates are generally as likely to over-estimate as to underestimate future currency prices. The absence of any significant tendency towards overestimation or underestimation suggests that forward rates are unbiased predictors of future rates. An unbiased predictor has no net tendency towards either underestimation or overestimation but may nonetheless be typically inaccurate. Perfect accuracy of any forecast is impossible since not all circumstances that will affect an exchange rate can be foreseen. The most that can be hoped for is that the market for forward foreign exchange is efficient. An efficient market is one that utilizes all available information in the determination of prices and in which the price adjustments are made quickly. If the markets for forward currency are not efficient there may be scope for obtaining better forecasts from other sources, for example when other sources utilize all the available information.

Forecasting services

If forward exchange rates do not fully utilize all the available information then there is scope for professional exchange rate forecasters to provide more accurate forecasts by making more effective use of the available information. Also, if a forward exchange rate differed from the expected future spot rate because of a risk premium or transactions costs there would be scope for professional forecasters to provide a better prediction than that obtained by observing the forward exchange rate. In the view of many, including the present authors, any suggestion that professional forecasts tend to be more accurate than forward rates must be regarded as not proven. Indeed, if it were the case that professional forecasts were better predictors of rates because they made better use of the available information it is to be expected that the process of obtaining speculative profit would pull forward rates into line with the forecasts thereby eliminating the superiority of the forecasts.

Selective cover

Companies often use forecasts of exchange rates in deciding whether to hedge. If the forecast rate is more favourable than the forward or futures rate they may choose not to hedge. A more sophisticated variant of this approach would be to hedge a portion of an exposure with that portion being dependent upon the forecast and the confidence held in it. The more favourable is the forecast rate relative to the forward or futures rate, the smaller is the portion of the exposure hedged, and the more confidence there is in the prediction, the smaller will the hedged portion be (in the case of a forecast rate less favourable than the forward or futures rate most of the exposure would be hedged and the hedged portion would be yet higher if the forecast was held with confidence).

Incomplete hedging of positions entails risks and it is arguable that an incompletely hedged company is involved in speculation. There are gains if forecasts prove to be correct, but losses can be made if forecasts are inaccurate. Exchange rate forecasts are highly unreliable. Interest rate forecasts are probably even more so.

Forecasting interest rates

This forecasting should be based on an understanding of how interest rates are determined. Considering this matter from a UK perspective the question subdivides into two: What determines world interest rates? What causes UK rates to deviate from world rates? Since the US dollar is so dominant in the world economy, 'world' interest rates can be seen as being synonymous with 'dollar' interest rates. Figure 7.1 superimposes sterling rates on Eurodollar rates and thereby suggests that the analysis of interest rate movements should emphasize the determination of dollar rates since there is an apparent tendency for sterling rates to follow the pattern set by the dollar rates.

The principle of interest rate parity suggests that sterling rates should bear a close relationship to dollar rates. According to this principle, interest rates around the world would tend to be equal when account is taken of expected exchange rate movements. Arbitrage, the process whereby money moves between financial centres in search of the highest return, brings interest rates into line. If sterling rates exceed dollar rates, money flows from dollar deposits to sterling and this lowers the return on sterling deposits relative to dollar returns. The qualification that account is taken of expected exchange rate movements is an important one.

If sterling is expected to depreciate against the dollar, sterling interest rates must exceed dollar rates by a margin sufficient to compensate for the anticipated exchange rate loss from holding sterling. For example, if sterling is expected to depreciate at 4 per cent p.a. against the US dollar the rate of interest on sterling deposits must be 4 per cent p.a. higher to compensate. In this way, expected returns on different currencies are equalized. Referring again to Figure 7.1 the tendency for sterling interest rates to exceed dollar rates prior to mid-1977 might be explained in terms of expectations of sterling depreciation. The mid 1970s was a period of persistent sterling weakness.

An interest rate can be looked upon as a price payable for loanable funds. Potential borrowers provide the demand for loans, and lenders the supply. Interaction of demand and supply determines the price (the interest rate). If borrowers outweigh lenders, interest rates will be bid up, conversely an excess supply of loanable funds leads to a fall in rates.

Government economic policy is an important factor in the determination of interest rates. A tight monetary policy will restrict the flow of funds to the banking system and hence limit the loans made available by it. This limitation on the supply of credit will force up interest rates. Fiscal policy is also important. An excess of government spending over revenues means that the government must enter the market to compete for loans with private borrowers. The government's demands for funds can add considerably to the pressure on interest rates.

Referring again to Figure 7.1 it can be seen that dollar interest rates have been higher in the 1980s than in the 1970s. A major explanation for this arises from the economic policies of the US government. A tight monetary policy has restricted the supply of loans from the banking system whilst the very large government budget deficit has involved the US government adding considerably to the demand for loanable funds.

The expected rate of inflation is one factor affecting the interest rate at which borrowers and lenders will transact. When inflation is expected, potential lenders will seek compensation for the anticipated erosion of the purchasing power of their assets and will correspondingly require higher interest rates. Borrowers, in anticipation of liabilities being eroded by inflation, may be prepared to pay higher rates. Thus the interest rate incorporates compensation for expected inflation. Falling inflation is probably the main reason for falling interest rates, throughout the world, in the mid 1980s.

Whilst US dollar interest rates probably constitute the main influence on sterling rates there are nevertheless UK specific factors that affect the extent of deviation of sterling rates from dollar rates. The tight monetary policy of the UK government would have contributed to the high rates experienced around 1980. British governments have also used interest rates for the purpose

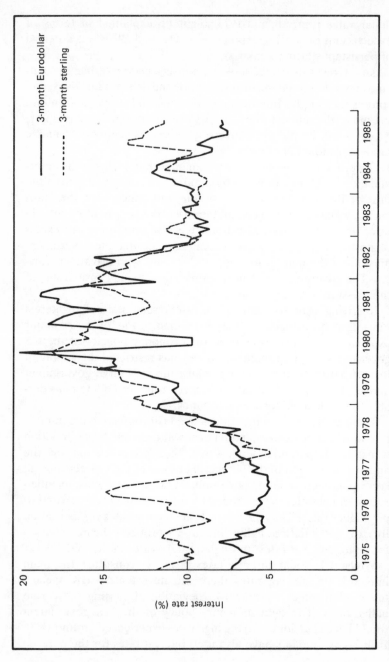

Figure 7.1 Comparison of sterling and Eurodollar interest rate movements (1975–85)

3-month Eurodollar
3-month sterling

Interest rate (%)

of exchange rate policy. The peaking of rates in the latter part of 1976 was aimed at supporting sterling in the face of considerable downward pressure on the pound in the international money markets. Conversely, the fall during 1981 might be explained in terms of attempts to dampen sterling's sharp appreciation against other currencies.

8 Currency futures

Financial futures markets emerged in response to a demand for instruments suitable for hedging and this should be regarded as their prime purpose. However, hedgers are not the only operators on the financial futures markets. Speculators and arbitrageurs also participate and, as will be explained later, are essential to the efficient operation of the markets.

The nature of financial futures

A financial futures contract provides a simultaneous right and obligation to buy or sell on a specific future date on terms agreed in the present. Currency futures involve future exchanges of currencies at rates of exchange determined at the time of entering the contracts.

These commitments are tradeable. For instance, a company that buys a contract that gives it the right and obligation to buy a particular amount of currency on a specified future date at an exchange rate determined in the present can subsequently close out that contract. It is desirable that the markets in such contracts are liquid so as to ensure easy trading conditions. Financial futures contracts are highly standardized so that there are sufficient quantities of each contract to provide liquid markets. The contracts traded on the London International Financial Futures Exchange (LIFFE, pronounced 'life') have just four maturity dates each year, these being in March, June, September and December.

The contract sizes are also standard, for example £25 000 for sterling currency contracts. This standardization limits the number of different contracts available and correspondingly increases the volume traded in each case.

The London International Financial Futures Exchange

LIFFE has operated since September 1982. It was not the first financial futures exchange, a number having previously been established with Chicago leading the way about a decade earlier. London was the first European city to obtain such an exchange and many would argue that such an innovation was necessary for the maintenance of London's role as a leading financial centre.

The currency futures traded on LIFFE involve sterling, Deutschmarks, yen and Swiss francs, each being traded against the US dollar.

Users of LIFFE must operate through a member. The members of LIFFE include banks, discount houses, money brokers, and stockbrokers. There are foreign as well as British members. The Bank of England exercises surveillance over the general conduct of LIFFE whilst the Board of the Exchange has responsibility for the day-to-day supervision of the exchange and its members.

The International Commodities Clearing House Limited (ICCH) is important to the operation of the exchange. ICCH is an independent clearing house owned by major UK banks. ICCH performs two crucial functions. One of these functions is the registration and confirmation of all transactions on the market each day, thus providing an up-to-date record of the current futures positions taken by members.

The other function is to become the counterparty to every futures position. Once two members have traded futures contracts with each other, ICCH substitutes itself for both counterparties. This eliminates the possibility of a holder of a contract suffering from default by the counterparty. Thus, buyers and sellers of contracts do not need to assess the creditworthiness of the other party to the deal. This allows the open outcry system to operate. Open outcry means that trades are solicited and agreed by means of dealers shouting and using hand signals. This apparently chaotic process takes place in areas of the exchange known as pits.

How customers execute transactions

A customer needs to open a futures trading account with a member of LIFFE. The choice of member to use as the broker is important. Brokers will vary considerably in terms of their financial requirements and the extent of the service provided. The customer places an order with a registered representative of a member firm. Once the member has checked that the order is acceptable the order will be confirmed to the customer orally. It is subsequently confirmed in writing, normally with a time stamp. As soon as the order is made, and found acceptable, it is transmitted to the member's booth on the floor of the exchange. Details are then written on a standard order slip, which is time-stamped. A copy of the slip is taken to a dealer in the pit whereupon the order is executed. Upon execution of the order, details of the trade are entered on the slip which is sent back to the booth. An official exchange clearing slip will be completed giving details of the transaction. Simultaneously, details of the transaction are communicated to the member, who informs the customer.

Hedging currency risk

The sterling futures will be discussed in this section since the volume of sterling futures contracts traded has been by far the largest amongst the currency futures.

Fluctuations in exchange rates produce risk. For example, suppose a British exporter sells goods to a US importer and the transaction is priced in US dollars. The British exporter is thus due to receive a sum of US dollars some time after the transaction is agreed upon. The exporter is then exposed to foreign exchange risk. A fall in the value of the US dollar relative to the pound sterling would reduce the sterling value of the receipts. This would reduce the profitability of the exports, and perhaps even render them loss-making. If the exporter wishes to avoid such a risk he could hedge. By hedging with financial futures he seeks to guarantee the rate of exchange at which he will buy the sterling. He wants to know in advance how much he will receive in terms of sterling. The guaranteed exchange rate might be less favourable than the current rate, but at least he is free of the risk that it might be so unfavourable as to render the sale unprofitable.

A hedger transfers his risk. If he buys futures someone else must sell them, that is his acquisition of the simultaneous right and obligation to buy currency on a specified date in the future at a price agreed upon in the present is matched by another user's right and obligation to sell that currency at that date and price. In the above example the risk that the US dollar may fall in value is transferred to the seller of sterling futures. If the dollar does fall this seller finds that he has committed himself to selling at a price that is lower than the spot rate available at the time that the currency actually changes hands. The seller of sterling futures would either be a hedger wanting to avoid the opposite risk, that is a rise in the US dollar relative to sterling, or be a speculator willing to take on the risk in the expectation of making a profit.

If neither of the hedgers had undertaken the futures transaction then one would have made a windfall loss and the other a windfall gain (unless, of course, the exchange rate remained unchanged). By locking-in the current exchange rate the two parties ensure that neither gains nor loses. One avoids a windfall loss whilst the other foregoes a windfall gain. The essential point is that both have reduced the risk that the exchange rate might move to their disadvantage. (If the exchange rate at which futures are traded differs from the current rate then the buying or selling of futures is in order to guarantee a particular exchange rate gain or loss. The fact remains that the uncertainty as to what exchange rate will be received has been reduced, insurance against unforeseen exchange rate movements has been obtained.)

It is likely that the value of the hedging required for one direction of exchange rate change is not perfectly matched by the amount of hedging required for the possibility of the opposite change. For example, transactors wishing to avoid losses from a rise in sterling against the US dollar may not find sufficient hedgers wanting to avoid the risk of a fall in the value of sterling. This is where speculators fulfil the function of making the market. Speculators buy and sell futures in anticipation of making profits. If the futures price is above what they expect it to become they will sell futures since they anticipate the opportunity of subsequently buying at a lower price. A futures price below their expectation would lead them to buy futures in the anticipation of being able to sell at a higher price later.

Such activities by speculators ensure that hedgers will be able to carry out their transactions. For example, suppose that hedgers want to sell more sterling futures than they want to buy. This will marginally reduce the futures price. The fall in the futures price will entice speculators to buy. Hence, speculators will take up the excess supply of sterling futures and thereby enable all exporters and importers to carry out their required hedging operations. By behaving in this way speculators render the futures market liquid, they ensure that desires to buy and sell futures can be realized. Speculators are often looked upon as unproductive and destabilizing. The above analysis indicates that, on the contrary, they serve a useful purpose. By making the market for futures liquid they allow exporters and importers to hedge.

Closing out

Hedgers do not need to hold contracts until maturity. They may close out contracts prior to maturity whilst still having successfully hedged their risks. Suppose that the British exporter anticipated the receipt of US dollars four months hence and wanted to hedge against the possibility of a fall in the value of the dollar in terms of sterling. He could buy six-months sterling futures rather than four-months futures. Indeed, since futures contracts relate to a small number of specific maturity dates in a year it is unlikely that a futures maturity date coincides with the date on which the dollars are to be received. For example, on 10 March the exporter may anticipate dollar receipts on 10 July and hedge by buying September sterling futures. If a rise in the value of sterling, in terms of the US dollar, by 10 July is matched by a rise in the price of September sterling futures then the hedge would be successful. The hedger could sell September futures on 10 July at a higher price than he bought them for in March. If he does so he will have made a profit from the purchase and subsequent sale of futures, a profit which is just enough to offset the loss on the US dollar receivables resulting from the exchange rate change. The hedger, by selling September futures in July, has closed out (that is, cancelled out) his long position in sterling futures. ICCH, being the counterparty to both the long and short positions, deems them to negate each other leaving the hedger with no outstanding position in futures arising from these contracts.

Basis

The manoeuvre in the above example will precisely offset the loss on the dollar receivables only if September futures prices move to exactly the same extent as spot prices. The price difference between the futures instrument and the cash instrument being hedged is known as basis. If September sterling futures have the same price, in terms of dollars, as spot sterling, basis is said to be zero. If basis were zero on 10 March and also on 10 July the futures prices would have moved precisely in line with spot prices and the hedge would have been perfect. However, if on 10 July the September futures had not risen to the same extent as spot sterling the profit on the futures transactions would have been insufficient to completely offset the loss on the dollar receipts. There would have been a change in basis. September futures prices would have risen less than spot prices and this change in basis would have rendered the hedge incomplete. The possibility of a change in basis is known as basis risk. Changes in basis may operate either to the hedger's advantage or against it. A hedger could be said to have substituted basis risk for the outright risk from an open (that is unhedged) position in foreign currency. Generally, basis risk is considerably less than outright risk.

Ticks

A tick is the smallest change in the price of a futures contract permitted by LIFFE. Each tick has a specific money value which is $2.50 for sterling and $12.50 for the other currencies. The face value of the sterling contract is £25 000. This means that sterling currency futures are traded in blocks of £25 000 each. The tick size is $0.0001 per £1 giving the value of $2.50 (0.0001 × 25 000 = 2.50). In the case of Deutschmark currency futures the face value of a contract is DM125 000 and the tick size $0.0001 per 1DM. This yields a tick value of $12.50 (0.0001 × 125 000).

Examples

The points covered thus far may be clarified by means of hypothetical examples. No example is given for the relatively straightforward case in which the hedger holds a contract until maturity and then takes delivery of, and parts with, currency. The two examples deal instead with the more complex, and far more frequent, procedure which involves the hedger closing out contracts before they reach maturity.

Example 1

A British exporter anticipates receipt of $1 million, on 1 May. The sale of goods is agreed upon on 3 February and the exporter wants to hedge against the risk that the dollar will depreciate against the pound before 1 May thus reducing the sterling value of the dollar receipts. The exporter might actually anticipate a fall in the dollar or may simply want to insure against the possibility of a weakening of the dollar. In either case the exporter could hedge by buying sterling futures.

Cash market	Futures market
3 February	
Exporter anticipates receipt of $1 million on 1 May. The spot exchange rate is £1 = $1.50 ($1 million = £666 666).	Buys 26 June sterling futures contracts, at £25 000 per contract, at an exchange rate of £1 = $1.50. Total value is £650 000 committing the exporter to a payment of $975 000 if the contract is held to maturity.
1 May	
The dollar has fallen so that the exchange rate stands at £1 = $1.60. The sterling value of the $1 million is now £625 000.	Sells 26 June contracts at £1 = $1.60. This gives the exporter the right to the receipt of $1 040 000 (650 000 × 1.60) upon maturity of the contracts.
Loss is £666 666 − £625 000 = £41 666 ($66 666).	Gain is $65 000.

The loss in the cash market, arising from the weakening of the dollar, is largely offset by the gain in the futures market. The offset is not perfect since the £666 666 in the cash market is coupled with only £650 000 in the futures market. Such a mismatch arises from the denomination of sterling futures contracts in units of £25 000 – perfect matching is impossible. Fortunately there is no change in basis. The exchange rate in the futures market moves in line with that in the cash market, and is indeed equal to it. The exchange rate for futures need not be equal to, nor move to the same extent as, the spot exchange rate. If the spot and futures rates change by different amounts there is a change in basis and a degree of imperfection enters the hedge. This possibility is illustrated in Example 2.

Example 2

This example differs from Example 1 only in the assumption that the rate of exchange for the June sterling futures moves to £1 = $1.58 rather than £1 = £1.60. Basis thus changes from zero to $0.02. As a result the hedge is imperfect.

Cash market	Futures market
3 February	
Exporter anticipates receipt of $1 million on 1 May. The spot exchange rate is £1 = $1.50 ($1 million = £666 666).	Buys 26 June sterling futures contracts, at £25 000 per contract, at an exchange rate of £1 = $1.50. $975 000 is due to be paid upon maturity.
1 May	
The dollar has fallen so that the exchange rate stands at £1 = $1.60. The sterling value of the $1 million is now £625 000.	Sells 26 June contracts at £1 = $1.58. This would yield $1 027 000 (650 000 × 1.58) upon maturity.
Loss is £666 666 − £625 000 = £41 666 ($66 666).	Gain is $52 000.

The change in basis results in a net loss of $14 666 ($66 666 − $52 000). The hedge is only partially successful. The hedger replaces outright risk with basis risk and consequently replaces a loss of $66 666 with a loss of $14 666.

Margins

ICCH seeks to avoid the risk of default by holders of contracts. It does this by means of margin requirements. When taking out a contract, whether as a buyer or a seller, it is necessary to deposit a sum of money with ICCH. This money is known as initial margin. It is returned to the contract holder when the contract matures or is closed out. If money is deposited it earns interest. Alternatively, other assets may be used as security, for example government stock may be lodged with the ICCH but will continue to earn interest for the contract holder. Bank guarantees are also acceptable. In the case of currency futures, initial margin is $1000 per contract. If prices move to the disadvantage of a transactor, such that closing out would involve a loss, the variation margin must be paid to the value of the loss. In this way the contract holder must ensure that, after every business day, the margin account balance is at least equal to the initial margin. Price movements in a contract holder's favour lead to gains that are credited to the margin account and can be withdrawn from that account. Should a contract holder be unable to pay the requisite variation margin, the ICCH has the right to close out his position. Outstanding losses will then be made good from the initial margin. Initial margin is set at a level which is very unlikely to be exceeded by the loss arising from the price movement of one day. In this way ICCH seeks to ensure that it will not make financial losses through the default of contract holders.

ICCH requires the members of LIFFE with which it deals to observe these margin requirements and stipulates that the members should impose conditions that are at least as strict on their customers. However, the process of revaluing all contracts on daily closing prices and paying or receiving variation margin payments, known as marking to market, would be administratively inconvenient for most customers. To avoid such inconvenience the customer could set up a futures margin account making use of the maintenance margin system. This is effectively a bank deposit with a minimum balance called the maintenance balance. The account is automatically debited or credited on a daily basis in respect of variation margin, initial margin, commissions, and any other resulting cash flows. The customer makes no payments unless the balance falls below the maintenance balance, in which case the customer is required to top up the account so as to restore the initial balance.

Interest rate parity

As with forwards it is to be expected that the relationship between spot and futures prices reflects the differential between the interest rates on the two currencies concerned. For example, if sterling interest rates exceed US dollar interest rates (on the Eurocurrency markets) by 2 per cent p.a. the price of sterling futures should show a 2 per cent p.a. rate of depreciation of sterling against the dollar. Thus if the spot value of sterling is £1 = $1.50 the futures price for a delivery date six months hence should be £1 = $1.485, representing a 1 per cent depreciation over six months.

The exchange rate that a hedger obtains will lie between the spot rate and the futures rate and will be dependent upon the timing of closing out. If the futures position is closed out immediately after being opened, the exchange rate obtained would be the spot rate, that is £1 = $1.50. If the contract was held to maturity, the rate obtained would be the futures rate ruling on the date of entering the contract, that is £1 = $1.485. Closing out on an intermediate date would attain an exchange rate between these two extremes, as indicated by Figure 8.1. The exchange rate obtained is a linear function of time. For example, if the futures contract is agreed at time t and closed out after four months the exchange rate obtained would be £1 = $1.49.

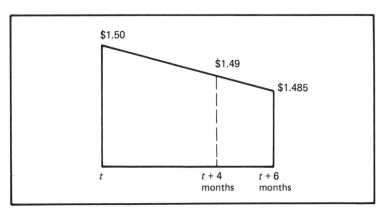

Figure 8.1   Guaranteed exchange rate as a function of time

The variation of the realized exchange rate with the passage of time can be explained in terms of changes in basis. Basis is initially $0.015 ($1.50 − $1.485) but after six months it will have eroded to zero – at maturity of a contract the futures and spot prices are identical. The difference between the spot and futures prices can be regarded as the rate of depreciation/appreciation required to offset the interest rate differential. As the time period shortens, the cash value of the interest rate differential falls proportionately and the corresponding depreciation/appreciation declines to match. Therefore, with just two months to maturity the cash value of a 2 per cent p.a. interest rate differential is one-third of its level when six months remained, and, correspondingly, the depreciation prior to maturity is $0.005 rather than the original $0.015.

As shown earlier in Example 2, a change in basis renders a hedge imperfect. Figure 8.1 shows that basis changes over time, beginning at $0.015 and declining to zero. This change in basis renders hedging imperfect, and the greater the period of time that elapses the more imperfect is the hedge. A contract that is closed out very quickly would entail little change in basis and the hedge would be nearly perfect – the exchange rate guaranteed would be very close to the spot rate when the contract was agreed. The more time that elapses before closing out, the greater is the change in basis and the larger is the divergence between the realized exchange rate and the spot rate ruling when the contract was entered into, as is illustrated by Figure 8.1.

The foregoing might give the impression that if hedgers know the date upon which the futures position will be closed out they know by how much basis will have changed and can take this into account when designing the hedging strategy. Indeed, a hedger might take such predictable changes in basis into account by adjusting the number of contracts so as to produce a futures gain sufficient to render the realized exchange rate equal to the initial spot rate of £1 = $1.50. However, basis would be deflected from the path suggested by Figure 8.1 if the interest rate differential were to change. For example, if at the date $t + 4$ months the interest rate differential had doubled to 4 per cent p.a. then the basis would be $0.01 rather than $0.005. Therefore, if basis risk were to be defined in terms of the possibility of unexpected (that is, excluding the predictable element) changes in basis it can be seen to emanate from the possibility of changes in the interest rate differential between the two currencies concerned.

Case study: an importing subsidiary

An American corporation manufacturing agricultural vehicles has a subsidiary in the UK. In addition to production of vehicles, the UK subsidiary has responsibility for the British sales of equipment produced by the parent company in the US. In order to avoid currency risk the parent requires the receipt of proceeds in US dollars. For a particular vehicle the parent requires $70 000 from the subsidiary for each one sold in the UK. At an exchange rate of £1 = $1.40 this implies a sterling price of £50 000, which is the list price in the UK. The UK subsidiary sells an average of four of these imported vehicles each month with the number rarely falling below two.

In the middle of March the dollar weakens to £1 = $1.50 and the June futures price follows suit. The cost of $70 000 is now £46 667, and this cost can be guaranteed into June by selling sterling currency futures. Believing that it is highly unlikely that less than six vehicles will be sold between the middle of March and the middle of June the treasurer of the UK subsidiary sells 12 June sterling currency futures contracts. As each vehicle is sold the treasurer closes out two futures contracts. The futures contracts insure against any deviation of the exchange rate from £1 = $1.50.

The subsidiary thus makes a profit of $5000 or £3333 on each imported vehicle sold. On the basis of six vehicles this amounts to $30 000 or £20 000 over the three-month period.

This is an example of an importing subsidiary profiting from a discrepancy between the intra-company exchange rate (£1 = $1.40) on the one hand and the spot and futures prices on the other. Importing subsidiaries can often profit by using the futures or forward markets in the event of such exchange rate discrepancies.

Appendix

Currency contract specifications on LIFFE

Unit of trading	£25 000	DM125 000	SF125 000	Y12 500 000
Delivery months	All currencies – March, June, September, December			
Delivery day	All currencies – third Wednesday of delivery month			
Quotation	US$ per £1	US$ per 1DM	US$ 1SF	US$ per 100 Yen
Tick size and value	0.01 cents per £1 ($2.50)	0.01 cents per 1DM ($12.50)	0.01 cents per 1SF ($12.50)	0.01 cents per 100 Yen ($12.50)
Initial margin	All currencies – $1000			
Contract standard	Currencies will be deliverable in the principal financial centres in the country of issue			

Unit of trading	US$50 000
Delivery months	March, June, September, December
Delivery day	Third Wednesday of delivery month
Quotation	DM per US$1
Tick size and value	DM0.0001 per US$1 (DM 5.00)
Initial margin	DM 2500
Contract standard	Currencies will be deliverable in the principal financial centres in the country of issue

Note: Specifications are subject to revision by LIFFE

9 Short-term interest rate futures

The basic principle of hedging with financial futures is that a futures position should be taken such that the feared interest rate change causes a gain on futures that compensates for the loss incurred on the assets or liabilities. Three-month sterling and three-month Eurodollar futures contracts are notional commitments to borrow or lend for three months on specified future dates at interest rates agreed upon at the time of undertaking the contracts. Futures interest rate movements tend to shadow the actual movements so an organization fearing, for example, a rise in interest rates should take up a futures position that would provide a gain from rising interest rates.

Both potential lenders and potential borrowers might find hedging desirable. Consider, for example, a company that anticipates receipts of £10 000 000 two months hence and intends to lend this money. The company treasurer might expect that interest rates will fall over the next two months and would like a means of ensuring that present interest rates, rather than those he expects to be available in two months' time, will be obtained on the proposed deposit. Alternatively, he may simply want to avoid the risk that interest rates might fall. Either way he wants to hedge, that is insure himself against the possibility of a fall in interest rates. On the other hand, a potential borrower could be worried about the possibility of an increase in interest rates by the time that he actually takes out the loan. He will want to avoid such a rise in interest rates, in other words he desires to hedge against the possibility that interest rates will increase.

Buying a financial futures contract simultaneously provides both the right and the obligation to buy the relevant financial instrument on a specified date in the future. Buying a June three-month Eurodollar time deposit contract notionally commits the buyer to the deposit of Eurodollars, for three months from the second Wednesday in June, at an interest rate determined in the present. The seller is simultaneously notionally committed to accepting the deposit for that period and to guaranteeing that interest rate.

Example 1

Cash market	Futures market
2 January	
Treasurer intends to borrow £500 000 on 1 February. Fears that interest rate will rise above the current 10 per cent p.a.	Sells a futures contract thereby notionally guaranteeing that £500 000 will be borrowed at 10 per cent p.a. on a future date.
1 February	
Borrows £500 000 at an interest rate of 12 per cent p.a.	Buys a futures contract thereby entering a notional commitment to lend £500 000 at 12 per cent p.a.

For the three months commencing 1 February the interest cost on the loan would be £2500 more than would have been the case had the interest rate remained at 10 per cent p.a. However, there is an offsetting gain from the futures position. For a future three-month period the hedger is committed to lending at 12 per cent p.a. and borrowing at 10 per cent p.a. This provides a gain equal to 2 per cent p.a. on £500 000 for three months, namely £2500.

There is no longer any depositing of money on the maturity date. Instead a cash settlement occurs whereby money changes hands between buyer and seller to the amount necessary to offset deviations of the actual interest rate on that date from the one agreed in the futures contracts. As with other futures contracts the vast majority of short-term interest rate futures contracts are closed out prior to the maturity date. By the time that closing out occurs the hedger should have received, or paid, variation margin adequate to offset movements in the interest rate. For example, a potential borrower having to pay more because of increased interest rates should have received, at or prior to maturity, a sum of money to compensate for the higher interest payments.

The pricing of short-term interest rate futures contracts

Short-term interest rate futures contracts on the London International Financial Futures Exchange (LIFFE) are quoted on an index basis. The index is equal to 100 minus the annualized interest rate; for example a three-month interest rate of 3 per cent giving an annualized rate of 12 per cent would mean that the contract would be priced at 88. It is to be emphasized that such prices are merely indices that are used in ascertaining gains and losses from futures trading and do not represent the money payable for contracts.

A tick is the smallest price movement recognized and recorded by LIFFE. In the case of short-term interest rate contracts it is 0.0025 per cent of the face value of a contract. The Eurodollar contracts each have a face value of $1 000 000 and so the value of a tick is $25, and three-month sterling deposit futures contracts are in units of £500 000 with a tick of £12.50. In terms of the pricing system outlined above, each tick is depicted by 0.01. Therefore a price change from 88 to 88.05 represents an increase of 5 ticks, amounting to $125 or £62.50. The difference between the 0.0025 per cent and the 0.01 arises because the index used for pricing is based on annualized interest rates whereas the interest actually payable is a quarterly one, so the annual interest rate must be divided by four. These points may be clarified by means of Example 2.

Example 2

A hedger buys, in December, a June three-month Eurodollar deposit contract at a price of 90 (annualized interest rate of 10 per cent). The following day the price rises by one tick to 90.01 (annualized interest rate of 9.99 per cent). Upon buying the contract the hedger guaranteed the receipt of 2.5 per cent over three months from the third Tuesday in June on a Eurodollar deposit of $1 000 000. A contract bought a day later would have guaranteed merely 2.4975 per cent (9.99 divided by 4). Thus the hedger has guaranteed the receipt of $25 000 whereas one day later he would have guaranteed only $24 975. On the day following his purchase he could close out his position by selling a contract and receive the value of one tick, $25, as his gain. In the absence of closing out, the $25 would be paid to him as variation margin.

Example 1 can now be rewritten using the pricing convention outlined above.

Cash market	Futures market
2 January	
Treasurer intends to borrow £500 000 on 1 February. Fears that interest rate will rise above the current 10 per cent p.a.	Sells a March three-month sterling deposit futures contract at a price of 90.
1 February	
Borrows £500 000 at an interest rate of 12 per cent p.a.	Closes out by buying a March three-month sterling deposit futures contract at a price of 88.
Loss is 2 per cent p.a. on £500 000 for three months, £2500.	Gain is 200 ticks at £12.50 per tick, £2500.

The transactions on the futures market have provided a perfect hedge to the cash market transaction. The cash market loss is precisely offset. The possibility that futures interest rates might change by different amounts than cash market interest rates produces basis risk. Such incomplete matching of interest rate changes can render hedging imperfect. This is illustrated by Example 3 which differs from Example 1 in that the futures interest rate rises by less than the cash market interest rate.

Example 3

Cash market	Futures market
2 January	
Treasurer intends to borrow	Sells a March three-month ster-

£500 000 on 1 February. Fears that interest rate will rise above the current 10 per cent p.a.

ling deposit futures contract at a price of 90.

1 February
Borrows £500 000 at an interest rate of 12 per cent p.a.

Closes out by buying a March three-month sterling deposit futures contract at a price of 88.50.

Loss is 2 per cent p.a. on £500 000 for three months, £2500.

Gain is 150 ticks at £12.50 per tick, £1875.

Basis has changed from zero (90 − 90) to −0.5 (88.00 − 88.5) and as a consequence the gain on futures trading is insufficient to completely offset the loss from cash market transactions – the hedge is imperfect. If basis had changed such that futures interest rates were greater than cash market rates the gain from futures trading would of course have been more than that required to offset the cash market loss.

Basis risk will be greater in the case of cross-hedging. Cross-hedging involves hedging a cash market position in one financial instrument with a futures market position in a different financial instrument. For example, if a cash position in American T-Bills were hedged by a futures position in Eurodollar deposits the basis risk would be greater than in the case of hedging cash market Eurodollar deposits with futures Eurodollar deposits. Cross-hedging that takes the form of using three-month deposit futures to hedge risk on instruments of different terms, for example six-month deposits, requires an appropriate adjustment in the number of futures contracts bought or sold. In the example of the six-month deposits, losses from a particular interest rate change would be twice as great as those suffered on three-month deposits. Correspondingly about twice as many futures contracts would be required for the hedging.

Case study – the use of futures by a local authority

A local authority has a £5 million loan at LIBOR plus $^{1}/_{4}$ per cent with six-month rollovers and faces a rate fixing on 2 April.

On 5 February LIBOR is 10½ per cent p.a. The local authority is concerned about the possibility that interest rates might have risen by 2 April.

A regression of changes in six-month LIBOR on changes in the rate implied by the three-month sterling interest rate futures gives a coefficient of 0.96. This suggests that the longer rate is subject to only 96 per cent of the variability of the shorter rate, so a correspondingly reduced number of contracts is required to hedge the six-month LIBOR risk.

The futures contract which is the first to mature after 2 April is the June contract. The appropriate number of June contracts is

$$\frac{£5\,000\,000}{£500\,000} \times \frac{6\,\text{months}}{3\,\text{months}} \times 0.96 = 19.2$$

The local authority decides to hedge by selling 19 June contracts, the current price of which is 89.10. By 2 April six-month LIBOR has risen to 11¼ per cent p.a. adding £18 750 to the cost of financing the debt over the 2 April to 2 October period. On 2 April the authority treasurer closes out by buying 19 June futures contracts at the new price of 88.33. There is a profit of 77 ticks per contract at £12.50 per tick:

$$77 \times 19 \times £12.50 = £18\,287.50$$

There is a net loss of £462.50 equivalent to an interest rate rise from 10.5 to 10.52 per cent p.a.

The hedge imperfection arises because 19 contracts do not completely cover the exposure, particularly since the realized coefficient between the rate changes of 0.974 implies that 19.48 contracts would have been needed for a complete hedge. The indivisible nature of futures contracts renders the avoidance of such hedge imperfection impossible.

The determination of futures prices

The prices of short-term interest rate futures are determined, for the nearer maturities at least, by arbitrage based on forward/forward calculations. For example, suppose that the three-month interest rate is 14 per cent p.a. whilst the six-month rate is 15 per cent p.a. A trader could borrow for three months and lend for six and thereby guarantee a profit from the 1 per cent margin during the first three months. However, he is at risk from a rise in the three-month interest rate by the commencement of the second three-month period. There is a three-month rate for the second period above which the loss on the second period will push the whole exercise into a loss. That is the forward/forward rate. Suppose that the trader lends £1 million for six months at 15 per cent p.a. and borrows it for three months at 14 per cent p.a. He will receive £1 075 000 at the end of the six-month period. Meanwhile he must pay £1 035 000 at the end of the first three months and must borrow £1 035 000 in order to repay the debt. A £40 000 interest payment on this second loan would mean that the trader breaks-even on the exercise, since the second debt could be repaid with the £1 075 000 from the £1 million originally lent. On a three-month loan of £1 035 000, £40 000 corresponds to a rate of interest of 15.46 per cent p.a.

This is the forward/forward rate and arbitrage would tend to ensure that the futures rate would approximate closely to it. If the futures rate were significantly below the forward/forward rate arbitrageurs would lend long and borrow short using the futures market to guarantee future short-term interest rates. This would involve selling futures (commitments to future borrowing) and the increased sales would push down their prices. The fall in futures prices corresponds to a rise in futures interest rates which move up and eliminate the gains from the arbitrage activity.

In the foregoing example, futures prices stood at a discount to cash prices. This is generally the case with upward sloping yield curves (longer-term interest rates higher than shorter-term ones). Downward sloping yield curves would involve futures prices standing at a premium to cash prices. This changeover occurs while the yield curve is still slightly upward sloping. A horizontal yield curve produces futures prices that are at a small premium to cash prices.

It follows that changes in the slope of the yield curve alter basis and are thus a source of basis risk. Example 4 illustrates a situation in which futures prices move from being at a premium to being at a discount with respect to cash prices (futures interest rates move from being lower to being higher than spot three-month rates).

Example 4

Cash market	Futures market
10 February	
Company plans to deposit $10 000 000 on 10 April. Current rate of interest on three-month Eurodollar deposits is 10 per cent p.a.	Buys 10 June three-month Eurodollar deposit futures contracts at a price of 90.5.
10 April	
Company deposits $10 000 000 at an interest rate of 9 per cent p.a.	Sells 10 June three-month Eurodollar deposit futures contracts at a price of 90.5.
Loss equals 1 per cent on $10 000 000 for three months = $25 000 (0.01 × 10 000 000 × 0.25).	There is no gain since the price is unchanged at 90.5.

In this example, basis changes by one percentage point. From a cash market interest rate 0.5 per cent above the futures rate there is a change to a cash market rate 0.5 per cent below the futures rate. As a result the overall loss is $25 000 – the attempt to hedge fails completely. Indeed, a fall in the futures price would have rendered the effects of the hedging attempt perverse (for example, a fall in the futures price to 90 on 10 April would have added a $12 500 futures loss to the $25 000 cash market loss).

It is worth bearing in mind that basis always reaches zero at maturity. This observation can influence the choice of maturity date when buying or selling futures contracts. If basis is close to zero at the time of buying or selling, then seeking the nearest possible maturity date would make sense. Maturity dates should fall after the date on which the risk to be hedged disappears (that is, the date on which a deposit is made or loan taken out) otherwise there would be a period during which hedging is absent. Using the earliest possible maturity date after the disappearance of the risk increases the probability that basis will be close to zero when the contract is closed out. If basis were close to zero when the contract was bought or sold then this procedure would minimize the likelihood of basis changing between entering and closing out contracts. In any event, the tendency for basis to converge towards zero as a contract approaches maturity implies that the closer a contract is to its maturity date the less susceptible it is to changes in basis arising from yield curve movements. For this reason it is advisable to choose futures contracts that mature early after the risk being hedged has passed.

It should be emphasized that cash and futures prices typically do exhibit reasonably close correlation so that basis risk tends to be much less than the outright risk of unhedged positions (so long as the instrument being hedged is not very different to the futures instrument).

Case study: hedging a Euronote

A corporate treasurer has issued a Euronote facility for US$50 million at a rate of LIBOR plus ¼ per cent with semi-annual rollovers on 15 June and 15 December. It is 15 March and current Eurodollar rates are:

3 month   6⅞–7
9 month   6⅞–7

whilst Eurodollar futures prices are:

June   93.20
September   93.10

The treasurer wants to hedge against the possibility of interest rates having risen by the June rollover date. The choice is between a forward/forward position and a futures strategy.

From the forward/forward expression

$$(1.06875)^{0.25} (x)^{0.5} = (1.07)^{0.75}$$

it is ascertained that $x = 1.070625$ which implies an annualized rate of interest of 7.0625 per cent, that is 7⅟₁₆ per cent. This is the forward/forward rate for 15 June–15 December.

Using the futures rates the expression

$$(1.068)^{0.25} (1.069)^{0.25} = (x)^{0.5}$$

yields $x = 1.0685$ implying an annualized interest rate of 6.85 per cent.

The treasurer thus ascertains that he can guarantee a lower interest rate with futures than with a forward/forward position.

Speculation

Risk may be transferred to a speculator rather than to another hedger. The speculator will accept the risk in the hope of making a profit. A speculator who believes that interest rates will probably rise would be prepared to sell futures in the anticipation of being able to buy at a lower price when interest rates have risen. If, for example, there is insufficient demand by hedgers for December three-month Eurodollar futures contracts then some of the would-be sellers could find themselves unable to carry out the futures transactions required for hedging. The excess supply would cause a fall (probably marginal) in the futures prices. Futures interest rates would increase. Such a rise in interest rates would cause some speculators to expect a fall back to what they consider to be a normal level. Expecting a rise in futures prices such speculators become ready to buy in the expectation of being able to sell at a higher price later. In this way speculators will fill any gap between futures sales and futures purchases.

Strips, rolls and spreads

Hitherto, only simple hedges have been considered. In the examples, short-term risk has been covered by a single futures position in each case. Borrowers and lenders may have longer-term anxieties.

Consider a rollover loan on which the interest is reassessed every three months. The borrower may face revisions of the interest rate on 1 May and 1 August. A strip hedge would involve taking out June and September futures contracts (there are four maturity dates each year, occurring in March, June, September, and December). This could prove difficult if there is inadequate liquidity in the more distant contract. Alternatively a rolling hedge could be employed. Rolling hedges always use the nearest futures contract (subject to the maturity date of the contract falling after the earliest interest rate reassessment date). A simple rolling hedge involves hedging only the earliest interest rate change. The borrower sells June futures contracts sufficient to match the value of the loan in order to hedge the interest rate risk of 1 May. This leaves the 1 August risk, and any subsequent risks, unhedged. A piled-up roll involves hedging more than one future interest rate change by using the nearest contract. The face value of the contracts would be a multiple of the value of the loan, for instance hedging for two interest rate reassessment dates would involve selling contracts with an aggregate face value of twice the value of the loan. Subsequent to 1 May, on which date the contracts would have been closed out, more contracts are sold in order to hedge the 1 August risk (effectively replacing previously-held contracts that hedged the 1 August risk). The advantage of piled-up rolls is that they avoid the liquidity problems that may arise from dealing in distant contracts whilst hedging risk on more than one future interest rate reassessment date. The disadvantages of piled-up rolls are that they involve a relatively large number of contracts and hence greater commission charges, and that they leave the hedger exposed to changes in the slope of the yield curve. Hedging distant interest rate changes with nearby futures contracts is effective if far and near rates move in line with each other, but if the near–far differential changes (that is, the slope of the yield curve changes) then the effectiveness of the hedge may be reduced.

Other currencies

The contracts on LIFFE permit direct hedging of short-term interest rate risks in sterling and Eurodollars. Although short-term interest rate contracts are not provided in other currencies it is possible to hedge short-term interest rate risk in other currencies by a more indirect technique. This makes use of the interest rate parity relationship.

A change in, say, Deutschmark interest rates could be broken down into two components. Firstly the change that is matched by Eurodollar rates and secondly the variation in the differential between Eurodollar and Deutschmark interest rates. The first component can be hedged with Eurodollar futures and the second can be hedged by means of a futures straddle or forward swap. A futures straddle involves buying futures for one delivery month and selling for another, both in the same instrument. Buying a Deutschmark currency straddle involves buying Deutschmark futures contracts and simultaneously selling the same number of Deutschmark futures contracts for a later delivery month. There would be a premium or discount between the two delivery months, that is the two futures prices would imply an appreciation or depreciation of the Deutschmark against the US dollar during the period between the two delivery dates. Selling the straddle entails selling contracts for the earlier delivery month and buying for the later delivery month.

Interest rate parity suggests that the rate of appreciation/depreciation implied by the futures prices represents the difference between dollar and Deutschmark interest rates between the two delivery months. Buying or selling a straddle thus provides a means of hedging changes in the interest rate differential.

Suppose that a potential borrower in Deutschmarks wishes to hedge against the possibility of a rise in short-term Deutschmark interest rates. The first step is to hedge interest rate changes that are common to Deutschmarks and Eurodollars. Since the fear is that interest rates might rise, the appropriate futures position is one that provides a gain from rising interest rates so as to offset the increased cost of borrowing. Eurodollar futures contracts would be sold. A rise in interest rates would cause a fall in futures prices so that the futures position could be closed out at a profit by buying contracts at a lower price than that at which they were sold. The potential borrower also needs to hedge the risk that Deutschmark interest rates might rise relative to Eurodollar rates. Given the interest rate parity relationship this is equivalent to hedging against the possibility that the rate of appreciation of the Deutschmark against the dollar might decrease (or rate of depreciation increase). This latter risk is hedged by selling a dollar–mark straddle.

Selling a dollar–mark straddle involves selling dollar–mark futures for a near delivery date and buying for a more distant date. If the implied rate of appreciation decreases (depreciation increases) the price of the near contract falls relative to that of the far contract. Closing out both contracts would entail a gain on the near contract that exceeds the loss on the far contract (or a loss on the near contract that is smaller than the gain on the far contract). So a decline in the Deutschmark premium (increase in the Deutschmark discount) provides a net gain from the futures transactions. This gain offsets the rise in Deutschmark interest rates relative to Eurodollar rates.

Example 5

Cash market

Futures market

10 March

Company intends to borrow DM10 million for three months on 1 May. Fears that Deutschmark interest rates will rise above the current 5 per cent p.a.

The June futures exchange rate is $1 = DM2.50. Sells four June Eurodollar futures contracts ($1 million each) corresponding to the DM10 million exposure. Price is 91.0. Sells a dollar–mark straddle, selling 80 June contracts and buying 80 September contracts ($50 000 each). June futures exchange rate is $1 = DM2.50 and September rate is $1 = DM2.475.

1 May

Borrows DM10 million at 8 per cent p.a. Incurs extra interest cost of DM75 000 (10 000 000 × 0.03 × 0.25 = 75 000).

Buys four June Eurodollar contracts at 90.0. Gain is 100 ticks per contract which is worth $10 000 (DM25 000). Buys a dollar–mark straddle, buying 80 June contracts and selling 80 September contracts. June futures exchange rate is $1 = DM2.50 and September rate is $1 = DM2.4875. There is neither a gain nor loss from the June contracts. The September dollars are bought at DM2.475 and sold at DM2.4875. Each contract provides a gain of 125 ticks at DM5 per tick. Total gain from straddle is DM50 000 (80 × 125 × 5 = 50 000).

Loses DM75 000   Gains   DM25 000   from   the
                                       Eurodollar   contracts   and
                                       DM50 000   from   the   dollar–
                                       mark straddle.

Short-term Deutschmark interest rates do rise as feared and this
causes interest payments to be DM75 000 greater than would have
been the case if the interest rate had remained at its 10 March
level. The futures hedge works perfectly, providing a total gain of
DM75 000 to offset the cash market loss. Part of the increase in
interest rates is common to Deutschmarks and Eurodollars, and
the cash market loss from this 1 per cent p.a. rise is hedged by
means of the Eurodollar contracts. The remaining 2 per cent p.a.
rise is hedged by the straddle.

On 10 March the futures markets implied a 4 per cent p.a.
appreciation of the Deutschmark against the dollar for the June to
September period, corresponding to the identical expectation for
the three-month period commencing on 10 March. By 1 May the
rate of appreciation had fallen to 2 per cent p.a. So on 10 March an
interest rate differential of 4 per cent p.a. was suggested by interest
rate parity, and was reflected in the 5 per cent p.a. Deutschmark
rate against the 9 per cent p.a. Eurodollar rate. By 1 May the
corresponding differential was just 2 per cent p.a., the rise in the
Eurodollar rate to 10 per cent p.a. was accompanied by a rise in
the Deutschmark rate to 8 per cent p.a. Selling the dollar–mark
straddle provided a futures gain (from the fall in the implied rate of
appreciation) which matched the increase in Deutschmark interest
rates relative to Eurodollar rates.

In addition to the dollar–mark futures which imply the purchase of US dollars with Deutschmarks, or the sale of dollars
for Deutschmarks, there are four other currency futures traded
on LIFFE. These are sterling, Deutschmarks, Swiss francs and
yen, all priced in US dollars against which they are traded.
There may be a need to hedge short-term interest rate risk on
a currency with no corresponding futures contracts on LIFFE, or
on one that is being traded with poor liquidity. One possibility
is to see if futures contracts in the currency are traded on
other futures exchanges such as those in Chicago, Philadelphia,

and Montreal. The alternative is to use forward exchange swaps.

Forward foreign exchange is available for a number of currencies for which there are no financial futures contracts. A forward exchange swap involves buying currency forward for one date and selling the same currency forward for a different date. A swap is thus similar to a futures straddle – they both involve advance purchases on one date and advance sales on another date (purchases do not necessarily precede sales).

A forward exchange swap could take the place of the futures straddle in the type of operation illustrated by Example 5, that is in hedging short-term interest rate risk in currencies for which short-term interest rate futures contracts are not available.

Appendix

Short-term interest rate contract specifications on LIFFE

Unit of trading	£500 000	US$1 000 000
Delivery months	Both contracts – March, June, September, December	
Delivery day	Both contracts – first business day after the last trading day	
Last trading day	Third Wednesday of delivery month	Two business days prior to the third Wednesday of delivery month
Quotation	Both contracts – 100.00 minus annualized rate of interest	
Tick size and value	0.01 (£12.50)	0.01 ($25)
Initial margin	£1000	$1000
Contract standard	Both contracts – Cash settlement, that is compensation for deviation of realized rates from the guaranteed rates rather than the provision of deposit facilities	

Note: Specifications are subject to revision by LIFFE

10 Long-term interest rate futures

The instruments available on LIFFE are based on long gilts, short gilts and US T-Bond contracts. They are sufficiently dissimilar to require attention to each although general principles relate to all of them and will, for the most part, be explained with reference to just one leaving the reader to extend the analysis to the others.

Gilt and US T-Bond futures

Gilt (US T-Bond) futures are commitments to buy or sell gilt-edged securities (US T-Bonds) during specified future months. There is a limited number of gilts (US T-Bonds) eligible for delivery in fulfilment of futures contracts and the seller has the choice as to the specific gilt (US T-Bond). Contracts are commonly not held until maturity but are closed out by means of the holder taking out an opposite contract, for example a buyer can close out by selling gilt futures in an amount and for a delivery month corresponding to those of the contracts previously bought. There is a cash settlement to reflect the change in futures prices between the dates of buying and selling. Long gilt futures contracts are based on a notional gilt-edged security which has a 12 per cent p.a. coupon yield (10 per cent for short gilt futures and 8 per cent for US T-Bond futures). Should a futures contract be held to maturity the gilts (US T-Bonds) eligible for delivery in settlement of the contract must approximate to this notional security.

Those using these financial futures for hedging may wish to safeguard either the value of securities or the cash flow arising from them.

Hedging the value of a portfolio

Portfolio managers may fear an increase in long-term interest rates, an occurrence that would reduce the price of gilts held in a portfolio. They could attempt to avoid this effect on the value of the portfolio by taking a position in futures that would provide an offsetting gain from a fall in gilts prices. To achieve this they would sell futures contracts. A fall in gilt prices should be accompanied by a fall in the prices of gilt futures. If a loss was made from a decline in the value of gilts portfolio managers could compensate by closing out the futures position. They would be able to buy gilt futures at a lower price than that at which they sold. In other words, their guaranteed selling price of gilts, for a specific month in the future, is greater than the agreed buying price for the same delivery month. The futures positions thus show a net gain and, in consequence, variation margin payments are received.

This process is illustrated by Example 1, which needs to be preceded by details of the specifications of the long-term interest rate futures contracts traded on LIFFE. Each long gilt contract has a nominal value of £50 000 (short gilt £100 000, US Treasury Bond $100 000) and the prices of contracts are expressed as pounds (dollars) per £100 ($100) nominal value. The price of the notional long gilt would be 100 when the long-run interest rate is 12 per cent p.a. but would rise above 100 when the interest rate is lower, vice versa for higher rates (corresponding relationships hold for short gilt and US Treasury Bond futures). The tick, the minimum price movement, is $\frac{1}{32}$ for long gilt and US T-Bond futures, and $\frac{1}{64}$ for short gilt futures.

In Example 1 a portfolio manager with gilts worth £1 million on 2 January is anxious about the possibility that interest rates might rise and thereby reduce the value of his gilts. He hedges by selling 20 long gilt futures contracts.

Example 1

Cash market	Futures market

Cash market
2 January
The 20-year interest rate is 12 per cent p.a. The £1 million gilt portfolio is vulnerable to an increase in long-term interest rates.

Futures market

Sells 20 March long gilt futures contracts. Futures price is 100, reflecting a 12 per cent p.a. interest rate.

15 February
The 20-year interest rate has risen to 15 per cent p.a. Correspondingly, the value of the gilt portfolio has fallen to £850 000 (this figure could be anywhere between £800 000 and £1 million dependent upon the maturities of the gilts held).

Closes out by buying 20 March long gilt futures contracts. The price of the contracts has fallen to $81^3/_{32}$ reflecting a 15 per cent p.a. futures interest rate.

There is a loss of £150 000 in the value of the gilt portfolio.

There is a gain of £189 000 from the futures position.

The portfolio manager has been more than successful in offsetting the fall in the value of his gilts. The reason for this over compensation is the fact that the average maturity of the gilts in his portfolio is less than 20 years (for the moment it will be assumed that the futures contract is based on a gilt with a 20-year maturity, whereas the maturity could be anywhere between 15 and 25 years). The value of a portfolio responds less to interest rate changes as the average maturity declines. In the light of this he could have chosen to hedge with fewer than 20 futures contracts, 16 would seem appropriate, particularly when it is borne in mind that with 20 contracts a fall in interest rates would have entailed a futures loss greater than the increase in the value of the gilt portfolio.

Anxiety about the volatility of interest rates may not be specific to a particular period. It is likely that portfolio managers are consistently nervous about the instability of interest rates and the possibility that it might involve a fall in the value of gilt portfolios. The holding of futures positions, to hedge against changes in the value of a portfolio, could thus be permanent with new futures positions being entered into as old ones are closed out.

Hedging cash flow

In this case, the hypothetical example is that of a corporate treasurer intending to raise money by the sale of securities with a fixed coupon yield. His anxiety is that interest rates might rise before the sale is made with the result that the raising of a particular sum of money would then entail a greater future cash flow commitment to the security holders.

Example 2

Cash market	Futures market
2 January	
The corporation intends to raise £1 million on 15 February by the sale of irredeemable debentures. The interest rate on undated stock is 12 per cent p.a. The treasurer wants to ensure that the cost of servicing the debt will be limited to £120 000 p.a.	Sells 20 March long gilt futures contracts. Futures price is 100, reflecting a 12 per cent p.a. interest rate on 20-year stock.
15 February	
The interest rate on undated stock has risen to 15 per cent p.a.	Closes out by buying 20 March long gilt futures contracts. Futures price is $81^3/_{32}$ reflecting a 15 per cent p.a. futures interest rate.
The cost of servicing a £1 million debt would now be £150 000 p.a.	There is a gain of £189 000 from the futures position.

The treasurer could use the £189 000 futures gain to reduce his borrowing requirement from £1 000 000 to £811 000 and hence reduce the annual servicing cost to £121 650. A perfect hedge would have provided a futures gain of £200 000 so that the cash flow required to service the debt returned to £120 000 p.a. The futures gain was less than £200 000 because the notional gilt is of a 20-year maturity (assumed for the purposes of this example) and only the price of irredeemable stock responds proportionately to interest rate changes. A more effective hedge would have been obtained by using 21 gilt contracts, which would have provided a futures gain of about £198 500.

In both Examples 1 and 2 the hedger would be able to ascertain the appropriate number of futures contracts required, 16 and 21 respectively, before undertaking the contracts. The ratio of the value of futures contracts required to the sum of assets or liabilities to be hedged is known as the hedge ratio. Even with the correct hedge ratio, hedging may not be perfect. Imperfections would arise if the cash market and futures interest rates did not change to the same extent. However, this basis risk tends to be much less than the outright risk of unhedged positions since the difference between cash and futures interest rates fluctuates less than cash market rates.

Delivery

The months during which the gilts (US T-Bonds) may be delivered are March, June, September, and December. The seller chooses the day of the month on which delivery takes place. Gilts with between 15 and 25 years to maturity are eligible for delivery upon maturity of the long gilt futures contracts (between 3 and 4½ years for the short gilt, and US Treasury Bonds with maturities in excess of 15 years for the US T-Bond contracts). The seller has to choose which gilt or US T-Bond to deliver.

Price (conversion) factor

The price factor will be described in relation to the long gilt futures contract, the description can readily be extended to the other two long-term interest rate contracts.

The long gilt futures contracts each have a nominal value of £50 000. Likewise, the gilts delivered when a contract matures must amount to £50 000 in nominal value. Gilts with the same nominal value may, however, have different market prices. A gilt with a coupon yield of 12 per cent p.a. would have a higher market value than one with a 10 per cent p.a. coupon despite identical nominal values. A £50 000 bond issued when the market rate was 12 per cent p.a. would provide a coupon of £6000 p.a. whereas a £50 000 bond issued at a rate of 10 per cent p.a. would yield £5000 p.a. The market value of bonds will vary according to the size of the coupon yield. A bond yielding £6000 p.a. is worth more than one with a coupon of just £5000 p.a. If the seller delivers high coupon gilts he expects to receive more money than if he delivers lower coupon gilts. To ensure that this happens, price factors are used in the calculation of the sums for which buyers are invoiced; the relevant adjustment is made by means of multiplying the futures price by a price factor.

To obtain the price factor for a long gilt, its price, if it were to have a gross redemption yield of 12 per cent p.a., is ascertained. This price is then divided by the nominal value of the gilt and the result is the price factor. Higher coupon yields are reflected in higher price factors and hence high coupon yield gilts are more expensive than lower coupon gilts.

If the bonds were perpetuities the price factor would equal the ratio of the percentage yields. The price factor for a 15 per cent p.a. bond would be 1.25 since a 15 per cent p.a. yield into perpetuity would render the bond 25 per cent more valuable than one yielding a perpetual 12 per cent p.a. However, most long gilts have maturity dates as does the notional gilt upon which futures contracts are based. Since the bonds are not perpetuities, the price factor tends to differ from the ratio of the percentage yields, with the factor approaching one as the period of maturity declines. This can be appreciated by reference to bonds with just one year to maturity. In such cases, value differences are approximately equal to the coupon difference. In the example above this amounts to £1500 (15 per cent p.a. on £50 000 minus 12 per cent p.a. on £50 000) which at 3 per cent of the nominal value is much smaller than the 25 per cent that arises in the case of perpetuities.

Invoice amount

The futures price upon which the invoice amount is based is known as the exchange delivery settlement price, which is the LIFFE market price at 11.00 a.m. on the second business day prior to delivery. The principal invoice amount is the exchange delivery settlement price multiplied by the price factor. The sum for which the buyer is invoiced is equal to the principal invoice amount plus accrued interest on the gilts. The resulting invoice amounts would normally differ from the market values of the deliverable bonds.

The cheapest to deliver gilt

The seller chooses which gilt to deliver in fulfilment of the contract. It is in the interests of the seller to deliver the gilt whose invoice amount exceeds the market price by the largest margin (or whose invoice amount falls short of the market price by the smallest margin). This is the cheapest deliverable gilt.

Cash and carry arbitrage

This refers to the process of simultaneously buying gilts spot and selling futures contracts. If the invoicing amount, inclusive of accrued interest, at maturity exceeds the sum of the purchase price and financing cost, arbitrage profits are available. Arbitrageurs can buy spot and simultaneously guarantee a profitable future selling price by selling futures contracts. Buying spot and selling futures raises the spot price, lowers the futures price, and thus tends to remove the scope for arbitrage profits. The arbitrage activity will bring about a situation in which the capital gain (loss) is equal to the excess (shortfall) of the cost of financing the long gilt position over the running yield on the gilt. If the yield on the gilt falls short of the financing cost of holding that gilt the spot price will be lower than the futures price since some capital gain will be necessary to offset the excess financing cost.

Thus cash and carry arbitrage serves to keep spot and futures prices close to each other, with the relationship between them being dependent upon the financing costs. Since the arbitrageurs would gain most by using the cheapest to deliver gilt it is this stock whose value is reflected by the invoicing amount for maturing futures contracts. This implies that the futures price itself is based on the cheapest to deliver gilt (since the price factor is unaffected by spot and futures prices the relationship between the cheapest deliverable gilt and the invoicing amount is matched by one between the gilt and the futures price).

The close correspondence between the futures price and that of the cheapest to deliver gilt implies that the futures contract effectively acquires the characteristics of the cheapest deliverable gilt in terms of coupon yield and maturity (adjusted by the price factor). It is to be expected that the cheapest deliverable is the gilt most accurately hedged by the futures contract. Changes in spot gilt prices may, however, change the cheapest to deliver gilt. The change from one gilt to another alters the implicit characteristics of the gilt futures and slightly undermines the effectiveness of the futures contract for hedging the first cheapest deliverable gilt. In fact the process of cash and carry arbitrage can be expected to tend to change the cheapest to deliver gilt since the additional demand for this stock would raise its price and make it less attractive, relative to other gilts, to the futures seller seeking the most profitable gilt to deliver upon maturity of the futures contract.

Basis

The market price of a gilt has two components, the clean price and the accrued interest. The latter refers to the right to interest receipts accumulated since the last interest payment date. A purchaser of a gilt realizes the interest receipts that accumulated while the seller was holding the gilt. The price paid for the gilt will include compensation for the accrued interest unrealized by the seller. The remainder of the price is known as the clean price.

Division of the clean price, per £100 nominal, by the price factor renders the price comparable with the futures price. The difference between the price thus obtained and the futures price is known as basis. In the case of the cheapest to deliver gilt, basis is determined by the difference between the yield on the gilt and the interest paid (or foregone) on the money required to finance the purchase of the gilt. Basis converges to zero as the maturity date of the futures contract is approached. As maturity is approached the period over which interest is paid and received shortens and hence the monetary value of the interest differential declines towards zero.

For example, suppose that it is 2 October and a December long gilt futures contract has been sold as part of a cash and carry arbitrage operation. The cost of financing the holding of the gilt exceeds the running yield obtained from the gilt. This implies that the arbitrageur will choose to deliver (the seller chooses the delivery date) at the earliest possible date (1 December) since there is a net loss to be expected from holding the gilt after that date. It also implies that the futures price is at a premium to the spot price.

If the clean price of the cheapest to deliver gilt is 121.00 and the price factor is 1.1 whilst the futures price is 112.00 then the basis will be given by

$$\text{Basis} = \frac{121}{1.1} - 112 = -2$$

Figure 10.1 illustrates the erosion of the expected basis over time.

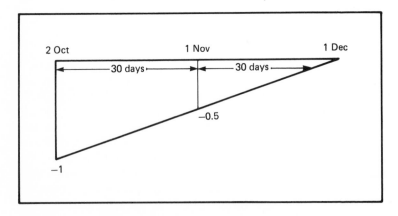

Figure 10.1   Expected erosion of basis over time

Thus basis is expected to change over time. This means that the price that a hedger seeks to guarantee may differ from the spot price at the time of taking out the futures contracts. The greater is the time lapse between agreeing the contracts and closing out, the higher will be the expected guaranteed price. Closing out soon after 2 October tends to provide a price close to the spot price, whereas closing out shortly before 1 December gives a price close to that implied by the futures price at which the contract was agreed.

A holder of a futures contract may hold it to maturity. By so doing he guarantees being able to buy or sell the cheapest to deliver gilt at the price implied by the price of the futures contract bought or sold. In most cases contracts are not held to maturity. This might be because the transaction being hedged may not fall in a delivery month or because the gilt (or other instrument) being bought or sold is not the cheapest to deliver gilt. If it is the cheapest deliverable gilt that is to be bought or sold, the locked-in price will lie somewhere between the current spot price and the price implied by the futures price.

If the proposed hedge occurs halfway between the present and the maturity date the guaranteed price will be the average of the spot and implied future prices, if it occurs after only a quarter of the time has elapsed the price guaranteed would equal three-quarters of the spot price plus a quarter of the price implied by the futures contract, and so on.

In the case of a gilt other than the cheapest to deliver, its value relative to that of the cheapest deliverable also affects basis. Variations in the relative values of the two gilts would cause movements in basis.

Cash flows

It is useful to consider what type of cash flows might be involved in producing an effective price of the cheapest to deliver gilt along the line shown in Figure 10.1. Consider two extreme possibilities.

First, suppose that the futures price corresponds to the expected price and that expectations prove to be correct. In such a case the sum paid for the gilt will change over time, whilst the futures price remains unchanged. If the price is expected to change in a linear fashion the profile shown by Figure 10.1 will indicate the amount payable at each point in time.

Second, suppose that the spot price is expected to remain constant and that expectations turn out to be correct. In this case the futures price does not represent an expectation but is merely based on the spot price, running yield, and financing costs. Whenever the contract is closed out the same spot price is paid. However, the futures price moves towards the spot price at a constant rate over time, becoming equal to it at maturity. This involves the payment (or receipt) of variation margin spread evenly over time. The spot price plus variation margin paid (or received) equals the price implied by the spot and original futures price, that is the price that lies on the straight line between the spot and original futures price drawn at the time that the contract was agreed. So, for example, if the contract were held to maturity the difference between the initial futures price and the unchanged spot price would have been paid (or received) in the form of variation margin.

Basis risk

As mentioned above, basis, the difference between the futures price and that derived from the spot price, reflects the financing cost relative to the yield on the gilt. A change in the interest rate on money borrowed to finance the purchase of a gilt in cash and carry arbitrage would alter the basis. Such a change in basis introduces a degree of imperfection into the hedge – the profile suggested by Figure 10.1 is deviated from. This possibility is known as basis risk. Fortunately, basis risk is likely to be low when the cheapest to deliver gilt is being hedged. As the characteristics of the instrument being hedged diverge further and further from those of the cheapest deliverable gilt, basis risk progressively increases. To the basis risk arising from the possibility of changes in financing costs must be added the basis risk from possible changes in the relative prices of the cheapest to deliver gilt and the instrument being hedged. The greater the difference between the cheapest deliverable gilt and the gilt (or other instrument) being hedged the greater is the basis risk arising from this latter source. When basis risk is so large that there is not a close relationship between changes in the futures price and changes in that of the instrument being hedged then this particular futures contract does not provide a suitable means of hedging.

Hedge design

The hedger must decide upon the number of contracts required to accomplish the desired hedge. This calculation is simplest when hedging the cheapest to deliver gilt.

$$\text{Number of contracts} = \frac{\text{Nominal value of gilt position}}{\text{Nominal value of a contract}} \times \text{Price factor}$$

The multiplication by the price factor is necessary to adjust for the price difference between the cheapest to deliver gilt and the notional 12 per cent p.a. coupon yield gilt. (It should be remembered that the corresponding coupon yields for short gilt futures are 10 per cent p.a. and for US Treasury Bond futures 8 per cent p.a.) At a discount rate of 12 per cent the price of the notional gilt is equal to its nominal value whereas the price of a gilt with a coupon yield greater than 12 per cent p.a. would be higher than the nominal value (vice versa if the coupon yield is less than 12 per cent p.a.). £100 nominal of a gilt with a coupon yield greater than 12 per cent p.a. is worth more than £100 nominal of a gilt with a coupon yield of 12 per cent p.a. The higher coupon yield gilt thus has a higher value to be hedged and will require a correspondingly larger number of contracts for the hedging.

Suppose that for the December 1985 contract month the cheapest to deliver short gilt was the Exchequer 12½ per cent 1990 whose price factor was 1.0858888. If the hedger wished to hedge £10 million nominal of this short gilt the necessary number of contracts would have been calculated thus:

$$\text{Number of contracts} = \frac{£10\ 000\ 000}{£100\ 000} \times 1.0858888 = 108.58888$$

The hedger would use either 108 or 109 short gilt futures contracts to hedge his position.

When hedging gilts other than the cheapest to deliver gilt, account must be taken of their relative volatility. This can be measured in terms of the money value of, say, a 1 per cent yield change per £100 nominal. If the gilt being hedged is more volatile than the cheapest to deliver, a correspondingly greater number of contracts will be required for the hedge (and vice versa for less volatile gilts). In this way the larger price movements of relatively volatile gilts are dealt with. The formula becomes:

$$\text{Number of contracts} = \frac{\text{Nominal value of gilt position}}{\text{Nominal value of a contract}} \times \frac{\text{Price factor of cheapest to deliver gilt}}{} \times \frac{\text{Relative volatility}}{}$$

Thus if the money value of a 1 per cent yield change per £100 nominal were £5 for the gilt being hedged and £3.50 for the cheapest to deliver gilt then the number of contracts necessary to hedge £10 million nominal of the gilts, in an example parallel to the previous one, would be

$$\text{Number of contracts} = \frac{£10\ 000\ 000}{£100\ 000} \times 1.0858888 \times \frac{5}{3.5} = 155.13$$

The appropriate number of short gilt contracts is 155. A large number of futures contracts is necessary so that the gains/losses on futures succeed in offsetting the relatively large losses/gains on the gilt being hedged. Without adjusting for relative volatility only £3.50 of every £5 price change would be offset. (Note that the difference between the price factor of the hedged gilt and that of the cheapest deliverable is reflected in the relative volatility. A relatively high price factor indicates a relatively expensive gilt – per £100 nominal – and this is reflected in a correspondingly larger price movement for each 1 per cent change in interest rates, vice versa for a low price factor gilt.)

Changes in relative volatility can reduce the effectiveness of the hedge. This occurs when the relative volatility experienced over the period of the hedge differs from that predicted from previous observations. Although this, together with basis risk, tends to reduce the efficiency of hedging an imperfect hedge is better than no hedge at all. Besides it is likely that these imperfections in hedging are not too serious when hedging diversified portfolios of gilts. In such cases the inefficiencies in hedging specific gilts tend to be offsetting.

Sterling bonds other than gilts can be hedged with gilt futures but the more dissimilar are the cheapest to deliver gilt and the bond being hedged the less effective is the hedge likely to be. The lack of similarity will tend to be greater in the case of bonds other than gilts.

Appendix

Long-term interest rate contract specifications on LIFFE

	Short gilt	Long gilt	US T-Bond
Unit of trading	£100 000 nominal value notional gilt	£50 000 nominal value notional gilt	US$100 000 par value notional US Treasury Bond
Delivery months	All contracts – March, June, September, December		
Delivery day	All contracts – any business day in delivery month (at seller's choice)		
Quotation	Per £100 nominal	Per £100 nominal	Per $100 par value
Tick size and value	£1/64 (£15.625)	£1/32 (£15.625)	$1/32 ($31.25)
Initial margin	£1000	£1000	$1250
Contract standard	Gilts with 3 to 4½ years to maturity delivered in multiples of £100 000 nominal (subject to certain restrictions)	Gilts with 15 to 25 years to maturity delivered in multiples of £50 000 nominal (subject to certain restrictions)	US Treasury Bonds with at least 15 years to maturity delivered in multiples of $100 000 par value (subject to certain restrictions)

Note: Specifications are subject to revision by LIFFE

Since the writing of this book Japanese Government Bond futures have been introduced by LIFFE.

11 Equity futures

In May 1984 LIFFE introduced a futures contract based on a stock market index, the *Financial Times* Stock Exchange (FTSE) 100 index. When using FTSE 100 futures to reduce stock market risk the anticipation is that any losses arising from movements in equity prices are offset by gains from parallel movements in futures prices. An investor might be anxious about the possibility that the prices of his equities might fall. He could reduce the risk of a reduction in the value of his portfolio by taking a position in the futures market that would provide him with a gain in the event of a fall in equity prices. In such a case the investor would take a short position in FTSE 100 futures contracts. By taking a short position he guarantees a notional selling price of a quantity of stock for a specific date in the future. Should equity prices fall and FTSE 100 futures behave in a corresponding fashion the notional buying price for that date would be less than the predetermined notional selling price. The investor could close out his short position in futures by taking a long position in the same number of contracts. The excess of the selling price over the buying price is paid to the investor in cash in the form of variation margin. This gain on the futures contracts is received on a daily basis as the futures price moves (a procedure known as marking to market). Had the prices of equities risen the investor would have gained from his portfolio of equities but lost on his futures dealings. In either case the investor has succeeded in reducing the extent to which the value of his portfolio fluctuates.

FTSE 100 contracts

The FTSE 100 futures contract is a notional commitment to buy or sell a given quantity of stock on a specified future date at a price determined at the time of taking out the contract. The quantity of stock is a basket of shares in 100 companies. With a few exceptions these are the largest 100 companies in the UK. The contribution of each company to the total is weighted in proportion to that company's size. The FTSE 100 index was given a base value of 1000 on 3 January 1984. Each futures contract is valued at £25 per full index point (so on 3 January 1984 the contract value was £25 000). There are just four delivery dates each year. These are the first business days following the last business days of the months of March, June, September and December.

Prices of FTSE 100 contracts are quoted as the FTSE 100 index divided by 10. So if the December 1985 delivery date was expected to have a FTSE 100 index of 1120 then the December 1985 FTSE 100 futures contract would be priced at 112. The tick is the smallest price movement allowed by LIFFE. Its size is 0.05. This is equivalent to 0.5 FTSE index points and has the value of £12.50.

The use of futures to hedge the risk of a fall in stock prices does not require any alteration of the original portfolio. It is thus preferable to any form of hedging that involves changing the composition of the portfolio, for example liquidating part of the portfolio. Also, futures trading is off balance sheet.

Example 1

In this example the portfolio holder fears a generalized fall in equity prices and wishes to avoid a fall in the value of his portfolio.

Cash market	Futures market
5 April	
Holds a balanced portfolio of equities valued at £500 000 but fears a fall in its value. The current FTSE 100 index is 1000.	Sells 20 June FTSE 100 contracts at a price of 100 each. He has thus committed himself to the notional sale of £500 000 of stock on the June delivery date

at the level of prices existing on 5 April (FTSE 100 index = 1000).

10 May

The FTSE 100 index has fallen to 950. Correspondingly, the value of the portfolio has declined to £475 000.

Closes out the futures position by buying 20 June FTSE 100 contracts at a price of 95. The notional buying price of each contract is thus 5 below the notional selling price. There is a gain of 100 ticks on each of the 20 contracts.

Loss on the portfolio = £25 000.

Gain from futures trading = £25 000 (100 × 20 × £12.50).

By 10 May the portfolio holder feels that the fall in equity prices is complete and chooses to close out his futures position. Should he wish to insure against adverse market movements on a permanent basis he could maintain a permanently open futures position, rolling-over contracts as they reach maturity. Of course this strategy is one that reduces variations in the value of the portfolio holder's assets. If, in Example 1, the FTSE 100 index had risen there would have been a cash market gain offset by a futures market loss.

Example 2

This example shows how a long position in futures can be used as a hedge. In this case a fund manager anticipates receipt of £1 million on 10 January and intends to use it to buy a balanced portfolio of UK equities. He fears, one month earlier, that stock prices will rise before the money is received.

Cash market

Futures market

10 December

Anticipates receipt of £1 million on 10 January. Current FTSE 100 index is 1100. Fears a rise in the index.

Buys 36 March FTSE futures contracts at a price of 110. He thereby notionally commits himself to paying £990 000 (36

	× £27 500) for stock on a future date.
10 January The new FTSE 100 index is 1150.	Closes out by selling 36 March FTSE futures contracts at a price of 114. He notionally guarantees a receipt of £1 026 000 (36 × £28 500) upon maturity of the contracts.
Requires an additional £45 455 in order to buy the quantity of stock that £1 million would have bought on 10 December.	Gain from futures of £36 000.

Futures prices did not move precisely in line with the FTSE 100 index and as a result the hedge was imperfect. In other words there was a change in basis, which had initially been zero. Of course, if basis had changed so as to establish futures prices in excess of cash market prices the fund manager would have gained more from the futures market than he needed for the hedge.

Cross-hedging

Cross-hedges involve hedging risk on one instrument with futures in another. For example, three-month sterling certificates of deposit might be hedged with three-month sterling deposit futures, or movements of a single share price might be hedged by using FTSE 100 futures. Cross-hedging is subject to greater basis risk and there is a level beyond which basis risk becomes unacceptable. Basis risk can be measured by correlating the relevant cash market and futures prices, or correlating the changes in the two prices. The nearer the correlation is to 1 the closer are the movements of the two instruments. A correlation coefficient of 1 indicates that the cash and futures instruments have moved precisely in line with each other so that changes in the price of the cash market instrument could have been hedged perfectly by the futures instrument. The correlation coefficient of 1 indicates an absence of basis risk in the past and that bodes well for the future. A correlation coefficient of 0 indicates that the two instruments have moved in completely unrelated ways in the past and therefore basis risk is high. Low values of the correlation coefficient suggest that the futures instrument is unlikely to be suitable for hedging risk on the cash instrument. A rule of thumb might be that a correlation coefficient of at least 0.6 is required to suggest that the hedging would be reasonably successful (a correlation coefficient of 0.6 indicates that the proportion of the risk eliminated is 0.36, that is $(0.6)^2$).

The more dissimilar are the cash market instrument and the instrument upon which the futures are based the lower would be the correlation coefficient and the higher the basis risk. Three-month sterling certificates of deposit and three-month sterling deposits are very similar and hence futures on the latter could safely be used to hedge risk on the former. There is less similarity between, say, a portfolio of shares in financial companies and the portfolio represented by the FTSE 100 so it may be expected that the correlation coefficient is lower and basis risk higher. Reasonable effectiveness of the hedge would be less certain.

Hedge ratios

Hedge ratios become necessary when the volatility of the futures contract is likely to differ from that of the instrument to be hedged. If the instrument to be hedged shows relatively large variations then it is appropriate to use more futures contracts than in the case of a more stable instrument. It is unlikely that a portfolio of equities, for which hedging is required, precisely corresponds to the composition of the FTSE 100 index. It is thus probable that it will show more or less volatility than the index.

The beta factor of a share is a measure of the extent to which it has moved in line with share prices in general. A balanced portfolio is likely to have a beta factor of about 1. A share with only half the movement of the market as a whole would have a factor of 0.5 whilst one with double the degree of change has a factor of 2. The beta factor of a portfolio of shares is the weighted average of the beta factors of the shares that constitute the portfolio. Beta factors can be obtained from research companies.

If the calculation indicated a beta factor of 1.2 then the portfolio tends to change by 20 per cent more than balanced portfolios of shares. Hedging the portfolio would require the value of the FTSE 100 futures contracts used to exceed the portfolio value by 20 per cent. The relatively large losses (or profits) arising from the high volatility require correspondingly large offsetting profits (or losses) from futures contracts, and this necessitates a relatively large number of futures contracts.

Determination of futures prices

In Chapters 8, 9 and 10 the prices of futures contracts were seen as being determined by arbitrage. Covered interest arbitrage to establish interest rate parity in the case of currency futures, arbitrage based on forward-forward calculations in the case of short-term interest rate futures, and cash and carry arbitrage in the case of long-term interest rate futures.

FTSE 100 futures prices are also affected by cash and carry arbitrage. This arbitrage activity tends to produce futures prices that are at a premium/discount against cash market prices that is dependent upon the yield on equities relative to the financing cost of holding those equities. However, it is to be expected that this arbitrage effect will be weaker in the case of FTSE 100 futures than in the case of long-term interest rate futures because of the expense of acquiring balanced portfolios of equities. Whilst the gilt arbitrageur needs to acquire only the cheapest deliverable gilt, the FTSE 100 arbitrageur needs to purchase a weighted portfolio of 100 different equities.

Thus factors other than arbitrage acquire significant influence in determining the prices of FTSE 100 futures contracts. Expectations of future share prices are likely to be important. If traders (speculators) expect share prices to be higher than those suggested by futures prices they will buy futures so as to make profits when futures prices rise into line with the expected share prices. These purchases of futures contracts will tend to pull up their prices towards the expected levels. Conversely, if equity prices are expected to be lower than those implied by futures prices, trading for the purposes of obtaining speculative profits would tend to pull down futures prices. Thus there will be some tendency for FTSE 100 futures prices to reflect expected share prices.

Indeed expectations of future cash market prices are likely to have some influence in the determination of the prices of other futures contracts. This is likely to be the case for the more distant delivery months. Arbitrage opportunities may be more fully taken in the nearer contracts than in the more distant ones so that the prices of the latter become more influenced by expectations of cash market prices. In fact, futures prices are often used as indicators of market expectations.

Arbitrage and expectations cannot provide a complete explanation of futures prices. Futures prices are established by demand and supply (offers to buy and sell in the pit). Arbitrage and trading based on expectations influence prices by way of their impacts on demand and supply. Anything that impacts on offers to buy and sell will affect prices. In the absence of substantial arbitrage and speculation the desired purchases and sales of futures contracts by hedgers would tend to determine futures prices.

Speculators and arbitrageurs

These types of transactor serve to render the market liquid and stable. It is unlikely that hedgers' demand for contracts will exactly equal hedgers' supply of contracts for a particular delivery month. Speculators (who might alternatively be described as market makers) and arbitrageurs fill the gap between demand and supply thereby ensuring the marketability of the contracts and reducing the price fluctuations that result from imbalances between demand and supply.

If there is a temporary excess demand for the contracts of a particular delivery month there would be a tendency for the price of those contracts to rise. The speculator would take a short position in those contracts in the anticipation of closing out by taking a long position when the price has fallen back to its normal level. He thus sells at the higher price and buys at the lower price. In so doing he fills the gap between the long and short positions desired by hedgers. Speculators thus help to ensure that hedgers can take the positions required and simultaneously prevent the abrupt price movements that might otherwise result from mismatching of desired short and long positions.

Arbitrageurs may operate between the futures market and the market for the underlying financial instrument. By doing so they help to create liquidity in the futures market and dampen excessive divergences between futures prices and the prices of the underlying financial instruments. Thus if hedgers sought to take a net long position for a particular delivery month there would be a tendency for the price of the contract to rise. The arbitrageur could sell futures and buy equities with a view to subsequently closing both positions and making a profit. Such might be the case, for example, if the premium of the futures price over the cash market price gave a return that exceeded the excess of the financing cost of holding equities over the running yield of those equities. Thus tendencies for futures prices to diverge from the underlying equity prices would be tempered by arbitrage. This means that arbitrage reduces basis risk.

This arbitrage process is likely to be less than complete for several reasons. Firstly, the arbitrageur faces uncertainty in the equity market. He may incur costs represented by the difference between interest paid on money borrowed to finance the equity purchases and the return on the equities, which takes the form of dividend receipts. These costs are subject to considerable uncertainty arising from the possibility of unexpected changes in dividends. The arbitrageur would therefore look for a risk premium. Secondly, buying a portfolio of equities that correlates strongly with the FTSE 100 is likely to prove expensive since a large number of individual purchases would be involved. Furthermore it is unlikely that they could all be purchased simultaneously with the sale of the futures contracts. The arbitrageur faces the risk of price movements whilst making his purchases. Unit trusts with a balanced portfolio of UK equities might provide the means to circumvent these problems but are subject to large front-end transactions costs. An arbitrageur seeking to take a long position in the futures market and a short position in the cash market faces the additional problem of how to sell something that he does not have. So arbitrage might operate only weakly in the opposite direction.

Appendix

FTSE 100 contract specifications on LIFFE

Unit of trading	£25 per full FTSE 100 index point
Delivery months	March, June, September, December
Delivery day	First business day after the last business day in the delivery month.
Quotation	FTSE 100 index divided by 10
Tick size and value	0.05 (£12.50)
Initial margin	£750
Contract standard	Cash settlement (that is, compensation for deviations of the realized FTSE 100 index from the futures index agreed when buying/ selling the contract) rather than equities being delivered upon maturity

Note: Specifications are subject to revision by LIFFE

12 Trading with financial futures

Trading, which might alternatively be referred to as market making, corresponds to what the layman would call speculating. It is necessary for the effective operation of the market. It provides greater depth, that is it adds to the volume of transactions, and it provides liquidity. Traders play an important role in ensuring the liquidity of futures markets. There are long-term traders who hold contracts for days, weeks, or even months in order to gain from price movements. There are day traders who may hold contracts for several hours but will always close out positions before the end of the business day. Finally, there are scalpers who keep positions open for merely seconds or minutes in order to make profits from small price movements occurring in short periods of time. If, for example, sales of March sterling futures contracts tended to outnumber purchases there would be a tendency for the price of such contracts to fall. Traders seeing a divergence between the normal price and the weakened price will enter the market to buy such contracts. They would do so in the anticipation of making a profit when the price returns to normal. They buy at the lowered price with a view to selling when the price has risen to what they see as its normal level. Thus the excess supply of March sterling futures contracts is taken up by traders. In this way other sellers (and buyers) of contracts can be assured of readily finding buyers (and sellers).

Trading can be divided into position trading and spread trading. Position trading involves buying or selling contracts in the anticipation of closing out at a profit when the price has moved in the expected direction. Position traders aim to make profits from changes in the prices of futures contracts. Spread traders seek to profit from changes in the relationships between the prices of futures contracts.

Spread trading

A spread is the purchase of one futures instrument coupled with the simultaneous sale of a different futures instrument. For example, short gilt futures contracts might be bought simultaneously with the sale of long gilt futures contracts. A straddle is a particular type of spread which involves the contracts relating to the same underlying instrument but being for different maturity months. For example, a June sterling currency contract might be bought simultaneously with the sale of a September sterling currency contract. Example 1 illustrates a straddle spread which is held by a trader who takes the view that the June sterling currency futures price will rise relative to that of the September contract.

Example 1

10 April
Buys a June sterling currency futures contract at £1 = $1.45.
   Sells a September sterling currency futures contract at £1 = $1.47.
10 May
Closes out by selling June sterling currency futures contract at £1 = $1.46.
   Closes out by buying a September sterling currency futures contract at £1 = $1.46.

The trader makes a profit equal to 1 cent per £1 (100 ticks) on each of the two contracts. Since the contract size is £25 000 the profit is $250 on each of the two contracts. The trader took a view on the relative price of the June and September contracts. Any price movement common to both contracts would make no difference to the profitability of the trade.

Example 2

Example 2 differs from Example 1 in exhibiting a price movement common to both contracts.

10 April
Buys a June sterling currency futures contract at £1 = $1.45.

   Sells a September sterling currency futures contract at £1 = $1.47.

10 May
Closes out by selling a June sterling currency futures contract at £1 = $1.43.

   Closes out by buying a September sterling currency futures contract at £1 = $1.43.

The trader makes a loss of 2 cents per £1 on the June contract and a profit of 4 cents per £1 on the September contract. A net profit of $500 is obtained as in Example 1. Despite the difference in the final exchange rates between the two examples the profit is the same. This is because they both exhibit the same relative price change. It is the relative price change that affects profits, a price change common to both contracts has no effect on profits since a gain from one of the contracts would be offset by an equal loss on the other.

Spread positions, particularly straddle spreads, often display less volatility than pure open positions. In recognition of this, straddles on LIFFE involve lower initial margin requirements than pure open positions. For example, at the time of writing, the initial margin for a sterling currency futures contract was $1000 but for a straddle in that contract the initial margin was only $100. The maximum likely day-to-day common price movement is seen as being far higher than the corresponding relative price movement.

A trader is said to buy a straddle when the nearest (earliest maturity) futures contract is the one being bought. If the nearest contract is being sold the trader is said to be selling the straddle. The size of the straddle spread is the price of the first maturing futures contract minus that of the later maturity contract.

If the size of the straddle spread becomes more positive or less negative the spread is said to strengthen. Conversely, if it becomes less positive or more negative it is weakening. If a straddle spread is expected to strengthen it should be bought, if it is expected to weaken selling is appropriate. In Examples 1 and 2 the straddle was expected to strengthen and was therefore bought. The subsequent strengthening of the straddle resulted in a profit for the trader.

Example 3

This example illustrates the case in which a trader sells a straddle spread based on the long gilt futures contract since he expects the spread to weaken.

10 April
Sells a June long gilt futures contract at 91.00.
  Buys a September long gilt futures contract at 90.00.
10 May
Closes out by buying a June long gilt futures contract at 92.00.
  Closes out by selling a September long gilt futures contract at 92.00.

The spread does weaken as expected. There is a loss of 32 ticks on the contract sold on 10 April (recall that the long gilt tick is $1/_{32}$) and a profit of 64 ticks from the contract bought on 10 April. There is thus a net profit of 32 ticks, which amounts to £500 (32 × £15.625) from selling the spread and subsequently closing out by buying the spread.

Inter-contract spreads involve the simultaneous purchase and sale of futures contracts relating to different underlying instruments. The underlying instruments need not even be on the same exchange, for example the spread might involve the three-month Eurodollar interest rate contract on LIFFE and the domestic certificate of deposit contract on the International Monetary Market (IMM) in Chicago. It is possible for the contracts being bought and sold to have the same maturity months in the case of inter-contract spreads.

Inter-contract spreads are subject to greater risk than straddle spreads. There is greater likelihood of divergent price movements, and the more unrelated are the two instruments the larger is the risk. A LIFFE three-month Eurodollar straddle is less risky than an inter-contract spread between LIFFE three-month Eurodollar and IMM domestic certificate of deposit contracts. The risk on the latter would in turn be less than that between LIFFE three-month Eurodollar and Chicago Board of Trade (CBOT) US Treasury Bond contracts. Since inter-contract spreads are riskier than straddles, all the contracts involved in an inter-contract spread require payment of the full initial margin; there is no reduced initial margin as occurs in the case of straddles.

A more complex type of spread is the butterfly. Whereas in the case of the spreads hitherto described the trader takes a view on the relationship between two prices, in the case of butterfly spreads the view is on the relationship between two spreads. A butterfly is a spread of spreads.

For example, suppose that three-month Eurodollar futures contracts have the following prices for the next three maturity months.

June: 92.00
September: 90.50
December: 90.00

The value of a spread is obtained by subtracting the farther price from the nearer price. Within the butterfly the nearby spread is 150 ticks whilst the deferred spread is 50 ticks. The value of the butterfly spread is therefore 100 ticks (150 − 50).

The rule of thumb for butterfly spreads is the same as that for ordinary spreads. If the butterfly spread is expected to strengthen (more positive/less negative) then the butterfly spread is bought, in the opposite case the butterfly is sold.

Example 4

This illustrates a case in which the expectation of a strengthening of a butterfly spread leads a trader to buy that spread. It is based on three-month Eurodollar futures.

Prices on 5 July
   September: 90.50
   December: 90.00
   March: 89.00
Prices on 25 July
   September: 90.50
   December: 89.75

March: 89.00

On 5 July the nearby spread is −50 ticks and the deferred spread is 100 ticks. So the value of the butterfly is 50 ticks. The trader expects that the nearby spread will increase relative to the deferred spread. In other words, the butterfly spread is expected to strengthen. On 5 July he buys a butterfly spread.

Buy one September contract at 90.50
Sell two December contracts at 90.00
Buy one March contract at 89.00

On 25 July he closes out by selling the butterfly spread. Selling a butterfly spread involves selling the nearby spread and buying the deferred spread.

Sell one September contract at 90.50
Buy two December contracts at 89.75
Sell one March contract at 89.00

There is a profit of 25 ticks on each of the two December contracts, which at $25 per tick is a profit of $1250. The trader was correct in expecting that the butterfly spread would strengthen. The nearby spread increased from 50 to 75 ticks and the deferred spread fell from 100 to 75. So the butterfly strengthened from −50 to zero.

Types of order

The most common type of order is the market order which is an order to buy or sell at the best price available at the time. A trader might also provide his broker with limit orders. Limit orders can be used for the purpose of taking profits and limiting losses. A holder of a contract might give his broker a 'take profit' limit order to sell if the price rises to a particular level and a 'stop loss' limit order to sell if the price falls to a particular level. These orders reflect the need for discipline in trading. They are necessary for ensuring that profits are not removed through the price reversing direction and for avoiding very large losses.

Another form of limit order is the time limit. A day order is an order to buy or sell at a particular price that lasts for just one day. If by the end of the day the transaction has not been carried out the order is cancelled. A 'fill or kill' (FOK) order involves an offer or bid at a specified price being made three times. If after the third attempt it has not been taken up, it is cancelled. A 'good 'til cancelled' (GTC) order specifies a price and remains in force until it is executed or countermanded. A 'market if touched' order turns into a market order as soon as there has been one transaction in the market at the price limit stipulated. 'Market on opening' and 'market on close' orders are for execution as market orders during the opening and closing periods.

13　Using currency options

Forwards and futures are techniques for guaranteeing a specific exchange rate for a future date or for obtaining compensation for deviations of actual rates from predetermined rates. A currency manager using a forward or futures position avoids losing from adverse movements of rates but also fails to gain from beneficial movements. An option is an instrument that contains elements of both hedging and position taking. It is a suitable tool for the currency manager who has a view as to future exchange rate movements but is not absolutely certain that the direction of change will be as he anticipates and wishes to reduce the losses arising in the event of the forecast being incorrect.

For example, suppose that US dollar receivables are due. Pure hedging would involve attempts to lock-in a particular exchange rate for the date on which the dollars will be received. This could be achieved with forwards or futures and the guaranteed exchange rate would be closely related to the spot rate at the time of taking out the forward or futures contract. A currency manager who forecasts an appreciation of the dollar against sterling may wish to back his forecast. Forwards and futures hedging would deny the manager the anticipated gains from an appreciating dollar.

Options may be more appropriate than forwards or futures when it is possible that competitors are not hedging. If an importer locks in a particular exchange rate whilst competitors do not, either because they do not hedge at all or because they hedge with options, he would suffer a competitive disadvantage in the event of the exchange rate moving to the competitors' advantage. By hedging with options he too can gain from a favourable currency movement and hence avoid the competitive disadvantage.

A possible procedure would be not to hedge at all. By leaving the dollar receivables exposed, the gains from the expected rise in the dollar would be obtained. However, should the dollar depreciate, the sterling value of the dollar receivables would decline. There may be a desire to prevent, or limit, this loss. A currency option protects the company from such a depreciation whilst allowing it to gain in the event of an appreciation. It is equivalent to a forward contract on the downside combined with an exposed position on the upside.

For this 'heads I win and tails I don't lose' opportunity a premium is paid. It is frequently likened to an insurance premium. Payment of the option premium guarantees compensation in the event of the dollar falling in value. If use of currency options is to be compared with not hedging at all then the insurance analogy is appropriate. If the use of such options is to be compared with hedging with forwards or futures then the premium appears to be more analogous to a gambling stake. The premium is the bet put on the currency and should the currency move in the anticipated direction the company takes its winnings.

Corporate treasurers would find it easier to convince their board of directors of the necessity of options if they use the insurance analogy rather than the gambling analogy. In fact the idea of insurance might be more appealing to the directors than the idea of hedging. A pure hedging strategy involves attempting to guarantee a particular exchange rate. This involves losing benefits of favourable movements as well as avoiding the costs of unfavourable movements. Treasurers might find it difficult to explain to their board currency management actions that result in gains from favourable exchange rate movements being lost. The less financially sophisticated members of the board might not understand that the losses on the futures market were incurred in the cause of hedging.

The purchase of an option gives the buyer the right, but not the obligation, to buy or sell the relevant currency on, or before, a specified expiry date at a price determined at the time of buying the option.

Options divide into calls and puts. A call option gives the holder the right to buy currency at a particular price. The price is known as the exercise, or strike, price and is decided upon at the time of buying the option. A put option provides the buyer of the option with the right to sell currency at a price agreed when the put is purchased. In neither case is the buyer of the option obliged to buy/sell currency at the exercise price.

On the other hand the seller, often referred to as the writer, of the option has no choice as to whether the option is exercised. If the buyer of a call option decides to exercise it the writer must sell the currency, likewise if the buyer of a put option chooses to exercise it the writer of that option must buy the currency. So the decision lies with the buyer of the option who will exercise the option if it is to his benefit and ignore it if it is not. This gives the advantage to the buyer of the option who must pay a premium to the writer for this advantage. The premium could be looked upon as an insurance premium, providing the option buyer with cover against adverse foreign exchange movements.

For example, suppose that someone buys a call option for the purchase of sterling with US dollars at an exercise price of £1 = $1.40. An increase in the value of sterling, say to £1 = $1.50, would provide the option buyer with a gain of $0.10 per £1 at the expense of the option writer. The option buyer would be in the position of buying sterling at the price of $1.40 instead of $1.50. On the other hand, should the foreign exchange value of sterling fall below $1.40, the option buyer would not exercise the option to buy at $1.40 but would buy at the lower price.

A further distinction to be drawn is between 'European-type' and 'American-type' options. The former can be exercised on one date only – the expiry date. The latter may be exercised on any business day up to the expiry date. American-type options provide greater flexibility, and the choice of date increases the likelihood of a gain being made. Correspondingly it is to be expected that an American-type option would involve a higher premium than that required in the case of a European-type option.

Simple currency option positions

Options can be used to limit unfavourable exchange rate movements whilst retaining the benefits of favourable movements.

Consider, for example, a British exporter anticipating the receipt of $1 million three months hence and anxious about the possibility of a weakening of the dollar (strengthening of the pound) prior to the receipt of the money. The exporter could buy a sterling call option allowing him to purchase sterling in three months' time at a price determined in the present. If the chosen exercise price were £1 = $1.33⅓, for example, then the exporter would have the right to exchange $1 million for £750 000. The exporter thereby puts an upper limit to the price to be paid for sterling. He is insured against the price of sterling being greater than $1.33⅓, since if it is greater he can exercise his option to buy at $1.33⅓. In the event of sterling being cheaper than $1.33⅓, the option would be ignored and the sterling bought at the lower price. Thus the exporter is able to gain from a favourable movement of the exchange rate, in this case a weakening of sterling (strengthening of the US dollar).

The profit/loss profile arising from the purchase of a call option is illustrated by Figure 13.1. It is assumed that the chosen exercise price is £1 = $1.40 whilst the exchange rate at the time of buying the option is £1 = $1.39. The premium payable is $0.02 (2 cents) per £1. If the exchange rate is less than $1.40 per £1 on the date that the option would be exercised, or when it expires, the option holder would choose not to exercise the option but instead to buy sterling at the cheaper price. In such an event the option buyer would make a net loss equal to the value of the premium paid, namely 2 cents. This is the maximum loss that the option holder can incur. On the other hand, should the price of sterling be greater than $1.40 when the option is to be exercised there would be a gain from exercising the option. It pays the option holder to exercise the right to buy at $1.40 if the price of sterling is greater. If the exchange rate is £1 = $1.42 there would be a gain of 2 cents per £1 from the exercise of the option. This would exactly offset the 2-cent premium paid, so $1.42 is the break-even price. At rates less than $1.42 there is a net loss incurred, whilst at higher rates there is a net gain. The possible extent of gain, the upside potential, is unlimited since the price of sterling could conceivably be at any level. The option buyer is thus in a position in which the extent of loss, the downside potential, is limited to the premium paid whilst the upside potential is unlimited.

The writer of the option faces the opposite situation. The maxi-

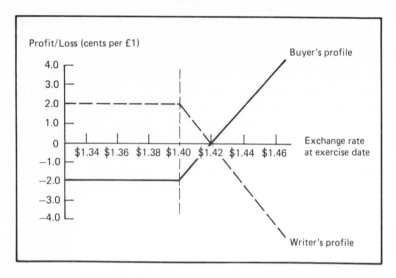

Figure 13.1   Profit/loss profiles for a call option

mum gain is the premium, this gain being fully made in the event of the option not being exercised. The writer's scope for loss, the downside potential, is unlimited. A very high price for sterling would put the writer in the position of paying a high price for sterling which he is obliged to sell at a mere $1.40 per £1. The writer's profit/loss profile is a mirror image of the buyer's profile.

The buyer of the option guarantees a maximum price of sterling of $1.40 per £1 at the cost of a premium of $0.02 per £1. Taking account of the premium the exchange rate is effectively limited to £1 = $1.42.

The option could be bought by either a hedger or a trader. A hedger would be concerned with fixing a limit to the exchange rate. For example, an exporter awaiting the receipt of US dollars might want to set an upper limit to the price to be paid, in dollars, for sterling. Such an exporter might buy sterling call options at an exercise price of $1.40 per £1 so as to ensure that $1.40 is the highest price that he could have to pay for the sterling. Options could also be used by traders (that is speculators) seeking to profit from exchange rate movements. A sterling call option might be bought by a trader with a bullish view as to the future movement of sterling. A trader expecting sterling to rise well above £1 = $1.40 might buy sterling call options at an exercise price of $1.40.

Subsequently, if the trader's anticipations are borne out, he buys sterling at $1.40 by exercising the options and sells that sterling at the higher price so as to realize a profit.

Hedging and trading are not always distinct activities. The exporter mentioned above is more likely to hedge against an increase in the dollar price of sterling if he expects sterling to appreciate than if he expects a fall in its value. When the decision to hedge, and how to hedge, is influenced by the view taken as to future exchange rate movements the hedging is effectively mixed with trading. A pure hedge would be unaffected by expectations. The simultaneity of hedging and trading can also be seen in the case of a company that hedges the tender for a contract.

Options are ideal for hedging tenders since if the tender is unsuccessful the option need not be exercised. A British exporter tendering for a contract in US dollars faces exchange risk from the date of making the tender. A weakening of the US dollar relative to sterling would undermine the profitability of the trade. Although the purchase of options would be primarily for the purpose of hedging exchange rate risk it is unlikely that, in the event of the tender being unsuccessful, the exporter would simply allow an option to expire if the exercise or sale of the option would produce a gain. If sterling had strengthened by the date on which the tender is rejected, a call option to buy sterling at $1.40 could be exercised and the sterling thus purchased in turn sold to give a profit. In the case of traded options the potential profitability of the options would give them a high sale value. Thus in the case of covering tenders, the possibility that the tender might be unsuccessful means that the option user is trading as well as hedging.

A hedger or trader buying an option is faced with a decision as to what exercise price to choose. This choice determines the profit/loss profile and is made in the light of the buyer's tolerance of risk and his view as to future exchange rate movements. This view encompasses not only the direction of change but also its extent, speed, and probability of occurrence. Figure 13.2 shows hypothetical call option profit/loss profiles at three exercise prices. It is assumed that the exchange rate is currently £1 = $1.39.

Strategy C, buying a call option to buy sterling at £1 = $1.45, involves the greatest risk in terms of potential adverse exchange rate movements since a hedger would be unprotected against a

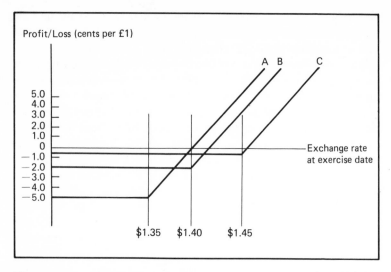

Figure 13.2   Profit/loss profiles for call options with differing exercise prices

rise in the dollar price of sterling between $1.39 and $1.45 per £1. However, at 0.5 cents per £1 the premium cost of strategy C is the lowest. Strategy C would be favoured by a hedger willing to bear a high degree of risk and/or feeling that it is unlikely that sterling would strengthen. If the hedger anticipates that it is likely that sterling will weaken or rise by only a very modest amount he would be reluctant to pay a high premium (such as 2 cents for a $1.40 call) to hedge against the possibility of sterling appreciation. A hedger with such a view as to future exchange rate movements would prefer to merely insure against an extreme appreciation of sterling (beyond $1.45) and correspondingly economize on the premium paid.

A hedger with a firmly-held view that there will be a considerable appreciation of sterling would be more likely to choose strategy A and buy the $1.35 call option. This strategy provides the highest net gain in the event of a substantial increase in the dollar price of sterling. The importance of the view taken as to future exchange rate movements in determining the choice of exercise price underlines the observation that hedging tends to contain elements of trading.

A trader's choice of exercise price would also be influenced by his attitude towards risk, expectations of exchange rate changes, and confidence in his expectations. Whilst the hedger seeks to reduce risk, the trader seeks to profit from his forecasts of exchange rate movements. Correspondingly, a hedger may insure against an appreciation of sterling even if he considers it more likely that the pound will fall, but a trader will buy a sterling call option only if he expects a sterling appreciation. If he is very confident that the dollar price of sterling will rise and has a high tolerance of risk he might choose a low exercise price, such as £1 = \$1.35. This maximizes his potential gain from a rise in the value of the pound. Strategy A, however, involves relatively high risk. The trader has paid a high premium, 5 cents per £1, and stands to lose this in the event of a sharp fall in sterling. If the trader is less confident about his expectation of a sterling appreciation or is more risk averse he may choose a higher exercise price. Although strategies B and C show smaller gains from a strengthening of the pound, the lower premiums ensure that there is less to be lost should the expectation of a substantial sterling appreciation prove to be incorrect.

Although the exposition thus far has concentrated on the buying of call options, similar analyses apply to the purchase of put options. A British importer needing to make a future payment in US dollars may be anxious about the possibility that sterling will depreciate against the dollar and hence render the necessary dollars more expensive. He could buy sterling put options and thereby obtain the right to sell pounds at a particular dollar exercise price. If the dollar price of sterling fell below this exercise price the importer could exercise the option to exchange sterling for dollars at that exercise price. The importer would thus have successfully hedged against a sterling depreciation by setting a lower limit to the dollar value of sterling (and hence an upper limit to the sterling value of the dollar). This is illustrated by the following example.

Example

A UK importer invoiced in US dollars needs to obtain \$1 500 000. He buys sterling puts at an exercise price of £1 = \$1.50, thereby acquiring the right to sell £1 000 000 for \$1 500 000. The spot exchange rate is £1 = \$1.50 and the premium is 2.5 cents/£ = \$25 000.

Outcome 1
The pound strengthens to £1 = $1.65. $1 500 000 is bought for
£909 091. Option not exercised.
Outcome 2
The pound weakens to £1 = $1.35. £1 000 000 would buy only
$1 350 000. Option to sell £1 000 000 for $1 500 000 is exercised.

A trader expecting a sterling depreciation might also buy a
sterling put option thereby guaranteeing a minimum selling price
of sterling. An actual price below the chosen exercise price would
allow the trader to make a profit by buying at the actual price and
selling at the exercise price.

Hedging and trading – the profiles

It is useful to visualize a hedger as seeking to make gains from
options in order to offset cash market losses. When the option is
looked upon in isolation (which is the way that a trader would see
it) the profit/loss profile is the opposite to that which emerges
if the option and the cash position being hedged are combined.
Figure 13.3 considers the case of a call option.

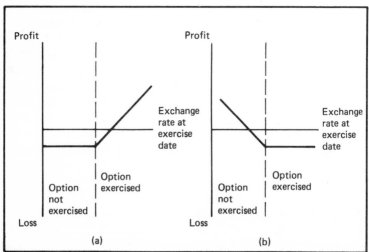

**Figure 13.3   A call option: (a) in isolation; (b) combined with
hedged cash position**

Figure 13.3(a) depicts the situation of a trader. Profits are made when the option is exercised and losses when it is not. Figure 13.3(b) illustrates the position of a hedger. Since the hedger faces a cash market loss in the event of a price rise, the options gain merely serves to offset this loss. A fall in price brings a cash market gain which is not offset by an options loss (other than the premium paid).

In the case in which the option is combined with a cash position being hedged the effect is to guarantee a particular exchange rate in the event of a rise in the price of the currency. This is the case whether there is delivery of the currency at the predetermined price, in which case there is no loss from the exchange rate movement, or whether there is compensation to offset the unfavourable price paid in the money market.

14   Writing currency options

In the preceding chapter the emphasis was on the buying of options. The buyer of an option obtains the right, but not the obligation, to buy or sell currency at a specific price. The writer (that is, the seller) of the option has no right to buy or sell but must transact with the option buyer in the event of the buyer choosing to exercise the option. The writer of a call option must sell currency if the buyer exercises the option, whilst the writer of a put option has a corresponding obligation to buy from the option buyer should the latter choose to exercise the option.

The question arises as to what circumstances would cause someone to decide that option writing is worthwhile. The answer can be obtained from observing the conditions under which the writer of an option makes a profit. Figure 14.1 illustrates the profit/loss profiles of a call writer and a put writer.

The premium paid to the call writer is 2 cents per £1 and the exercise price is $1.40 per £1. At spot prices below $1.40 the call option buyer would not exercise the option, but instead choose to buy sterling at the lower price. Therefore at spot prices less than $1.40 per £1 the call option writer makes a profit of 2 cents per £1. When the spot price is above $1.40 it is possible for the option buyer to exercise the option and thereby buy at a price below the spot price. In the event of the option being exercised the option writer would have to obtain sterling at a price above $1.40 in order to sell it at $1.40. At a spot price of $1.42 the loss made on the currency transactions exactly cancels the 2 cents per £1 premium received.

If the option is exercised when the spot price is above $1.42 the option writer makes a net loss. Since the price of sterling could, conceivably, be at any level above $1.40 the potential for loss is unlimited whereas the maximum profit is equal to the premium of 2 cents per £1, received in the event of the option not being exercised.

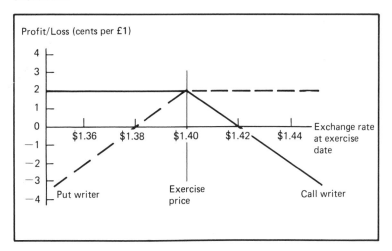

Figure 14.1   Profit/loss profiles of option writers

Again it is assumed that the premium paid to the put writer is 2 cents per £1 and that the exercise price is $1.40. At spot prices above $1.40 the put option buyer would not exercise the option, preferring to sell sterling at the higher price. Therefore the option is not exercised and the put writer makes a profit of 2 cents per £1. At spot prices below $1.40 the option would be exercised by the buyer. Break-even occurs at $1.38 with the writer's loss on the currency transaction, buying at $1.40 and selling at $1.38, exactly offsetting the premium received. At spot prices below $1.38 the transactions loss per £1 exceeds the 2 cents per £1 premium leaving the writer with a net loss. The potential for loss is unlimited whilst the maximum profit is 2 cents per £1.

The call writer gains if the price of sterling remains below $1.42 per £1 prior to the expiry date, therefore someone might write the call option if he expects the price of sterling to remain below $1.42. The question then arises as to why a trader with such an expectation should choose to write a call option rather than buy a put, after all buying the put gives unlimited profit potential whilst writing the call provides a profit of only 2 cents per £1 at most. Writing the call is more profitable than buying the put if the price of sterling remains in the band $1.36 to $1.44. Buying a put at an exercise price of $1.40 involves losses unless the price of sterling falls below $1.38, whereas writing a call provides a profit at all prices below $1.42. For at-the-money (that is, spot price equals exercise price) options, writing a call is a suitable strategy for a trader who expects the exchange rate to undergo little change, but feels that a sterling depreciation is more likely than an appreciation.

The put writer gains if the price of sterling remains above $1.38 until the expiry date. Reasoning similar to that used in the case of the call writer above leads to the conclusion that put writing is an appropriate strategy for a trader who expects the exchange rate to be persistently close to £1 = $1.40 with any deviation being towards a higher dollar price of sterling.

The writer of an option needs to decide on the premium that he requires, whilst the buyer of the option should have an idea of the appropriate premium (or 'fair price'). Although premiums are typically determined by highly-complex statistical formulae it is informative to consider the factors that such formulae take into account.

Determination of premiums

An important determinant of an option premium is the relationship of the exercise price to either the spot price or the forward price. In the case of a call option, a spot or forward price above the exercise price would provide the buyer of the option with an automatic profit. If a sterling call option were bought at an exercise price of $1.40 per £1 whilst the spot price was $1.43 per £1 then the buyer of the option could make an immediate profit by exercising the option, thereby buying sterling at $1.40, and simultaneously selling sterling at $1.43 (the profit referred to is, of course, not net of the premium paid). If the call option were bought at the exercise price of $1.40 per £1 whilst the forward exchange rate was $1.45 per £1 there would again be scope for automatic profit.

Upon buying the option the holder could sell sterling forward at $1.45 and when the forward delivery became due obtain the necessary sterling by exercising the option, thereby buying at $1.40. The excess of the spot price or the forward price over the exercise price, whichever difference is the greater, determines a minimum value that the option premium could take.

In the case of a put option, a spot or forward price below the exercise price would provide the opportunity for an automatic profit. It would be possible to buy cheaply and sell at a higher price. The difference between either the spot or forward rate, whichever difference is the greater, and the exercise price determines a lower limit to the premium.

The currency options traded on the London Stock Exchange and the London International Financial Futures Exchange are American-type options, allowing the holder to exercise the option at any time up until an expiry date. This is in contrast to the European-type options which permit the holder to exercise on the expiry date only.

The premium payable for an American-type option is affected by the volatility of the exchange rate and the length of time to the expiry date. Both of these factors are relevant to the likelihood of the option holder being able to exercise his option at a profit. For example, in the case of a sterling call option a relatively high degree of volatility would increase the probability that the dollar price of sterling would exceed the exercise price at some stage prior to the expiry date of the option. This probability would also increase as the time period to expiry is lengthened.

An option premium can be subdivided into two components, these being known as 'intrinsic value' and 'time value'. Intrinsic value refers to the gain to be made from exercising the option immediately after buying it. In the case of a call option it is the excess of the spot price over the exercise price and for a put option it is the excess of the exercise price over the spot price. When intrinsic value exists the option is said to be 'in-the-money'. The call buyer could profit by exercising the option, thereby buying currency relatively cheaply, and simultaneously selling the currency at a higher price. The put buyer profits by purchasing currency cheaply in the spot market and selling it at a higher price by means of exercising the option. Intrinsic value provides a lower limit to the premium payable for an in-the-money option.

If a call option exercise price is above the spot price the option
is said to be 'out-of-the-money' and intrinsic value is zero. A put
option exercise price below the spot price would also offer no
immediate profit and hence be deemed to be out-of-the-money,
with intrinsic value again being zero.

The difference between a premium and its intrinsic value
is referred to as its time value. Time value, which cannot be
negative, reflects the volatility of the spot exchange rate and the
length of the period to expiry. In Figure 14.2 time value for a call
option is represented by the vertical distance between the intrinsic
value boundary, OBC, and the broken line showing the premium
at each spot price. The exercise price is at B.

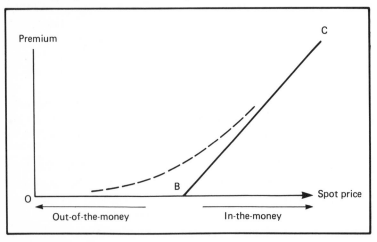

**Figure 14.2 Call option premiums and the intrinsic value
            boundary**

At spot prices below B there is no intrinsic value and hence the
intrinsic value boundary coincides with the horizontal axis. Above
B, intrinsic value increases, cent for cent, with the spot price of
sterling so the intrinsic value boundary slopes upwards at 45° from
point B. This intrinsic value boundary sets limits to the value of the
premium, which cannot fall below the boundary.

Figure 14.3 illustrates, in a parallel fashion, the case of a put
option. Again, the exercise price is at B. At spot prices below B
the put option buyer can buy at a lower price than that at which
he has the right to sell. In this case the intrinsic value boundary is

represented by CBA. Two option premium curves are depicted, labelled X and Y. They illustrate the effects of volatility and period to maturity on the time value and hence the premium. Greater volatility and a longer period to maturity increase time value and raise the option premium curve, for example from X to Y.

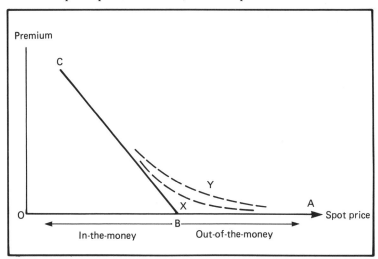

Figure 14.3 The effects of expected volatility and period to maturity on option premiums

When the exercise price is equal to the spot price the option is said to be 'at-the-money'. Time value is always at its greatest when an option is at-the-money. The further into or out of the money the option moves, the lower the time value becomes. This is illustrated in Figures 14.2 and 14.3 by the tendency for the option premium curves to approach the intrinsic value boundary as the spot price moves further away from the exercise price.

It is possible to obtain an intuitive insight into why time value behaves in this way. Consider first the out-of-the-money option. As the option moves further out-of-the-money the likelihood of it moving into the money prior to expiry reduces because the necessary movement of the spot rate becomes progressively greater and hence less probable. Thus the further out-of-the-money that the option becomes, the smaller is the chance that the holder of the option will be able to profit from exercising the option. The option becomes less and less valuable to the holder whilst the risk of loss to the writer declines so that the premium required for taking on the risk diminishes.

In the case of the in-the-money option, the decline in time value is to be explained in a different way. An in-the-money option has an intrinsic value and this intrinsic value is vulnerable to erosion in the event of the spot price moving towards, or beyond, the exercise price. The option buyer has paid for the intrinsic value and runs the risk that the intrinsic value might be in part, or in whole, lost. The further in-the-money an option is when bought the greater is the potential loss. This is to be compared with an at-the-money option which has no intrinsic value and hence provides no risk of losing an intrinsic value already paid for whilst it provides the same opportunity as the in-the-money option for gain arising from movements (deeper) into the money. The in-the-money option buyer is compensated for this potential loss of intrinsic value by a reduced time value with the compensation rising as more intrinsic value is paid for in the premium. On the other hand, the writer selling the option that is in-the-money receives a premium containing intrinsic value and a movement of the spot price towards, or beyond, the exercise price would provide a gain to the writer since the loss incurred by the writer from buying and selling currency when the option is exercised falls below the intrinsic value, and hence the premium. Thus the option writer stands to gain from an erosion of intrinsic value. This potential for gain is reflected in a reduced requirement for time value in the premium payable to the writer for in-the-money options. This reduction in time value becomes greater as the option moves further in-the-money, a movement that enhances the opportunity for gain by the writer.

Time value is subject to decay. In other words, time value declines as the option approaches its expiry date. This is consistent with the observation made earlier that time value is greater when there is a relatively long period remaining to expiry. Time value decay does not occur at a constant rate. The rate of decay is initially slow but becomes progressively more rapid as the expiry date is approached. Figure 14.4 illustrates the type of path that the time value decay follows.

Time value is proportional to the square root of the length of time remaining to the expiry date. Thus the time value when 100 days remain will be twice that which exists when just 25 days remain. Time value declines by as much during the last 25 days

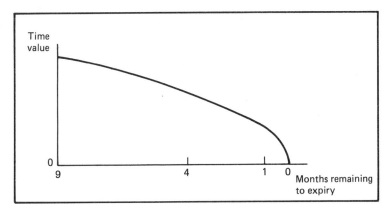

Figure 14.4 The decay of time value over time

as it does during the first 75 days. This is the type of accelerating decline illustrated by Figure 14.4.

Option premia

Some examples of option premia are shown by Table 14.1. These premia are expressed in cents per £1. They are taken from LIFFE and are the premia available for sterling call options at the close of business on 6 February 1986. The closing spot rate for sterling on that day was very close to $1.40 ($1.3995 to be precise), so the $1.40 options were very close to being at-the-money.

Table 14.1
Examples of option premia

Strike price	Month in which expiry date falls				
	Feb	Mar	Apr	June	Sept
1.35	5.04	5.25	5.83	6.36	7.00
1.40	1.31	2.24	3.10	3.90	4.74
1.45	0.11	0.70	1.42	2.21	3.07

In Table 14.1 the options with a strike price of $1.35 are in-the-money since the guaranteed purchase price of sterling is lower than the spot price. Sterling could be bought at the guaranteed price and immediately sold spot at a profit. The options with a strike price of $1.45 are out-of-the-money since the guaranteed purchase price of sterling is higher than the spot price.

In-the-money options are more expensive than at-the-money options since the potential immediate gain (intrinsic value) must be paid for. At-the-money options are more expensive than out-of-the-money options since the latter involve the hedger accepting some of the risk. The buyer of a $1.45 call option receives no compensation for a rise in the price of sterling to $1.45, so he absorbs that part of the risk himself.

Options with more distant expiry dates are more expensive than the closer ones. Longer time spans provide more opportunity for the spot price to move above the strike price.

Case study: zero cost options

A British exporter anticipates the receipt of US$3 000 000, two months from the present. The spot exchange rate is £1 = $1.45. The company budgeted for an exchange rate of £1 = $1.50, at which rate margins are tight. The exporting company is reluctant to lock-in an exchange rate with forwards or futures since the company treasurer forecasts a strengthening of the dollar and wishes to benefit in the event of his expectations proving to be correct. Nevertheless, the treasurer wants to limit the effective cost of sterling to £1 = $1.50, should his forecast prove to be badly in error.

One solution would be to buy $1.50 calls and finance them by writing puts. The treasurer ascertains that sterling option premiums on the London Stock Exchange for the first maturity date following the receipt of the dollars are:

Strike price ($)	Calls	Puts
1.35	10.20	0.20
1.40	6.00	1.02
1.45	2.00	2.05
1.50	0.98	6.03
1.55	0.15	10.25

By buying $1.50 calls and selling an equal number of $1.40 puts there is a net gain of 0.04 cents per pound.

Alternatively, the treasurer might approach banks to see if he can obtain an over-the-counter zero cost option (sometimes known as a cylinder or collar). It might be deemed worthwhile to accept a bank's offer of a $1.4050 to $1.5000 option with a zero net premium to cover the full exposure in preference to using traded options.

15 Complex strategies with currency options

A vast number of different profit/loss profiles can be constructed by combining option contracts. This chapter shows the construction and purposes of some of the more popular option strategies that use combinations.

Vertical spreads

Vertical spreads, which may be used for either hedging or trading, involve the simultaneous buying and writing of options with different exercise prices. Figure 15.1 illustrates a bullish call spread (bullish since it would be undertaken by a trader expecting the price of sterling to rise) – spot exchange rate £1 = $1.22, buy $1.25 call at a premium of 2 cents, write (that is, sell) $1.30 call at a premium of 0.5 cents. This spread might appeal to a trader with a very specific view of the future exchange rate. He expects that sterling will strengthen to around $1.30 but feels it is unlikely that it will rise beyond this. The trader is thus prepared to forgo any profit that might arise due to the spot price of sterling rising above $1.30 in order to reduce his premium payments, and hence risk, by 0.5 cents per £1. This latter attribute of the spread increases its attraction to more risk averse traders.

Such a spread might also appeal to a hedger who seeks insurance against a rise in the spot price of sterling above $1.25 whilst feeling that a strengthening of sterling beyond £1 = $1.30 is unlikely. This latter view leads to the writing of the $1.30 call so that, beyond $1.30, gains from the $1.25 call would be offset by losses on the $1.30 call, but with the benefit that the premium paid is reduced by 0.5 cents per £1. This stance further illustrates how hedging can involve elements of trading; the hedging strategy is affected by the view taken as to future exchange rate movements. Selling the $1.30 call adds an element of trading based on the view that sterling will not strengthen beyond £1 = $1.30.

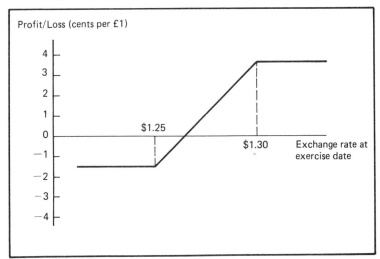

Figure 15.1   A bull call spread

Figure 15.2 illustrates a bearish put spread (bearish because it would be used by a trader expecting a fall in the price of sterling) – spot exchange rate £1 = $1.22, buy $1.20 put at a premium of 2.5 cents, write $1.15 put at a premium of 0.6 cents.

At spot prices above $1.20 neither option would be exercised and the transactor makes a net loss equal to the balance of the premiums – 0.6 − 2.5 = −1.9 cents. As the value of sterling falls below $1.20 there is a potential gain from selling sterling at the exercise price of $1.20 and buying it more cheaply. This potential gain increases until it reaches 5 cents per £1 when the exchange rate is £1 = $1.15. The net gain at $1.15, taking account of the net premium, is 5 − 1.9 = 3.1 cents. As the price of sterling falls

below $1.15 the $1.15 put will be exercised obliging the transactor
to buy at $1.15 whilst selling at a lower price. Thus as the price of
sterling falls below $1.15 the additional gains from exercising the
$1.20 put are cancelled by the losses on the $1.15 put leaving the
net profit at a constant 3.1 cents per £1.

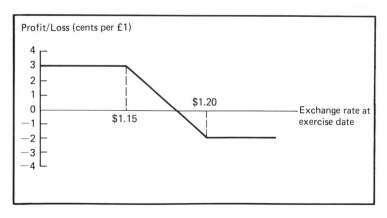

Figure 15.2   A bearish put spread

A bearish put spread might appeal to a trader who feels confident that the price of sterling will fall towards $1.15 but considers it
unlikely that the decline will go beyond this. Also a hedger wanting
to insure against the possibility that sterling will depreciate beyond
£1 = $1.20 but holding the view that the depreciation could not go
beyond £1 = $1.15 would buy such a put spread. He reduces the
net premium payable from 2.5 to 1.9 cents per £1 at the cost of
foregoing protection from depreciation beyond $1.15. Again this
hedging strategy contains an element of trading. The writing of the
$1.15 put amounts to adding a trade to the hedge. The 'hedger'
backs his expectation that sterling will not decline below $1.15 and
seeks to profit by 0.6 cents per £1 in the event of his expectation
turning out to be correct.

In addition to the bullish call spreads and bearish put
spreads there are bullish put spreads and bearish call spreads.
A speculator expecting sterling to strengthen relative to the US
dollar might seek to profit from such a strengthening by buying
a put option with a low exercise price (and consequent low premium) and writing a put option with a higher exercise price (and

higher premium). This is a bullish put spread. A rise in the price of sterling could produce a profit equal to the difference between the two premiums, since neither option would be exercised if the price exceeds the higher exercise price.

A bearish call spread involves buying a call option with a high exercise price (and low premium) and writing a call option with a low exercise price (and high premium). In the event of the price of sterling falling below the lower exercise price neither option would be exercised and the difference between the premiums accrues as profit.

Volatility trades

It is possible to make profits from trades based upon expectations about volatility. The trader takes a position as to whether exchange rates will or will not remain within a specific range. Three strategies that might be used are straddles, strangles and butterflies. Figure 15.3 illustrates straddles, which involve either buying calls and puts at the same exercise price and for the same expiry date or writing simultaneous calls and puts.

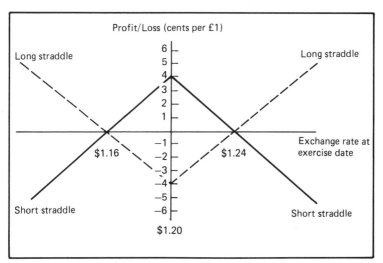

Figure 15.3   Long and short straddles

A trader expecting low volatility would sell a straddle. The profit/loss profile of this strategy is illustrated in Figure 15.3 by the unbroken line. The trader simultaneously writes (sells) a call and a put, both at the exercise price of $1.20. The total sum received in premiums is 4 cents per £1. Should the exchange rate be so stable that it remains at £1 = $1.20 then the trader will make a profit equal to the sum of the premiums. Should either option be exercised the net profit will be less than 4 cents per £1. So long as the price of sterling is between $1.16 and $1.24 on the exercise date the loss on the currency transaction is less than the sum of the premiums, and the seller of the straddle makes a net profit. The closer the exchange rate remains to £1 = $1.20, that is the lower the volatility, the greater is the profit made by the seller of the straddle. Therefore a trader who anticipates a stable exchange rate might be inclined to sell a straddle.

A trader taking a bullish view as to volatility would be inclined to buy a straddle. His worst possible outcome would be a persistence of the exchange rate at £1 = $1.20. A total of 4 cents per £1 would have been paid in premiums and no offsetting gains from currency transactions would be available. If the price of sterling deviates by more than 4 cents from $1.20 the straddle buyer stands to make a net gain.

Strangles involve buying or writing simultaneous calls and puts for the same expiry date, but with different exercise prices. Long and short strangles are illustrated by Figure 15.4. In the case of the long strangle, represented by the broken line, the trader buys a call option with an exercise price of $1.23. He simultaneously buys a put option with an exercise price of $1.17. The sum of the two premiums paid is 2 cents per £1. If the price of sterling remains within the range $1.17 to $1.23 the trader makes a net loss equal to the sum of the premiums. Movement of the exchange rate outside this range provides a potential gain, from currency transactions, that offsets the cost of the premiums. A price of sterling outside the $1.15 to $1.25 range on the expiry date provides a net profit. For example, a spot price of $1.26 would produce a profit of 3 cents per £1 from the $1.23 call option and that is more than necessary to offset the 2 cents per £1 cost of the premiums. A trader who anticipates considerable volatility would be inclined to buy a strangle.

A trader with a bearish view of future volatility might sell a strangle. This strategy is illustrated by the unbroken line in Figure

15.4. The trader sells a call and a put option, with respective exercise prices of $1.23 and $1.17, and receives a total of 2 cents per £1 in premiums. If the price of sterling remains in the range $1.17 to $1.23 the trader makes a profit equal to the sum of the two premiums. Sufficient departure of the price of sterling from this range renders the trader liable to a net loss.

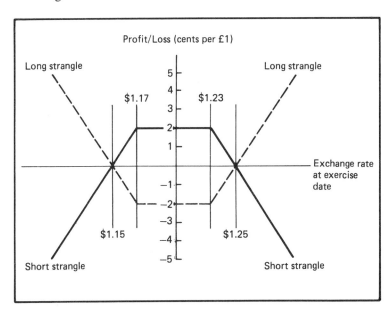

Figure 15.4 Long and short strangles

Butterfly spreads are illustrated by Figure 15.5. Buying a butterfly involves buying an in-the-money call, writing two at-the-money calls, and buying an out-of-the-money call with the same maturities. For example, when the spot exchange rate is $1.20, buy a $1.16 call at a premium of 5.0 cents, write two $1.20 calls at a premium of 2.5 cents each, and buy a $1.24 call at a premium of 1.0 cent. The profit/loss profile of this long butterfly is shown by the broken line in Figure 15.5. At spot prices below $1.16 none of the options is exercised and the trader makes a loss of 1 cent per £1, the excess of the premiums paid over those received. As the spot price rises from $1.16 to $1.20 there is a cent for cent gain from the currency position leading to a net profit of 3 cents per £1 at a spot price of $1.20. As the price of sterling rises further, from $1.20 towards $1.24, the cent for cent losses on the two options written outweigh the gains from the $1.16 long call. At a spot price of $1.24 the 8 cent gain from the $1.16 long call is precisely offset by the two 4 cent losses arising from the $1.20 short calls with the result that the net position is back at a loss of 1 cent per £1. As the price rises beyond $1.24 the $1.24 long call is exercised. There are then cent for cent gains from two long calls and corresponding losses from two short calls. In consequence the net outcome remains at a loss of 1 cent per £1 for all prices above $1.24.

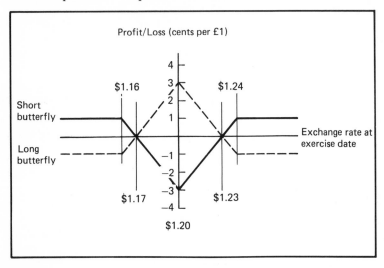

Figure 15.5   Long and short butterfly spreads

Selling a butterfly involves writing an in-the-money call, buying two at-the-money calls, and writing an out-of-the-money call. The profit/loss profile of a short butterfly spread is represented by the unbroken line in Figure 15.5. The short butterfly has a profile that is a mirror image of that of the long butterfly.

Figure 15.6 provides a comparison of the three volatility trade strategies described. A choice between the three types of spread is made in the light of the trader's expectations as to volatility and his attitude towards risk. Straddles are preferred to strangles by traders whose expectations are of particularly low volatility and who hold those expectations with confidence. Strangles are less

risky than straddles, they provide profits over a wider range of
spot rates and involve slightly lower losses in the event of volatility
being higher than expected. The price of the lower risk is the lower
prospective profit to be obtained if volatility turns out to be very
low. The long butterfly could be seen as providing the least risk
since there is a lower limit to the potential losses whereas the other
strategies are capable of producing unlimited losses in the event
of high volatility. Again, the reduced risk is attained at the cost of
lower potential profits.

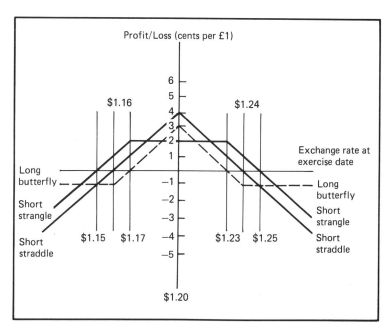

**Figure 15.6   Comparison of the straddle, strangle and butter-
fly strategies**

Users of complex strategies that involve writing options need
to be able to control the timing of the exercise of the options that
they have written. Traded options are particularly suitable in this
regard since sellers can readily close out their positions by buying
identical contracts, a procedure that is an effective alternative to
exercising and which provides similar results.

16   Traded currency options

An 'over-the-counter' (OTC) option is typically provided by a bank and is tailor-made to meet the requirements of the customer. The customer can stipulate the amount of currency, the strike (exercise) price, the expiry date and whether the option is of the American or European type. American-type options can be exercised on any business day up to the expiry date whereas European-type options can be exercised on the expiry date only.

Traded options are standardized. There is limited choice as to amount, strike price, and expiry date. The customer must also accept an American-type option. For example, the sterling option traded on the London International Financial Futures Exchange (LIFFE) must be traded in blocks of £25 000, the exercise prices available are at 5 cent intervals (for example $1.30, $1.35, $1.40 per £1), and there are just five expiry dates available at one time.

Standardization is necessary to ensure adequate liquidity in traded options markets. It is not surprising, however, that it leads corporate users to prefer OTC options for the most part. Traded options tend to be used by banks, including those seeking to offset the OTC options provided for customers. Corporate users may find that the traded options are cheaper, if they are willing to accept the standardized terms.

Hedging and trading without exercising options

A hedger may choose to sell the options that he holds rather than exercise them. This is particularly likely in the case of traded options. The procedure is illustrated by the following hypothetical example.

Suppose that the spot exchange rate is £1 = $1.25 and an exporter anticipates receipt of dollars in two months. He buys sterling call options with an exercise price of $1.25 at the cost of a premium of 2 cents per £1. On the date of receiving the dollars, he finds that sterling has strengthened to £1 = $1.30. He could exercise the options and pay $1.25 per £1. Taking into account the 2 cents per £1 option premium he would be paying a total price of $1.27 per £1 for sterling. Alternatively he could sell the options. The increase in the price of sterling from $1.25 to $1.30 would raise the market value of $1.25 call options. The premiums might rise, for example from 2 cents to 5.5 cents per £1. The hedger could sell his options at a profit of 3.5 cents per £1 and then buy sterling at the new spot price of $1.30. Taking account of the profit on the options, the price effectively paid for sterling is $1.30 − $0.035 = $1.265 per £1.

Table 16.1
Selling versus exercising options ($)

Spot price	Premium		Effective price if option sold	Effective price if option exercised
	Intrinsic value	Time value		
1.250	0.000	0.010	1.260	1.270
1.260	0.010	0.009	1.261	1.270
1.270	0.020	0.008	1.262	1.270
1.280	0.030	0.007	1.263	1.270
1.300	0.050	0.005	1.265	1.270
1.350	0.100	0.002	1.268	1.270
1.400	0.150	0.001	1.269	1.270

For traded options, such as those of the London Stock Exchange and LIFFE, it is to be expected that hedgers would sell options rather than exercise them. This is because time value cannot be

negative. Table 16.1 shows a hypothetical set of values that illustrates this point. It is assumed that the chosen exercise price is
$1.25 per £1 and that a premium of 2 cents per £1 has been paid.

As long as an option is sold prior to the expiry date some time
value is likely to remain. In Table 16.1 the time value of 2 cents per
£1 which made up the 2 cents premium for the $1.25 at the money
call option has eroded as the time left to expiry has been reduced
(see Figure 14.4 on p. 145). The time value for a $1.25 at the money
call option is now 1 cent per £1. Time value further declines as the
option moves into the money, but intrinsic value increases cent for
cent. If the option is sold for the new premium and sterling bought
at the existing spot price the effective price paid for sterling is given
by:

$$\frac{\text{Spot}}{\text{price}} + \frac{\text{Original}}{\text{premium}} - \frac{\text{New}}{\text{premium}} = \frac{\text{Effective}}{\text{price}}$$

The original premium is $0.02 and the new premium is equal to
the sum of the intrinsic and time values. For example:

$$\$1.28 \ + \ \$0.02 \ - \ \$0.037 \ = \ \$1.263$$

It can be seen from Table 16.1 that as long as some time value
remains there is an advantage in selling the option and buying
sterling at the spot rate rather than exercising the option. The
difference between the two alternative effective prices of sterling
is equal to the time value.

Trading

The facility of selling options previously bought provides scope for
making profits. Already a number of ways in which options can be
used for trading have been indicated. The ability to sell options
previously bought allows for trading based upon views as to future
changes in market expectations of volatility and views on the speed
of movement of exchange rates.

As mentioned earlier, one factor determining premiums is the
expected volatility of the relevant exchange rate. Greater volatility
increases the likelihood that options will be profitably exercised

and hence causes option writers to require higher premiums. Simultaneously, the enhanced chances of profit render option buyers prepared to pay higher premiums. A trader who anticipates that market expectations of volatility will rise can buy options and subsequently sell them for higher premiums when market expectations of volatility have increased.

Views as to the speed of exchange rate movements can also provide scope for profitable trading. For example, suppose that the spot exchange rate is £1 = $1.25 and that the premium for a $1.30 out-of-the-money call option is 1 cent per £1. If the exchange rises to, say, $1.28 within a few days the premium on the $1.30 call option would rise, perhaps to 1.75 cents per £1. The trader can then sell the option at a profit of 0.75 cents per £1, whereas an identical appreciation which is not accomplished until the expiry date, or close to it, might leave the trader with a loss.

In the foregoing example a profit was made on an option that remained out-of-the-money. In fact use of out-of-the-money options for trading can provide higher percentage returns to traders than use of in-the-money options. Although an increase in the price of sterling would add more to in-the-money call option premiums than to out-of-the-money call option premiums the fact that out-of-the-money premiums are lower could mean that the percentage return on the money paid in premiums is higher in the case of out-of-the-money options.

The possibility of greater percentage returns from out-of-the-money options is also present when the source of profit is the extent, rather than speed, of change in the price of sterling. Again, although the absolute gain on the option if it is out-of-the-money at the initial price of sterling is less than the absolute gain from the option that starts from being in-the-money, the lower cost of the out-of-the-money option could mean that the percentage return obtained on the funds invested is greater.

The fact that it is more profitable to sell traded options than to exercise them means that the writers of options can assume that exercise of the options will not occur prior to the expiry date, even when the options are of the American type traded on the London Stock Exchange and LIFFE. This means that hedgers and traders can use complex strategies that involve writing options – such as the vertical spreads, straddles, strangles and butterflies discussed in Chapter 15 – without fear of the strategies being undermined by options written being exercised before the dates on which the writers choose to close them out.

Delta hedging

In addition to traded options, which are standardized (as to size, expiry date and available exercise price), there are OTC options written by banks. An OTC option is tailor-made to a customer's specific requirements in terms of size, expiry date, and exercise price. The writing of OTC options subjects banks to risks that can be offset by delta hedging (alternatively known as ratio hedging) with traded options.

It is necessary at this stage to explain what is meant by deltas and to introduce the concept of fair value. The delta of an option is the ratio of the change in its premium to the change in the price of the underlying financial instrument. For example, if the dollar price of sterling rose by 1 cent and as a result the premium on a sterling call option increased by 0.4 cents the delta of the option would be said to be 0.4.

The fair price of an option is the premium that would be expected in the light of the magnitudes of the variables that determine its value – for example the spot price of sterling, the exercise price, time to expiry, and the expected volatility of the dollar price of sterling. Fair prices are calculated by means of mathematical models.

A bank writing OTC options might wish to avoid losses arising from increases in premiums. If option premiums rise subsequent to a bank writing an option for an agreed premium that bank could be in what is effectively a loss-making position. If the fair price of the option written exceeds the premium agreed, the balance of probabilities is that the option will be exercised at a net loss to the bank. This loss-making position might alternatively be explained in terms of the bank needing to pay more, for an option that exactly offsets the one that it has written, than it receives for the option that it has written.

Suppose, for example, that a bank has written an OTC option for the purchase of £1 million. The spot exchange rate and exercise price are both $1.23, so the option is at-the-money. The bank charges a premium of 3 cents per £1 but calculates that the fair price would have been 2.9 cents per £1. The bank is in the position of having made a net gain of 0.1 cents per £1, that is $1000. The bank wishes to protect this profit from the possibility of the fair price rising. It does this by buying traded options. It looks for traded options with characteristics as close as possible to those of the OTC option, that is options similar in respect to expiry date and exercise price. If the fair price of the written option were to rise, so too would the premiums on traded options, and hence there would be a profit on the traded options to compensate for the loss on the OTC option. However, a perfect offset could occur only in the event of the traded options being identical in the relevant attributes to the OTC option.

The differences between the OTC option written by the bank and the traded options used to hedge risks arising from the OTC option would tend to cause the deltas to differ. For example, the delta of the OTC option (as calculated from mathematical models using the same variables as the models used to estimate fair prices) might be 0.54 whereas the delta of the relevant traded options is 0.60. The fact that the traded options premiums show greater sensitivity to exchange rate movements than the OTC option fair price means that correspondingly fewer traded options are required for the hedge.

If the hedger chooses options traded on LIFFE he would find that they are traded in units of £25 000, each unit being known as a contract. Hedging a £1 million OTC option might appear to require 40 traded option contracts. However, the higher delta of the traded options means that fewer than 40 are required. The requisite number is found with the use of the ratio of the deltas:

$$\frac{\text{Required}}{\text{number}} = \frac{\text{Value of OTC option}}{\text{Value of each option contract}} \times \frac{\text{Delta of OTC option}}{\text{Delta of traded options}}$$

In the current example the numbers are:

$$36 = \frac{£1\ 000\ 000}{£25\ 000} \times \frac{0.54}{0.60}$$

The fact that the responsiveness of the fair price of the OTC option to exchange rate movements is only 90 per cent of the responsiveness of the traded options means that the optimal number of traded options contracts is 36. Use of a greater number of contracts would probably involve gains (or losses) on the traded options being greater than those on the OTC option, so that hedging could be expected to be imperfect.

A delta hedge needs to be continuously monitored. Deltas change in response to variations in exchange rates, expectations of volatility, and time remaining to expiry. The ratio of the deltas could change as a result so that the number of contracts may need to be altered.

Valuation trading

If the market price of an option differs from its fair price there will be scope for making profits from valuation trading. A valuation trader would estimate fair prices of options contracts using a mathematical model and his own assessment of expected volatility. If the market price of a contract is below the fair price calculated then it could prove profitable to buy the contract with a view to selling it when the market price moves up into line with the fair price. Similarly, an options contract with a premium in excess of the fair price might be sold in anticipation of the premium subsequently falling into line with the model based estimate. The success of valuation trading depends crucially on the validity of the mathematical model, and the trader's assessment of expectations of volatility, used in the calculation of fair prices.

A valuation trader will need to hedge his position so as to avoid the risk of making losses from changes in exchange rates and volatility expectations. A contract bought with a view to profiting from a rise of the premium into line with the fair price could prove loss-making if, due to exchange rate movements or a decline in market expectations of volatility, the fair price were to fall (along with option premiums). The valuation trader would hedge by means of taking short positions to offset long ones, and vice versa. An ideal strategy might be to simultaneously buy underpriced options and sell (write) overpriced options so that two potentially profit-making positions hedge each other.

The mechanics of transacting in options

The procedures whereby money changes hands between people who deal in traded options will be illustrated by means of the practices followed when using the options traded on LIFFE. It is useful to begin with an introduction to the margin arrangements.

Any transactor in LIFFE options, whether buyer or writer, is required to put up an initial margin. This is a sum of money deposited with the International Commodities Clearing House (ICCH) and is ultimately returnable to the transactor. The initial margin is equal to the initial margin on the corresponding LIFFE futures contract multiplied by the delta of the options contract. Therefore, if the initial margin on a LIFFE sterling currency futures contract were $1000 (as it is at the time of writing) and the delta of a particular option were 0.64 then the required initial margin would be $640. The delta is recalculated daily and hence the initial margin is subject to daily variation.

As option premiums vary from day to day, gains and losses are incurred as a result. The daily calculation of profits and losses is known as marking to market. After each business day those incurring losses must realize them by paying variation margin, correspondingly profit-making option positions are rewarded in the form of variation margin. The purpose of initial margin is the provision of a source of funds from which variation margin can be drawn in the event of an option position-taker being unable to meet the variation margin requirements. Such a transactor would be compelled to terminate his options position so as to avoid losses that cannot be met.

It is through the medium of variation margin that hedgers normally obtain their compensation for exchange rate movements and traders realize their profits and losses. Option buyers and writers typically do not expect options to directly result in the exchange of currencies. The buying and selling of currencies will usually take place on the foreign exchange spot market. Although a buyer of an option may choose to exercise the option, such a procedure is unlikely since the time value component of the option premium would thereby be lost (the time value would be realized if the option were instead closed out by means of a sale). In the event of an option being exercised the premium is payable when the option is exercised, and is the premium at the time of exercising rather than the premium on the date of buying the option (the variation margin received compensates for the difference between the two premiums).

For example, a sterling call option is bought with an exercise price of $1.25 per £1 at a premium of 2 cents per £1 when the spot price of sterling is $1.25 per £1. On the date of selling the option the spot price of sterling is $1.30 and the option premium is 6 cents. The seller of the option realizes a net gain of 4 cents per £1. He will have received this by means of variation margin payments over time as the option premium rose. He will not actually have paid the 2 cents per £1 premium upon buying the option but the 4 cents per £1 received in variation margin is equivalent to buying the option at 2 cents and selling at 6 cents per £1. The effective price of sterling is $1.26 ($1.30 spot price minus 4 cents compensation). This is better than the $1.27 guaranteed by the purchase of the option ($1.25 exercise price plus 2 cents premium) since the transactor has been able to sell remaining time value at 1 cent per £1 (time value = premium minus intrinsic value, 1 cent = 6 cents minus 5 cents, the intrinsic value of 5 cents being the excess of the spot price over the exercise price).

The person to whom the option is sold obtains an option with an exercise price of $1.25 when the spot price of sterling is $1.30. Although the option premium stands at 6 cents per £1 this new buyer does not make any payment at the time of buying the option. Suppose that the new buyer holds the option until its expiry date, at which time the spot price of sterling stands at $1.35. At the expiry date there is no time value, but the intrinsic value of the option is $1.35 − $1.25 = $0.10. While the new buyer was holding the option the premium rose from 6 cents to 10 cents per £1, correspondingly he will have received 4 cents per £1 in variation margin. He buys sterling at the spot price of $1.35 and receives 4 cents compensation so that his effective exchange rate is £1 = $1.31. The final outcome is equivalent to having paid 6 cents per £1 premium for a call option with an exercise price of $1.25. His effective price of sterling is equal to his guaranteed maximum price of $1.31.

During this process the writer of the option will have paid a total of 8 cents per £1 in variation margin. This is equivalent to honouring a $1.25 call option when the spot price of sterling is $1.35 after receiving 2 cents per £1 by way of a premium payment.

Factored hedging

The tendency for time value to decay slowly at first but to accelerate as the expiry date is approached has implications for hedging. A hedger who buys an option and subsequently sells it prior to its maturity date faces a decline in time value arising from the passage of time. This loss of time value is minimized if options with distant expiry dates are used, since time value decays slowly when the expiry date is distant. The hedger would be avoiding the rapid loss of time value that is experienced close to the expiry date.

A consequence of this strategy is that the premium is likely to contain considerable time value and this causes substantial exposure to the risk of time value loss arising from exchange rate movements. Time value peaks when an option is at-the-money and declines as it becomes in-the-money with the decline continuing as it moves deeper in-the-money. A hedger requiring a gain from an option becoming in-the-money (or deeper in-the-money) would be faced with a loss of time value that partially offsets the gain from rising intrinsic value. In order to generate adequate gains from options the hedger will need to hold an increased number of options. In other words, the option position must be factored up. Options that are far from expiry have relatively high time value and hence exhibit greater time value loss from currency price movements. Consequently the option position must be factored up to a greater degree. This increase in the number of options, together with the high time value, increases the option holder's time value loss in the event of the options becoming out-of-the-money (or moving deeper out-of-the-money).

Options contracts available

Traded currency options are available on a number of exchanges and for several currencies. For sterling against US dollars, options are traded on the following exchanges (the contract size – the amount of sterling to which each contract relates – appears in brackets following the respective exchanges): LIFFE (£25 000), London Stock Exchange (£12 500), Philadelphia Stock Exchange (£12 500), International Options Clearing Corporation in Montreal (£100 000), European Options Exchange in

Amsterdam (£5000), International Monetary Market in Chicago (£25 000).

Other currency options are traded (all against the US dollar) on the Philadelphia Stock Exchange (Deutschmarks, Swiss francs, yen, Canadian dollars, French francs and ECUs), the London Stock Exchange (Deutschmarks), the International Monetary Market in Chicago (Deutschmarks, Swiss francs), the Montreal Exchange (Deutschmarks, Swiss francs, yen, Canadian dollars), and the European Options Exchange in Amsterdam (Deutschmarks, guilder).

LIFFE also has a dollar–mark currency option which is based on buying/selling US dollars against Deutschmarks.

Appendix

Currency option specifications on LIFFE

Unit of trading	£25 000 traded against US dollar	$50 000 traded against Deutschmark
Expiry months	Three nearest months followed by the earliest month in the March, June, September, December cycle followed by that cycle	
Expiry day	Three business days before third Wednesday of expiry month	
Quotation of premium	US cents per £	pfennigs per US dollar
Tick size and value (minimum change in premium)	0.01 cents per £ ($2.50)	0.01 pfennigs per US dollar (DM5.00)
Contract standard	Delivery of the currency at the exercise price (in the event of exercise)	

Note: Specifications are subject to revision by LIFFE

Currency option specifications on the London Stock Exchange

Unit of trading	£12 500 traded against US dollar	DM62 500 traded against US dollar
Expiry months	March, June, September, December	
Expiry day	Friday before third Wednesday of expiry month	
Quotation of premium	US cents per £	US cents per Deutschmark
Minimum price movement	0.05 cents per £ ($6.25)	0.01 cents per Deutschmark ($6.25)
Delivery	Delivery of the currency at the exercise price (in the event of exercise)	

Note: Specifications are subject to revision by the London Stock Exchange

17 Interest rate options

By taking out an option hedgers obtain the right to borrow (or lend) at a particular rate of interest for a particular period of time, commencing on a specific future date or beginning during a period starting from the present. They are not, however, obliged to borrow (or lend) at that rate.

Consider, for example, a company intending to borrow £1 million at some point in the future. The current interest rate may be 10 per cent p.a. and the potential borrower may fear that interest rates might rise by the date of taking out the loan. An interest rate option is then taken out at an exercise (strike) rate of 10 per cent p.a. This means that the company acquires the right to borrow at 10 per cent p.a. for the relevant period. The counterparty to the contract, the writer, is committed to providing a loan at 10 per cent p.a. should the borrower wish to exercise the option. If the interest rate on the date at which the loan is to be made is 10 per cent p.a. or lower then the borrower would choose not to exercise the option. If the rate were above 10 per cent p.a. then the option would be exercised and money borrowed at 10 per cent p.a. The option allows the borrower to fix an upper limit to the interest rate whilst preserving the right to borrow at a more favourable rate should interest rates fall.

For this facility the borrower pays the writer of the option a premium. The premium will be dependent upon the relationship of the exercise rate to the current rate, the expected volatility of interest rates and the maximum length of time prior to the exercise of the option. If the exercise rate, the guaranteed rate, is below the current rate the premium will tend to be high since it is probable that the option will be exercised at a loss to the writer. If the exercise rate is below the current rate then the option is in-the-money. This gives rise to the intrinsic value component of the premium, the intrinsic value being the gain to be made from immediate exercise of the option. If the exercise rate is above the current rate the option is out-of-the-money and there will be no intrinsic value component to the premiums; the only component will be time value. Converse relationships exist where the holder of an option is a potential lender rather than borrower.

The further in-the-money an option is, the higher the premium. If the chosen exercise rate renders the option out-of-the-money the premium will be lower and the further out-of-the-money it is the lower will be the premium. Greater volatility of interest rates and more distant exercise dates increase the likelihood of options being exercised and hence would determine higher premia.

The buyer of an option, whether to lend or to borrow, can lose no more than the premium paid. He is said to have limited downside risk. The potential for gain is unlimited, that is upside potential is unlimited. If the would-be borrower buys an option to borrow at 10 per cent p.a. and the interest rate turns out to be lower, then he borrows at the lower rate and the cost incurred is the premium. If the interest rate is greater than 10 per cent p.a. then the differential is a gain to the borrower, with a net gain if the differential exceeds the premium. In principle, the interest rate could be at any level so that the net gain is potentially unlimited. On the other hand, the writer of the option has a limited potential for gain – limited to the premium paid. His scope for loss is unlimited. A very high interest rate, such as 20 per cent p.a., would put him in the position of having to borrow at 20 per cent p.a. (or forgo this rate on funds) in order to lend at 10 per cent p.a.

Parallel considerations apply to a buyer of an option to lend. In return for the payment of the premium the buyer obtains the right to lend at a particular rate of interest on a particular date or up to a particular expiry date. He has a downside risk limited to the premium paid. Should the interest rate turn out to be higher than the guaranteed rate then the buyer ignores the option and lends at the higher rate. An interest rate lower than that guaranteed would induce the lender to exercise the option and lend at the guaranteed rate. The actual rate could be considerably below the exercise rate, providing the lender with a considerable gain from using the option. Conversely, the writer of the option has a potential for gain limited to the value of the premium, with this maximum gain being obtained in the event of the holder of the option deciding not to exercise it. The writer's loss potential is much greater. He could find that the guaranteed rate at which he is committed to borrow is considerably above the rate of interest at which he can lend.

It should be noted that although the chapter has thus far talked in terms of the option writer's commitment to lend or borrow it may be the case that the option writer does not lend or borrow in the event of the option being exercised. An alternative procedure would be for the writer to compensate the buyer of the option for the interest rate deviation from the exercise rate. So, for example, if the buyer takes out an option to borrow £1 million for three months at 10 per cent p.a. and exercises the option when the relevant rate is 12 per cent p.a. then the option writer would compensate the buyer for the extra 2 per cent p.a. to be paid. This would amount to about £5000 being paid by the writer to the buyer. (The amount may be somewhat less than £5000 since the extra interest is payable by the borrower at the end of the three months whilst the compensation is paid at the beginning of that period and can earn interest in the meantime, so the compensation necessary would be somewhat less than £5000.)

In addition to the over-the-counter interest rate options available, primarily from banks, there are also some traded options. LIFFE provides interest rate options in the form of options on some of its interest rate futures – the three-month Eurodollar deposit, long gilt, and US Treasury Bond futures. The London Stock Exchange trades options on gilts, both short and long, and also trades options based on the FTSE 100 index. The same basic principles apply to all of these instruments, so the following section will focus on just one of them – the options on three-month Eurodollar futures.

Options on Eurodollar futures

The buyer of a Eurodollar futures call option obtains the right to buy a Eurodollar futures contract, on any business day up to the expiry date, at an exercise price chosen at the time of buying the option. Similarly the buyer of a Eurodollar futures put option acquires the right to sell a futures contract at a particular exercise price. Traded options give the buyer a choice of exercise prices. On LIFFE the exercise prices are available at 50 basis point (0.50 per cent) intervals, for example 10.00, 9.50, and 9.00 per cent.

Call option buyers seek to guarantee a maximum futures price and thereby a minimum rate of interest at which to deposit dollars whilst retaining the right to invest at higher rates. (The price of a Eurodollar futures contract is equal to 100 minus the annualized futures interest rate.) Put option buyers seek to obtain a ceiling to the interest payable on a loan, by guaranteeing a minimum selling price of futures contracts, whilst allowing themselves to obtain cheaper funds if available.

The use of a Eurodollar futures option, compared with using a straightforward futures contract, is shown by Figure 17.1. This

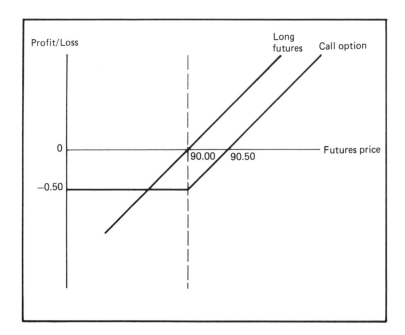

Figure 17.1 Futures options versus futures

figure shows futures prices rather than futures interest rates – it is conventional to use futures prices rather than the corresponding interest rates.

Figure 17.1 compares buying a futures contract at a price of 90.00 with buying a call option with an exercise price of 90.00. In this example the premium payable for the option is 0.50, which has a monetary value of $1250 per contract. (Each futures contract is for the investing/borrowing of $1 million for three months – $1250 is equal to 0.50 per cent p.a. for three months on $1 million.) For futures prices above 90.00 the call option produces profit levels that are consistently 0.50 below those obtained from the straightforward long futures position, in other words the net profit is reduced by the value of the premium paid.

Below the futures price of 90.00 the long futures position produces a loss that is equal to the difference between the purchase price of 90.00 and the current futures price. On the other hand, the call option shows a loss of 0.50 at each futures price below 90.00. At futures prices less than 90.00 the option holder would choose not to exercise the right to buy at 90.00 and the only loss suffered would be the premium paid.

Thus buying a call option produces a result similar to a long futures position with the effective price being 0.50 higher (that is, net profits are lower by the value of the premium) and an automatic stop-loss order coming into play when the current futures price falls below 90.00. The potential for loss is limited at the cost of reduced profit opportunities. The scope for loss, the downside potential, is limited to the premium paid whilst the scope for profit, the upside potential, is limited only by the maximum price of 100.00 for Eurodollar futures contracts.

Options on Eurodollar futures guarantee maximum or minimum prices of futures contracts but this does not necessarily involve the guarantee of minimum and maximum rates of interest. The interest rate can be guaranteed if the option is exercised on the maturity date of the futures contract, otherwise basis risk renders the interest rate guarantee less than absolute. Basis risk refers to the possibility that futures interest rates and cash market interest rates move to different extents so that gains/losses on futures positions do not precisely offset losses/gains arising in the cash market.

The benefits of selling

The purchaser of a LIFFE Eurodollar options contract has three possible courses of action:

(a) sell the option
(b) exercise the option
(c) let the option expire.

The first of these three is likely to be the most attractive, unless the interest risk to be hedged occurs on the expiry date of the option. This is because selling a contract provides the holder with the time value remaining on the contract, whereas exercising the option would not.

If the risk being hedged arises on the expiry date of the option there will be no time value to be obtained and the option holder would allow it to expire if it is out-of-the-money, or exercise it if it is in-the-money. In fact, on LIFFE in-the-money options are automatically exercised on behalf of the holder on the expiry date.

The exercise of an option provides the holder with a Eurodollar futures contract. Since exercise would occur (if at all) at the time that the risk arises, and the hedging would be accomplished by the receipt of money arising from the holding and exercising of the options, there would typically be no purpose served by the holding of the futures contracts. The futures contracts received at the time of exercising options would be immediately closed out. In fact the expiry date of the options coincides with that of the futures so that when options contracts are held to the expiry date and then exercised the futures contracts received would automatically be closed out.

The mechanics of transacting in options

As options premiums vary from day to day, gains and losses are incurred as a result. The daily calculation of profits and losses is known as marking to market. After each business day those incurring losses must realize them by paying 'variation margin', correspondingly profit-making option positions are rewarded in the form of variation margin. It is through the medium of variation margin that hedgers obtain their desired compensation for interest rate movements, and traders realize their profits and losses.

For example, a call option is bought with an exercise price of 90 at a premium of 2 when the futures price is 90. The option is subsequently sold when the futures price is 92.5 and the option premium is 3.5. The seller of the option realizes a net gain of 1.5. He will have received this by means of variation margin payments over time as the option premium rose, that is he would have received the monetary value of 1.5 per cent p.a. on $1 million for three months for each contract ($3750 per contract). He will not actually have paid the premium upon buying the option but the money received in variation margin is equivalent to buying the option at a premium of 2 and selling at a premium of 3.5. The effective futures price is 91 (92.5 minus 1.5 compensation). This is better than the 92 guaranteed by the purchase of the option (exercise price of 90 plus premium of 2) since the transactor has been able to sell the remaining time value of 1.

Caps and collars

A cap sets an upper limit to the interest payable on a floating rate loan. The agreement may be with the bank providing the loan or with another bank that undertakes to compensate the borrower should interest rates rise above a specified level. For this guarantee the borrower pays a fee to the bank. The fee could be reduced by using a collar rather than a cap. A collar sets a lower as well as an upper limit to the rate of interest. Since the bank stands to gain in the event of the interest rate falling below the minimum, the fee required from the borrower would be correspondingly less.

These instruments can be looked upon as forms of option. Caps are borrowers' options that are automatically exercised when in-the-money and which can be exercised on numerous occasions. Caps differ from ordinary options in being automatically exercised, being capable of exercise on more than one date, and in providing fixed interest rates for periods that are indeterminate at the time of agreeing to the cap.

Collars can be viewed as the simultaneous buying and writing of caps. The buying of a cap guarantees the borrower a ceiling to the rate of interest. Writing a cap, at a lower interest rate, provides an interest rate floor. Writing the cap involves selling the bank a lender's option. The bank obtains the notional right to lend to the customer at the minimum interest rate. Should rates decline below this minimum there is a loss for the customer that offsets the benefits of a falling interest rate, and a gain to the bank. The cost of the collar to the customer is the difference between the premiums (notionally) charged for the two caps.

Hedging and trading

The basic principles underlying interest rate options are the same as those upon which currency options are based. Consequently the previous discussions of hedging, trading, writing, premium determination, complex strategies, and the operation of traded options in relation to currency options could be reproduced in a parallel form for interest rate options.

Appendix

Interest rate option specifications on LIFFE

Unit of trading	One Eurodollar futures contract	One long gilt futures contract
Delivery months	March, June, September, December	
Expiry day	Two business days prior to the third Wednesday of delivery month	Six business days prior to the first business day of the delivery month
Quotation of premium	Multiples of 0.01	Multiples of 1/64
Tick size and value	0.01 ($25)	1/64 (£7.8125)
Contract standard	Assignment of one futures contract for the delivery month at the exercise price (in the event of exercise)	

Note: Specifications are subject to revision by LIFFE

Interest rate option specifications on the London Stock Exchange

Unit of trading	£50 000 nominal
Deliverable stocks	Treasury 11¾ per cent 1991 Treasury 11¾ per cent 2003/2007
Expiry days	Last business day in February, May, August, November
Minimum premium movement	1/32 (£15.625)

Note: Specifications and deliverable stocks are subject to revision by the London Stock Exchange

FTSE 100 index option specifications on the London Stock Exchange

Unit of trading	£10 per index point
Expiry months	Next four months
Expiry day	Last business day of month
Quotation of premium	1p per £10 of premium (for example, a premium quotation of 10p corresponds to £100 of payable premium)
Delivery	Cash value of difference between exercise price and FTSE 100 index value on the exercise date (NB the exercise price is a FTSE 100 index value)

Note: Specifications are subject to revision by the London Stock Exchange.

Since the writing of this book options on FTSE 100 Index futures have been introduced by LIFFE.

18 The accounting treatment of financial futures and options

It is difficult to write with authority on this subject since there is no Statement of Standard Accounting Practice dealing specifically with this matter. There are, however, several published standards, such as SSAP 20 on *Foreign Currency Translation* and SSAP 2 on *Disclosure of Accounting Policies*, which have relevant contributions to make on the accounting treatment of financial futures and options. In addition, there are the disclosure requirements laid down in the various Companies Acts. It is also relevant to take account of current best practice particularly in relation to disclosure, although the variations in interpretation and application of certain standards in this area often leave much to be desired.

However, before considering what use can be made of the existing standards and disclosure requirements so as to assist in the accounting treatment of financial risk exposure, it would be prudent to bear in mind the limitations of the accounting standards programme itself. The Accounting Standards Committee (ASC), the body responsible for the setting of accounting standards in the UK, is suffering considerable criticism, to the extent that there is a grave danger that its authority is being seriously undermined, thereby damaging the entire accounting standards programme. Indeed, the ASC is under such pressure in relation to its existing standards that it has announced that it sees its work in the next few years as being based upon the consolidation and improvement of existing standards rather than upon the development of new standards. It is therefore extremely unlikely that a standard dealing with financial futures and options will evolve in the near future.

The ASC has come under attack for a variety of different reasons. Firstly, it has been accused of failure to develop a conceptual framework upon which a logical sequence of accounting standards could be based. The consequence of this has been the development of conflicting and inconsistent standards which inevitably make it more difficult to achieve one of its major declared objectives – namely the narrowing of areas of difference and variety in accounting practice. In relation to financial risk exposure, as will be seen shortly, there is a major conflict of interest between the accruals or matching concept and the prudence concept. Moreover, this conflict of interest has been compounded by the ASC's adoption of a pragmatic problem-solving approach to standard setting. Indeed, this approach was illustrated at the very outset of the standards setting process when the desire to deal with the urgent problem of the accounting treatment of mergers in the late 1960s meant that SSAP 1, dealing with the problem of *Accounting for the Results of Associated Companies*, preceded SSAP 2 dealing with the *Disclosure of Accounting Policies* despite the fact that the latter laid down the basic accounting concepts relevant to all standards.

The view of many in the profession is that statements of standard accounting practice should not continue to be produced on an *ad hoc* problem-solving basis since it is likely to produce more contradictions and inconsistencies. Moreover, these problems, along with the controversy surrounding particular standards (such as the inflation accounting standard), have enabled companies to become more flexible in their interpretations of standards and have made non-compliance a more regular occurrence. Indeed, an ex-member of the ASC, Professor Michael Bromwich, in his book *The Economics of Accounting Standard Setting*, argues that the authority of the Committee has been so undermined that immediate action must be taken if the profession is to maintain its influential role. It is against this controversial background that the relevance of existing standards to the accounting treatment of financial futures and options will be examined.

The fundamental accounting concepts

As with any area of accounting in which there is no specific standard to act as a guideline, best practice is usually based upon an attempt to apply the fundamental accounting concepts laid down in SSAP 2. The four basic concepts laid down by that standard are as follows:

1   *The going-concern concept* – this assumes that the business entity in question will continue to exist operationally for the foreseeable future.
2   *The accruals concept* – this states that revenues and costs should be accrued, matched and dealt with in the accounting period to which they relate, rather than on a cash flow basis.
3   *The consistency concept* – this states that there should be consistency of treatment of similar items within each accounting period and from one period to the next.
4   *The prudence concept* – this argues in favour of the different treatment of expected profits and losses in that revenue and profit should not be anticipated but should be recognized only when it is realized, whereas full provision should immediately be made for known or expected liabilities or losses.

In so far as financial futures and options are concerned, the going-concern concept and the consistency concept do not pose any problems. However, there is an inherent conflict between the accruals concept and the prudence concept, which is of particular importance in this area. The accruals concept, based as it is upon the principle of matching, advocates the recognition of unrealized profits whereas the prudence concept clearly states that unrealized profits should not be recognized.

Before making a judgement about which of these two fundamental accounting concepts (accruals or prudence) is most relevant in the case of financial futures and options, it is worth considering standard practice in relation to other areas in which these accounting concepts come into conflict. It should be pointed out that the ASC stated in SSAP 2 that if a situation of conflict arose between matching and prudence, then the prudence concept should take precedence. However, this viewpoint has not been consistently applied by the ASC in its standard setting.

Classic examples of this conflict of interest between accruals and prudence have arisen in relation to SSAP 13 on *Accounting for Research and Development*, and SSAP 9 dealing with *Stocks and Work in Progress*. In the original exposure draft 14 (ED 14), on accounting for research and development, the prudence concept was very strictly interpreted in that it was recommended that all research and development costs should be written off against income in the period in which they were incurred. Thus, there was very little matching since the costs of research and development were incurred in one accounting period while the hoped for resulting revenues did not accrue until future accounting periods. This proposal was strenuously criticized by many professional accountants who argued that some degree of matching should be allowed. The ASC relented under this pressure so that with the eventual publication of SSAP 13 certain development expenditures fulfilling fairly stringent conditions were allowed to be carried forward and matched against the revenues of future accounting periods. Although prudence still plays the major role in SSAP 13, this is certainly not the case with SSAP 9 on stocks and work in progress which places heavy emphasis upon matching. Indeed, with the exception of losses upon long-term contracts, matching takes a high precedence over prudence in SSAP 9.

It is against this background of conflict between the accruals and prudence concepts that the accounting treatment of financial futures and options is considered.

Application of the fundamental accounting concepts: accruals versus prudence

The best practice so far in accounting, for both financial futures and options, seems to be based upon the dominance of the accruals concept which advocates the matching of costs and revenues. However, where the outcome of a situation is likely to be uncertain, it is recognized that the prudence concept may also be of some relevance.

There would appear to be two main accounting issues involved here. The first is to determine whether a profit or loss has arisen on the contract and the second is to consider in which accounting period the profit or loss should be recognized. Each of these issues will now be considered in turn.

The calculation of profit or loss

The recommended practice for the calculation of profits or losses arising from a financial futures or options contract is based upon the accruals or matching concept rather than upon the prudence concept. The basic assumption underlying this policy is that in an active, liquid market an open position is basically the same as a closed position, since an open position can be closed out at any time. The implication of this is that the unrealized profits or losses arising from an open position should be treated similarly to the realized profits and losses emanating from a closed position. In effect, unrealized profits and losses (from an open position) can be turned into realized profits and losses (from a closed position) simply from closing out. Such a policy of recognizing unrealized profits is clearly at odds with the prudence concept which advocates that unrealized losses but not unrealized profits should be recognized.

The crux of this issue is the valuation of open positions, since it is these positions which give rise to unrealized profits and losses. In effect, the recommended policy is that open positions should be revalued at market value, a policy which is referred to in both the UK and US as a policy of 'marking to market'. If this revaluation of open positions is accepted, then the calculation of profit or loss is fairly straightforward, even where there are a large number of open contracts. At any point in time, the profit or loss on open positions will simply be the aggregate market value of open positions less the aggregate value at their contracted prices. The total profit or loss position is then simply obtained by adding this amount to the aggregate profit and loss on closed positions.

There are a number of reasons why the accruals concept should take precedence over the prudence concept in the valuation of open positions. In the first place, the objective of using any accounting policy is to ensure that a true and fair view is given in the accounts. To deny the use of the marking to market policy would be to deny the true nature of the financial futures and options market. In particular, it would deny the fact that an effective financial futures market requires that profits or losses should be instantly realizable. Indeed, it is precisely because a firm can close out a position at any time that a movement of market rates will instantly record a realizable profit or loss without the firm having to take the decision to close out. Moreover, the payment or receipt of variation margin on a daily basis in response to market rate movements adds further credence to the view that these profits and losses have actually been realized. It could also be contended that the valuation of open positions on a marking to market basis is entirely consistent with the approach taken by banks and other institutions in their accounting treatment of forward foreign exchange transactions.

In addition to these arguments in favour of the use of the accruals concept and the marking to market policy in the treatment of financial futures and options, there is also an extremely good reason why the alternative application of the prudence concept to this situation is likely to be undesirable. This is that the prudence concept, even though it might have been applied consistently, will give management the scope to vary its profit and loss results by selectively choosing which contracts it wishes to close. This is demonstrated in Example 1, which assumes for simplicity purposes that a firm has only two contracts open at the end of its accounting period, one showing a profit of £50 000 and the other showing a loss of £10 000. If the firm was to take a strict interpretation of the prudence concept then it would have to make provision for the loss-making contract, irrespective of whether it remained open or whether it had been closed out. However, the profit or loss declared would then be dependent upon the firm's decision to keep open or close out the profitable contract, since the prudence concept requires that profit will only be recognized when it has been realized (that is, closed out). Thus, the firm in our example could either declare a loss of £10 000 or a profit of £40 000, dependent upon whether it closes out the profitable contract. Hence the accounting profit or loss arising from the financial futures contracts could be manipulated by management even though they have applied the prudence concept consistently.

Example 1

Contract 1   Loss £10 000

Profit (loss) declared as a result
of an accounting policy to
provide for all losses (prudence)
(£10 000)

Contract 2   Profit £50 000   −

Accounting results	
If both contracts open	(£10 000)
If contract 1 only closed	(£10 000)
If contract 2 only closed	£40 000
If both contracts closed	£40 000

Moreover, the application of the marking to market policy for the same firm with the same contracts as shown in Example 2, clearly illustrates that there is no such scope for the firm's management to manipulate the accounting results by selectively deciding which contracts to close out. Whether both contracts remain open, the loss-making contract only is closed, the profit-making contract only is closed, or both contracts are closed, the accounting result will be the same in each case − a profit of £40 000. Given the all powerful requirements that the accounts should present a true and fair view, the valuation of open positions on a marking to market policy would seem to be much the best policy.

Example 2

	Profit (loss) declared as a result of an accounting policy to value open contracts at market value
Contract 1 Loss £10 000	(£10 000)
Contract 2 Profit £50 000	£50 000
Accounting results	
If both contracts open	£40 000
If contract 1 only is closed	£40 000
If contract 2 only is closed	£40 000
If both contracts closed	£40 000

However, the recommendation in favour of the marking to market policy is based on the assumption that the financial instruments in question are easily valued and highly liquid in that they are traded on a reputable financial futures market. Thus the prices quoted on an exchange such as LIFFE ensure that no difficulty arises in the valuation of traded options.

This ease of valuation and high liquidity of traded options contrasts with over-the-counter (OTC) options where the market is likely to be much less liquid and where valuation can often only be established by asking the original writer of the option. In such cases, the accruals approach should be used only with considerable caution.

When should a profit or loss be recognized?

Having established the size of the profit or loss on a futures or option contract, in the way suggested above, the next problem is to decide in which accounting period it should be recognized. In this respect, the underlying basis of any accounting policy should be that the accounting treatment of any business transaction should reflect, as closely as possible, the economic effects and objectives of the transaction. Since the underlying economic reasons for trading and hedging transactions differ, it will be necessary to distinguish between such transactions for the purposes of determining when a profit or loss should be recognized.

Recognition of profit or loss on hedging transactions

A hedging transaction has the objective of reducing the risk of loss arising from adverse movements in prices or interest rates. It is achieved by taking up positions in financial futures or options contracts which cover existing or expected cash market positions. Hedging positions include such diverse transactions as protecting the value of a currency in which receipts or payments are to be made, guaranteeing an investment income yield or the interest cost of borrowing over a certain period, or even preserving the value of an asset or restricting the amount of a liability which is denominated in a foreign currency. The important point in each of these cases is that the hedger is attempting to protect himself from the impact of price changes on an underlying asset or liability. Since such protection is the economic basis of the hedged transaction, it is therefore important that the accounting treatment of the events in the futures market should closely mirror what is happening to the underlying asset or liability.

This is most easily demonstrated by means of the following example.

Example 3

A corporate treasurer has $100 million worth of short-term loans outstanding which currently on 1 October carry an interest rate of 11 per cent. These loans are on a six-monthly rollover basis which are due to be renewed on 1 December. The corporate treasurer believes that interest rates will rise significantly above the current rate of 11 per cent and wishes to take action to protect the company from having to pay higher rates of interest on its outstanding loans. He notes that the current rate of interest on three-month Eurodollar contracts is $11^{1}/_{2}$ per cent which is $^{1}/_{2}$ per cent above the current spot rate, reflecting the market's perception that interest rates will rise. However, the corporate treasurer believes that interest rates will rise much higher than this and therefore takes the following action to try and immunize the company from paying higher interest costs:

1 With contract values fixed at $1 million, he sells 200 December three-month Eurodollar interest rate contracts on 1 October. (Note that 200 $1 million three-month contracts are necessary to cover $100 million for a six-month period.) The price of the December three-month Eurodollar interest rate contracts is 88.5 reflecting an interest rate of $11^{1}/_{2}$ per cent on these futures contracts.

2 If the corporate treasurer has guessed right and by the rollover date of 1 December interest rates have risen substantially, then he will buy 200 December three-month Eurodollar interest rate contracts thereby closing out his position. If, for example, the interest rate on three-month Eurodollar interest rate contracts has risen to 15 per cent then the corporate treasurer will be able to buy them at a price of 85.

In this example, the corporate treasurer has been substantially successful in protecting the company from the impact of higher interest rates, since the higher interest costs are substantially offset by the profit made from the difference in the selling and buying prices of the Eurodollar interest rate contracts. The movement in prices in the futures market from 88.5 to 85 represents 350 ticks which at $25 a tick and over 200 contracts amounts to $1 750 000. This profit in the futures market is counterbalanced by the higher interest costs in the cash market. If it is assumed that on the day of the loan rollover (1 December) the six-month Eurodollar interest rate is 14.75 per cent, then the additional interest cost will be $6/12 \times (14.75\% - 11\%) \times \$100$ million which equals $1 875 000. Thus $93\frac{1}{2}$ per cent of the additional interest rate cost will have been successfully hedged by the profit in the futures market. (Note that the hedge was not 100 per cent effective because of the movement in basis.)

From an accounting point of view, what is important is that this is a genuine hedged transaction in the sense that the action taken in the futures market is designed to exactly offset what is happening in the cash market. Then it becomes particularly important that the accounts should provide a symmetrical treatment of the hedge profit alongside the additional cost of borrowing. Thus, if the accounts were made up to 31 December, since the interest cost of the rollover loan taken out on 1 December will only show one month's interest, so also only one month of the hedged profit should be recognized in the profit and loss account. The interest cost of the rollover loan for six months is

$$\frac{6}{12} \times 14.75\% \times \$100 \text{ million} = \$7\,375\,000$$

Thus the profit and loss account treatment of the above example would be shown as follows:

Profit and loss account extract at 31 December
Interest cost of six-month rollover 1–31 December
    $1/6 \times \$7\,375\,000$ (1 229 167)
Amortized profit on hedging 1–31 December
    $1/6 \times \$1\,750\,000$ 291 667

Reserves   (937 500)

In a similar fashion, if the accounts had been made up to the end of February then half of the gain on hedging in the futures market would have been recorded in the profit and loss account to counteract the additional cost of borrowing over this three-month period.

To the extent that the gain on hedging in the futures market has not been released to the profit and loss account, it will be carried forward as a deferred gain in the balance sheet. For the above example, the balance sheet extracts up to 31 December would therefore read as follows:

Balance sheet extract at 31 December

Cash (profit on hedge)	1 750 000
Accrued liability (interest cost for December)	(1 229 167)
Deferred profit on hedging	
$^5/_6 \times \$1\ 750\ 000$	(1 458 333)
Reserves (as in profit and loss extract)	(937 500)

The illustrated profit and loss and balance sheet extracts above provide classic examples of the matching of profits on a hedge with the corresponding expenditure on the underlying transaction. The accounting policy involved was that of carrying forward profits in the balance sheet as a deferred gain to be recognized at a later date. However, symmetrical treatment of the futures transaction and the underlying asset also implies that in the event of a loss in the futures market, the loss will be carried forward in the balance sheet until it is matched with the income from the underlying asset. If, for example, the corporate treasurer had judged wrongly and interest rates had fallen, the accounts to 31 December would have shown that, in the profit and loss account, the one month December loss on the futures market would have been matched against the one month December gain from paying lower interest charges. Similarly, in the balance sheet, a five months deferred loss in the futures market would be carried forward against the reduced liability on interest charges. This provides a striking example of the accruals concept taking precedence over the prudence concept and it is consequently of vital importance, if losses are to be carried forward, that the transaction be unambiguously identified as a hedge. (The criteria for identifying a hedge will be examined later.)

It should be recognized that deferral of profits and losses should only take place to enable symmetrical treatment of the underlying asset or liability being hedged. If the underlying asset or liability is itself a futures or options contract then there is no case for deferral since the underlying contract itself would have been treated on a mark to market basis with instantly realizable profits. An example of such a hedge would be where an option writer decides to hedge his risk by buying an option with similar characteristics to the one he has written. In such a case, there is no question of deferral and for accounting purposes the transaction should be regarded as a trade and dealt with as recommended in the following section.

The recognition of profits or losses on trading transactions

The objective of a trading transaction is not to reduce risk but to make a profit out of the futures market by correctly anticipating which way interest rates and futures prices are going to move. Futures positions which are judged correctly will lead to profits while those which are judged wrongly will lead to losses.

There is no underlying asset or liability to offset the futures position and therefore the accounting treatment is completely different. In the case of trading transactions there is no controversy over the deferral of profits and losses, since the simple rule to observe is to measure profits and losses on the mark to market basis, and to recognize the whole of that profit or loss immediately. This reflects the underlying economic objective of the futures transaction which is to make a profit, such profits and losses arising being recognized immediately, irrespective of whether they are closed out.

Thus, if the futures transaction undertaken in Example 3 above had been a trading transaction which was unrelated to the interest cost liability in the cash market, then the profit and loss account would have recognized the whole of the futures profit immediately on a mark to market basis and there would have been no deferred gain in the balance sheet. The entries in the profit and loss account and the balance sheet would then appear as follows:

Profit and loss account extract at 31 December
Interest cost of six-month rollover 1–31 December

$1/_6 \times \$7\ 375\ 000$	(1 229 167)
Realized profit on futures market	1 750 000
Reserves	520 833

Balance sheet extract at 31 December
Cash (profit on hedge)   1 750 000
Accrued liability (interest cost for December)   (1 229 167)

Reserves (as in profit and loss account)   520 833

Which transactions should be classified as a hedge?

Given the underlying basis of accounts to provide a true and fair view, and given the substantial difference in the way that trading and hedging transactions are treated for accounting purposes, it therefore becomes of paramount importance to identify which transactions are trading transactions and which are hedging transactions.

Although the UK does not have an accounting standard dealing with this issue, considerable guidance can be obtained from the US Financial Accounting Standard on *Foreign Currency Translation* (FAS 52) which advocates that a hedge transaction should be both 'designated' and 'effective' as a hedge.

To be designated as a hedge can be interpreted as meaning that the underlying economic intent of the futures transaction is to counteract adverse price movement of an underlying asset or liability. For control purposes it is therefore particularly important that the specific underlying asset or liability is identified and documented at the time at which a futures contract is taken out, so that there can be no ambiguity about which futures transaction is 'designated' to hedge which particular asset or liability.

On the issue of 'effectiveness', it is necessary to identify those characteristics which will enable a hedge to be effective in the sense of substantially covering the risk involved. Hence the major principle here is one of a high degree of correlation between the price movements in the futures market and the price movements of the underlying asset or liability. For a hedge to be judged to be effective it must also involve similar values as the item to be hedged and similar maturity dates. However, although the standardized nature of futures contracts sometimes makes this impossible, technical problems of this nature should not disqualify a transaction from being regarded as a hedge.

While business practice in the UK appears to agree with the American criteria of designation and effectiveness, there is rather more controversy over a third criteria related to the 'certainty' of the commitment. This controversy relates to potential commitments such as a British firm wishing to hedge against foreign exchange exposure while tendering for a large overseas fixed-price contract which it may or may not get. The position in the US is that options transactions taken out against such potential commitments would be regarded as trading transactions and not hedging transactions and therefore all profits and losses would be regarded as instantly realized. The position in the UK appears to be somewhat different in that such potential commitments may be regarded as eligible for hedge transactions so long as there is a reasonable chance that the commitment will materialize.

Complications in practice

While the aforementioned criteria provide some guidelines with which to classify transactions, there are in practice likely to be a whole range of complicating factors which make, for accounting purposes, the identification of which transactions to treat as hedges rather more difficult. Typical of these complications are the cases of general hedges, rolling hedges and discontinued hedges which are considered below.

The assumption so far has been that the accounting treatment of a particular futures transaction should be symmetrical to the treatment of the particular asset or liability being hedged. However, cases may arise in which the company will wish to take out general hedges against a whole aggregate of assets and liabilities. This seriously complicates the control and identification of hedges compared to the situation when hedges are taken out against specific assets and liabilities. Nevertheless, this does not disqualify such transactions from being treated as genuine hedges, although great care needs to be taken to ensure that they are closely monitored and related to the underlying assets and liabilities.

A further complication is provided by the case of rolling hedges in the form of successive futures contracts. Such rolling hedges may be necessary where there are different maturity dates in the cash and the futures markets. Again it is reasonable to treat such rolling hedges as a genuine hedge transaction so long as it is clear that this is the intent of the transaction.

More problems are created by the existence of discontinued hedges. The accounting treatment of these is likely to depend upon the reason why they are discontinued. If they are discontinued because the hedged cash market transaction does not take place then there is a strong case for treating it as a trading transaction as soon as the cash market position becomes known. An example of this might be a manufacturer who has taken out an anticipatory hedge in the belief that he will import some raw materials in the future even though he is not yet sure whether he will place a firm order. As soon as it becomes clear that he will not place an order, then the hedge transaction should immediately be recategorized as a trading transaction with the appropriate accounting treatment.

However, hedges may also be discontinued because corporate treasurers may have altered their views concerning changes in interest rates or currency values. As long as the intentions of management on these issues are clear, it is argued that it is still possible to apply the accounting treatment of hedges to such transactions. However, great care should be taken to record and monitor these activities in this highly controversial area.

Conclusion

On the basic issue of calculating profit and loss, the nature of futures and options markets should be taken into account. Given the highly liquid nature of such markets the recommended policy is that of calculating gains and losses on a mark to market basis, since keeping positions open in such markets is in principle no different from closing them out.

On the related issue of when such profits and losses should be realized in terms of the accounting period to which they belong, the important principle is to match the activities in the futures and options markets to those of the underlying assets or liabilities to which they belong. Where there is no underlying asset or liability as in a trading transaction, or where the underlying asset or liability gives rise to instantly realizable profits or losses, then the profit or loss in the futures and options markets should be regarded as instantly realizable in the current accounting period. However, in so far as the revenue or expense associated with the underlying asset or liability arises in a future accounting period, then if such an asset or liability has been properly hedged, it becomes appropriate to defer the appropriate amount of profit or loss arising from the hedge transactions to achieve symmetrical treatment.

To conclude, since a policy of deferring losses on hedge transactions is in direct contradiction to the basic accounting concept of prudence, it therefore becomes particularly important that agreement of the company's auditors be sought upon which transactions it is appropriate to treat as hedges.

19 Taxation

The UK tax system has evolved somewhat haphazardly over the years. Its underlying principles were designed mainly to apply to manufacturing companies with simple accounting techniques and under a regime of stable exchange rates. It was subsequently developed to deal with the complexities of commercial and financial trades, but it has not yet been adequately extended to incorporate the effects of floating exchange rates. Indeed, the absence of such legislation at a time when increasing use is being made of foreign currencies means that taxation treatment has to rely upon tax principles which are often not suited to deal with the new range of financial instruments at the disposal of the corporate treasurer. The evolution of the current system of tax treatment of foreign currency gains and losses is thus heavily dependent upon the *ad hoc* decisions arising from case law, many of which appear to be contradictory. It is therefore perhaps not surprising that corporate treasurers are sometimes somewhat confused as to what the after-tax implications of their foreign exchange decisions will be.

The UK system of taxation, in common with all other countries, imposes a tax liability denominated in the home currency – in the case of the UK a tax liability denominated in sterling. The crucial issue then becomes the calculation of the taxable sterling profit or loss. In so far as foreign exchange profits and losses are concerned, the computation of taxable profit and loss is highly controversial in two important respects. The first is the extent to which the foreign exchange transactions are of a 'capital' or 'revenue' nature. Different tax schedules will apply to these two different transactions under existing tax law, with the result that various adjustments may need to be made to the profit and loss account if trading profits or losses for tax purposes are to be computed correctly. The second major issue is whether the sterling tax liability should be based upon a realized, conversion basis whereby the currency has actually been converted, or whether it also needs to include a figure for notional currency gains and losses on an unrealized translation basis. Both of these issues will be discussed in the sections on the *Marine Midland* case (see p.196), in the Provisional Statement of Practice, published by the Inland Revenue in January 1985 (see p.197), and in the subsequent full Statement of Practice of February 1987 (see p.204). However, it is first necessary to consider the different schedules under which foreign exchange transactions could, in principle, incur a tax liability or loss.

Taxation schedules applicable to financial futures and options

In principle, there are three different ways in which the profits and losses arising from financial futures transactions could be treated for tax purposes. These are as follows:

1   Schedule D, Case I which is levied upon trading profits.
2   Schedule D, Case VI which is levied upon various miscellaneous sources of profit or gain on an annual basis.
3   Capital Gains tax which is levied upon gains of a capital nature.

The current state of play as to when these various schedules will apply is discussed later under the heading of the 1985 Finance Act (see p.208) which introduced significant changes, particularly with respect to the applicability of Schedule D, Case VI and capital gains tax.

It is particularly important for the corporate treasurers to know under which schedule their foreign exchange transactions will incur a tax liability or loss. This is because there are considerable advantages to be gained from being taxed under Schedule D, Case I rather than under Schedule D, Case VI. Foreign exchange losses generated under Schedule D, Case I can usually be offset against all forms of other income in the same and previous year of assessment, and are also available to be carried forward and relieved against profit arising in future years. Companies, as opposed to individuals, also have the additional advantage under Schedule D, Case I of being able to relieve their foreign exchange losses under the group relief provisions.

This wide applicability of loss relief is in marked contrast to the treatment of foreign exchange losses arising under Schedule D, Case VI. In this case there is very limited loss relief – foreign exchange losses will only be available for offset in the current year against other Case VI profits. In the event that Case VI losses of the current year exceed Case VI profits of the current year, then the unrelieved part of the loss can only be relieved against future Case VI profits, and is not available for general relief as under Case I.

Schedule D Case I and Schedule D Case VI are concerned with transactions of a 'revenue' nature. In so far as the foreign exchange gain or loss arises from transactions of a 'capital' nature, then they become chargeable under the capital gains tax rules. However, under the capital gains tax rules, capital losses can only be relieved against capital gains of the same or subsequent accounting period so that loss relief is less generous than that available under Case I. Moreover, it is particularly important to note that the capital gains tax system applies only to assets and not to liabilities. Consequently, currency gains will only incur a tax charge if they relate to a sale of assets rather than liabilities. Similarly, currency losses will only be allowable if they relate to the sale of assets. Thus a long term capital liability in a foreign currency may mean that no relief is given in the event of a loss and, equally, no tax being incurred in the event of a gain.

Thus, different tax schedules will give rise to different tax treatment, particularly in relation to loss relief. Companies are particularly keen to avoid treatment under Case VI with its extremely limited provision for loss relief. The situation in which each Case will apply is dealt with later under the discussion of the provisions of the Finance Act of 1985.

The case of Marine Midland (*Pattison* v. *Marine Midland Limited* (1984) A.C. 362)

The case of *Marine Midland* is particularly important because it highlights the two major controversial issues raised above – namely, the distinction between 'capital' and 'revenue' transactions and the issue of conversion versus translation as the basis of tax assessment.

Marine Midland is the case of a UK resident bank which carried on business in international commercial banking. In order to make dollar loans to its customers, it borrowed $15 million in the form of unsecured loan stock which was redeemable in 10 years' time. These funds were then used to lend dollars short term to its customers. After five years the bank's customers repaid their loans and the proceeds were used to redeem the $15 million loan stock.

Over the five-year period while the dollar loan was outstanding, sterling had weakened in relation to the dollar, so that the sterling value of the loans to its customers increased while at the same time the sterling value of the bank's liability on its dollar loan stock had also increased. The position taken by the Inland Revenue in relation to these exchange rate fluctuations was that the exchange loss made by the bank on the redemption of its loan stock was a 'capital' loss arising from the repayment of a liability, and was therefore not tax deductible because capital gains tax does not apply to liabilities. On the other hand, the Inland Revenue claimed that the exchange gain made by the bank when its customers repaid their dollar loans was 'revenue' profits arising from circulating assets and was therefore taxable under Schedule D, Case I.

The importance of the *Marine Midland* case is that the general aim of the bank was to remain matched in each foreign currency and for the most part the dollar borrowings by the bank remained invested in dollar assets. At no time was any of the $15 million converted into sterling. Consequently, the House of Lords dismissed the Inland Revenue's case on the grounds that there could be no foreign exchange profit or loss when no currency conversion had taken place. In effect, it argued that there could be no taxable profit when a bank borrows $15 million, lends $15 million and eventually repays $15 million. As Lord Templeman pointed out:

The company did not make any income or other profit when it lent $15 million to its customers and was repaid $15 million. Between 12th October 1971 and 15th June 1976 the company made a profit which consisted of the difference between the interest paid to the loan stockholders and the interest received by the bank from its customers. This profit was brought into account in the computations of the profits upon which the company paid corporation tax.

The judgment of the House of Lords in this case centred upon the issue of conversion versus translation rather than upon the issue of 'capital' versus 'revenue'. The House of Lords decided *Marine Midland* on the primary issue that there was no realization of a currency gain so that the issue of fixed versus circulating capital remained unconsidered. Indeed, the Inland Revenue still maintain that the *Marine Midland* unsecured dollar loan was of a capital nature.

This case seems to imply clearly that when there is a fully-matched position and no physical conversion of the currency has taken place, a loss on a capital liability (the dollar loan stock) could be offset against a gain on current assets (the dollar loans to customers). It also seemed to imply that there could be no taxation without conversion so that mere translation gains are not taxable. Following the House of Lords judgment, the Inland Revenue acted quickly by publishing a 'Provisional Statement of Practice' in January 1985 which clearly restated that translation gains may be taxable and that where there are unmatched positions that the calculation of trading profits would be determined by reference to the capital and revenue nature of the currency assets and liabilities. This Statement of Practice is now discussed.

Inland Revenue Provisional Statement of Practice, January 1985

The Inland Revenue Provisional Statement of Practice lays down the Revenue's approach to the following main issues:

The capital revenue distinction and the calculation of trading profits

The first important point to note about the Inland Revenue Provisional Statement of Practice issued in January 1985 is that it is concerned only with how exchange rate fluctuations will affect the computation of a company's trading profits. In particular, it is concerned with the adjustments that need to be made to the computation of taxable trading profits when exchange profits or losses on 'capital' assets or liabilities have been included in the profit and loss account.

In so far as the 'capital' or 'revenue' issue is concerned, the Statement follows the judgment of *Marine Midland* and acknowledges that:

> where currency borrowings are matched by currency assets in circumstances that no exchange adjustments are made to the profit and loss account, the capital or current nature of the borrowing will no longer be relevant in determining whether such adjustments are to be made for the purposes of computing trading profits or losses for tax. In these circumstances exchange differences, whether profits or losses, arising on long term borrowings are not to be distinguished and adjusted in computing trading profits or losses for tax.

The Revenue also accepts that the same logic applies when currency fixed assets are matched by currency liabilities. Thus, where there is complete matching and no net exchange differences, there is no tax liability.

However, where currency assets are not matched, or not completely matched, with currency liabilities, so that net exchange differences arise, the Provisional Statement claims that those differences must be analysed according to the 'capital' or 'revenue' nature of the currency assets and liabilities involved. Indeed, the major part of the Provisional Statement is concerned with the procedure to be followed when currency assets and liabilities are not matched. The heart of the statement then is concerned with the adjustment required to eliminate the capital element from the trading results.

The recommended procedure to follow on unmatched or imperfectly matched positions is as follows. First consideration of the tax position starts with the net exchange difference on current items (column A in Table 19.1). Secondly, it is necessary to ascertain the net exchange differences on capital items (column B in Table 19.1). By adding the net exchange differences on current items (column A) to the net exchange differences on capital items (column B) we then obtain the net exchange difference shown in the profit and loss account (column C). Finally, the adjustment to the calculation of trading profits required in order to eliminate the unmatched capital element is shown by column D. Note that the figures in the table are used purely for illustration purposes in the examples that follow the table.

Table 19.1
Analysis of tax adjustments required

	A Net exchange difference on current items	B Net exchange difference on capital items	C Net exchange difference in profit and loss account	D Tax adjustment in computation of trading profits
1	Profit or loss	Nil	Profit or Loss	None
2	Profit £20 000	Loss (£80 000)	Loss (£60 000)	Add back smaller of B and C £60 000
3	Loss (£20 000)	Profit £80 000	Profit £60 000	Deduct smaller of B and C £60 000
4	Profit £60 000	Loss (£20 000)	Profit £40 000	None
5	Loss (£60 000)	Profit £20 000	Loss (£40 000)	None

The Provisional Statement provides a number of examples to illustrate how column D in the table is derived.

Case 1 in Table 19.1 indicates that no adjustment to the trading profits is needed for taxation purposes because there are no net exchange differences on capital items. This is illustrated in Example 1 below, taken from the Inland Revenue Provisional Statement.

Example 1

A company normally trading in sterling incurs a liability on a trade debt of $600 000 when $1.5 = £1. The liability is entered in the books in sterling as £400 000. By the accounting date sterling has fallen to $1.25 = £1, so that the sterling value of the liability has increased to £480 000. The exchange loss of £80 000 is charged to the profit and loss account.

There are no capital exchange differences. No adjustment is required for tax purposes because the transactions are wholly on revenue account. As can be seen, the entire £80 000 loss is allowable in the computation of trading profits. Similarly, if sterling had strengthened instead of weakened, the entire gain would have been included in taxable trading profits.

Case 2 in Table 19.1 indicates the action to be taken when there is a loss on the net exchange difference in both the profit and loss account and in capital items. In this case the smaller of the two losses is the amount to be disallowed in the tax computation as relating to capital items. Since it is a loss which is to be disallowed for tax purposes, it has to be added back in the computation of taxable trading profits. This is illustrated in Example 2 taken from the Inland Revenue Provisional Statement.

Example 2

A trading company borrows $600 000 on long-term capital account when $1.5 = £1. It retains $150 000 as current assets and converts the balance of $450 000 to £300 000. The books will then show the following entries:

Capital loan ($600 000)	£400 000	Current assets ($150 000)	£100 000
		Cash on hand	£300 000
	£400 000		£400 000

By the accounting date when sterling has fallen to $1.25 = £1 these become:

Capital loan ($600 000)	£480 000	Current assets ($150 000)	£120 000
		Cash on hand	£300 000
		Exchange difference to profit and loss account	£ 60 000
	£480 000		£480 000

The exchange difference on capital account is £80 000 (£480 000 – £400 000) but the tax adjustment is limited to the amount charged to the profit and loss account so that £60 000 is disallowed. This reflects the fact that $150 000 of the liability is matched with $150 000 assets. The whole of the exchange difference, £60 000, is attributable to the excess currency liability on capital account.

In this case the capital loss of £80 000 is only partially matched by the gain on current assets (£20 000) leaving £60 000 unmatched and therefore disallowed in the computation of trading profits.

Case 3 in Table 19.1 shows what action has to be taken when there is a profit on the net exchange difference in both the profit and loss account and on capital items. The smaller of the two profit figures is to be deducted in the calculation of taxable trading profits. This is because it is a non-taxable unmatched exchange gain on a capital item which is not taxable as part of the trading profit. This is illustrated by Example 3 taken from the Inland Revenue Provisional Statement.

Example 3

A trading company incurs a liability by way of overdraft on current account of $150 000 and borrows a further £300 000 as a capital loan when $1.5 = £1. It converts the £300 000 to $450 000 and acquires capital assets for $600 000. The books will then show the following entries:

Overdraft on current account ($150 000)	£100 000	Capital assets ($600 000)	£400 000
Capital loan	£300 000		
	£400 000		£400 000

By the accounting date, sterling has fallen to $1.25 = £1 and the book entries are as follows:

Overdraft on current account ($150 000)	£120 000	Capital assets ($600 000)	£480 000
Capital loan	£300 000		
Exchange difference to profit and loss account	£ 60 000		
	£480 000		£480 000

The net exchange profit of £60 000 in the profit and loss account comprises £80 000 profit on the assets and £20 000 loss on the liability. The net capital exchange difference is £80 000 (£480 000 − £400 000) but the adjustment for tax purposes is limited to the figure in the profit and loss account of £60 000. This reflects the fact that $150 000 of the assets are matched with the dollar liability. The non-taxable exchange profit is attributable to the excess capital assets, whose sterling value changed from £300 000 to £360 000.

In this case the capital profit of £80 000 is only partially matched by the exchange loss on the overdraft (£20 000), leaving £60 000 unmatched and therefore not included in the computation of taxable trading profits.

Case 4 in Table 19.1 provides an example where the net exchange difference on the capital items is a loss while the net exchange difference in the profit and loss account shows a profit. In this case no adjustment is necessary in the computation of taxable trading profits since the net capital loss has been more than offset by the exchange gains on current items, so that no further adjustment needs to be made for capital items. This is illustrated in Example 4 taken from the Inland Revenue Provisional Statement.

Example 4

A trading company borrows $900 000 on capital account and raises a further sterling loan of £200 000. It converts the £200 000 to $300 000 and buys capital assets for $750 000. At this time $1.5 = £1. The balance of $450 000 is retained as a current asset. The books show the following entries at this point:

Capital loan ($900 000)	£600 000	Capital assets ($750 000)	£500 000
Capital loan	£200 000	Current assets ($450 000)	£300 000
	£800 000		£800 000

By the accounting date the exchange rate alters to $1.25 = £1 and the book entries become:

Capital loan ($900 000)	£720 000	Capital assets ($750 000)	£600 000
Capital loan	£200 000	Current assets ($450 000)	£360 000
Exchange difference to profit and loss account	£ 40 000		
	£960 000		£960 000

The profit and loss account entry for the net exchange profit of £40 000 is made up of £160 000 profit on the assets and £120 000 loss on the liabilities. The net capital exchange difference is a debit of £20 000 ((£720 000 − £600 000) − (£600 000 − £500 000)) but the profit and loss account shows a net credit of £40 000. No adjustment is therefore required for tax purposes. This reflects the matching of the net capital liability of $150 000 with part of the dollar current assets. The taxable exchange profit of £40 000 is attributable to the balance of the dollar current assets, whose value increased from £200 000 to £240 000.

Case 5 in Table 19.1 is similar to Case 4 except that the net exchange difference on capital items is a profit whereas the net exchange difference in the profit and loss account is a loss. Again in this case no adjustment is necessary in the computation of taxable trading profits since the net capital gain has been more than completely offset by the exchange loss on current items, so that no further adjustment needs to be made for capital items. The reader can illustrate this by using Example 4 with the assumption that sterling strengthens instead of weakens.

In conclusion it should be noted that the amount of any tax adjustment is limited in each case to the credit or debit for net exchange differences in the profit and loss account. In Table 19.1 this means that the amount of the tax adjustment in column D cannot be larger than the figure in column C.

The issue of conversion versus translation

Despite the *Marine Midland* judgment, the Revenue continues to take the view that it is not necessary to abandon the current practice of bringing translation adjustments on unmatched positions into account for tax purposes. Indeed, the Provisional Statement points out that any attempt to deal with exchange profits and losses on unmatched positions only where there is conversion into sterling would present substantial problems of identification for both tax-payers and the Revenue.

Thus, the Revenue seems to be taking the view that from a practical point of view it would prefer to continue to bring translation adjustments on unmatched positions into account for tax purposes. However, it should be pointed out that existing case law does not prevent taxpayers from being taxed on a conversion basis if they so wish.

The issue of capital gains

The Statement is primarily concerned with the computation of taxable trading profits and not with capital gains tax. Nevertheless, it emphasizes that capital items excluded from the trading results will be treated in the usual way under the existing capital gains tax legislation.

Inland Revenue Statement of Practice February 1987

Following the issue of the Provisional Statement of Practice and the invitation to comment on its scope and content, the Inland Revenue received 28 responses from the major representative bodies and other interested parties. In the light of these comments, the Inland Revenue issued a full Statement of Practice to replace the Provisional Statement. Its position on the capital/revenue distinction and the translation/conversion issue remains fundamentally the same as in the original provisional Statement.

The capital/revenue distinction and the calculation of trading profits

The full Statement emphasises the view that the distinction between capital and current liabilities is based on principles well established in tax case law and reiterates its view that the liability in question in the *Marine Midland* case was of a capital nature. Nevertheless, the Inland Revenue Statement follows the judgment of *Marine Midland* and its own provisional Statement that the capital or current nature of the borrowing will be irrelevant where there is complete matching.

In general, the examples provided in the Statement are the same as those examined earlier in the provisional Statement. The major additions relate to the matching principles when there is more than one currency involved, and where the matching involves hedge transactions. These are examined in Cases 6 and 7 in Table 19.2, using the same analysis as provided in Table 19.1 illustrating the examples in the Provisional Statement.

Table 19.2
Examination of cases

A	B	C	D
Net exchange difference on current items	**Net exchange difference on capital items**	**Net exchange difference in profit and loss accounts**	**Tax adjustment in computation of trading profits**
6 Profit of £7000 on Deutschmarks	(a) Profit of £33 000 on Deutschmarks	Profit of £40 000 on Deutschmarks	Deduct £33 000
	(b) Loss of £50 000 on $	Loss of £50 000 on $	Add £50 000
			Add back
7 Loss of £30 000	(a) Loss of £120 000	Loss of £50 000	Add back
	(b) Profit on forward exchange contract of £100 000		£17 000 £20 000

Case 6 in Table 19.2 is an example of the Inland Revenue view that where there are transactions in more than one currency, each currency must be considered separately. Thus the $ exchange loss of £50 000 is entirely on capital account and should be added back to the tax computation. The Deutschmark capital profit of £33 000 is also entirely unmatched and should be deducted in the calculation of taxable trading profits. Thus the overall adjustment to the tax computation is an addition of £17 000 (£50 000 − £33 000).

Example 6

A trading company borrows $900 000 on long-term capital account and DM 300 000 on overdraft when £1 = $1.5 = DM3.0. It makes a loan of $600 000 to an associated company (not in the course of trade) and converts $300 000 into DM600 000. It loans DM500 000 to another associated company (not in the course of trade) and retains the balance of DM400 000 as a current asset. The books show the following entries:

Capital loan ($900 000)	£600 000	Capital assets ($600 000)	£400 000
Overdraft (DM300 000)	£100 000	Capital assets (DM500 000)	£167 000
		Current assets (DM400 000)	£133 000
	£700 000		£700 000

By the accounting date sterling has fallen to £1 = $1.20 = DM2.5 and the book entries are as follows:

Capital loan ($900 000)	£750 000	Capital assets ($600 000)	£500 000
Overdraft (DM300 000)	£120 000	Capital assets (DM500 000)	£200 000
		Current assets (DM400 000)	£160 000
		Exchange difference to profit and loss account	£ 10 000
	£870 000		£870 000

The net exchange difference of £10 000 comprises £50 000 loss on the dollar assets and liabilities offset by £40 000 profit on the Deutschmark assets and liabilities.

The dollar exchange loss is entirely on capital account and should be added back to the tax computation.

The Deutschmark exchange difference comprises £60 000 profit on the assets and £20 000 loss on the liability. The net capital exchange difference on Deutschmark assets and liabilities is a profit of £33 000 (£200 000 minus £167 000), so the adjustment for tax purposes is limited to £33 000. This reflects the fact that the overdraft is matched with Deutschmark current assets and the Deutschmark capital assets are unmatched.

Thus the overall adjustment to the tax computation is an addition of £17 000 (£50 000 minus £33 000).

In considering whether a 'trader' is matched in a particular currency, forward exchange contracts and currency futures entered into for hedging purposes may be taken into account, provided that hedging is reflected in the accounts on a consistent basis from year to year and in accordance with accepted accounting practice. This is illustrated in Case 7 in Table 19.2. In this particular case, the forward contract specifically hedges a capital loan, so that the net exchange loss on capital items is £20 000. Because this is less than the overall exchange loss of £50 000, the capital loss of £20 000 is disallowed for tax purposes.

Similarly, for the purposes of calculating trading profits or losses, the Statement accepts that where a trader enters into a currency swap agreement the two transactions in the original currency should be treated as matched. By contrast, in the Revenue's view, where currency assets or liabilities are hedged by transactions in currency options no matching can be said to have taken place and such transactions are unaffected by the *Marine Midland* decision.

Example 7

At the start of the accounting period the book entries are:

Capital loan ($600 000)	£480 000	Current assets ($150 000)	£120 000
Overdraft on current		Cash in hand	£500 000
account ($300 000)	£240 000	Exchange difference	
		brought forward	£100 000
	£720 000		£720 000

Three months from the end of the accounting period (there having been no transactions in the meantime affecting the assets and liabilities referred to in the example), when $1.18 = £1, the company enters a forward contract to purchase $600 000 at $1.20 = £1 in six months time, to hedge the capital loan which is repayable on the date the forward contract matures.

By the accounting date, when $1.0 = £1 the books show:

Capital loan ($600 000)*	£500 000	Current assets (£150 000)	£150 000
Overdraft on current		Cash on hand	£500 000
account ($300 000)	£300 000	Exchange difference	
		brought forward	£100 000
		Exchange difference to	
		profit and loss account	£ 50 000
	£800 000		£800 000

* translated at forward rate $1.20 = £1

or

Capital loan ($600 000)	£600 000	Current assets ($150 000)	£150 000
Overdraft on current		Cash on hand	£500 000
account ($300 000)	£300 000	Forward contract	£100 000
		Exchange difference	
		brought forward	£100 000
		Exchange difference to	
		profit and loss account	£ 50 000
	£900 000		£900 000

Because the forward contract specifically hedges the capital loan the net exchange loss on capital items on either basis is £20 000 (£500 000 minus £480 000: or £600 000 minus £480 000 less £100 000 profit on forward contract). Because this is less than the overall exchange loss of £50 000, the capital loss of £20 000 is disallowed for tax purposes.

The issue of conversion versus translation

On the issue of conversion versus translation the Inland Revenue rejected the view of some commentators that translation profits or losses should be ignored for tax purposes on the grounds that they have not been realized or incurred. Despite the *Marine Midland* case the statement argues that the wider body of case law generally supports the view that the calculation of annual profits and gains for tax purposes should start with a consideration of the accounts drawn up in accordance with the correct principles of commercial accounting. In general, the Inland Revenue view is that if the accounts of a business have been compiled in accordance with the Companies Acts and generally accepted accountancy principles and have taken account of translation profits and losses, then those profits and losses should normally be taken into account for tax purposes unless there are particular reasons relevant to the case in question for taking a different view. The Statement makes quite clear that if a taxpayer wishes to make use of a conversion or some other basis, it will be necessary for him to make out his case to the Inspector.

The 1985 Finance Act

Whereas the Inland Revenue statements were primarily concerned with the computation of taxable trading profits, the financial futures section of the 1985 Finance Act concentrates upon the issue of which tax schedule would apply in particular circumstances. The effect of the 1985 Finance Act was to substantially reduce taxation under Schedule D, Case VI by transferring many of the cases previously taxed under this schedule to the capital gains tax section. The major provisions of the 1985 Finance Act in so far as they affect the taxation of financial futures are as follows:

1   Where the taxpayer enters into financial futures or traded options transactions as part of a trade, any profits or losses will be liable as before to treatment under income tax for individuals, or corporation tax under Schedule D, Case I for companies.

   Much of course hinges upon the definition of trading. In reply to a parliamentary question about the tax treatment of futures, Mr John Moore, the Financial Secretary to the Treasury wrote as follows:

   Whether in any particular instance the activities of a taxpayer amount to trading will turn on the facts of the matter as well as on the law. But in general a taxpayer whether an individual or company, would not be regarded as trading in respect of transactions which are relatively infrequent or, for example, where the intention was to hedge specific investments; and an individual is unlikely to be regarded as trading as a result of purely speculative transactions in futures:

2   The main change in the 1985 Finance Act relates to those transactions in financial futures and traded options which are not part of a trade. Whereas previously these profits had been treated as income and taxed under Schedule D, Case VI, the Act stipulated that from 6 April 1985, Stock Exchange traded options and The London International Financial Futures Exchange (LIFFE) futures and options were to be taken out of the scope of Schedule D, Case VI and taxed under the capital gains tax legislation.

   LIFFE is the only futures exchange which has statutory

recognition for the purpose of excluding futures and traded options from the scope of Schedule D, Case VI. However, since the Finance Act received the Royal Assent on 25 July 1985, the Board of Inland Revenue has the power to designate futures exchanges anywhere in the world as also being recognized for this purpose. Since then, the following futures exchanges have been designated as recognized, with effect from 6 August 1985 (except where otherwise indicated):

Baltic International Freight Futures Exchange
International Petroleum Exchange of London
London Cocoa Terminal Market
London Coffee Terminal Market
London Gold Futures Market
London Gold Market (12 December 1985)
London Grain Futures Market
London International Financial Futures Exchange (6 April 1985)
London Meat Futures Market
London Metal Exchange
London Potato Futures Market
London Rubber Market
London Silver Market (12 December 1985)
London Soya Bean Meal Futures Market
London Sugar Terminal Market
London Wool Terminal Market
New York Mercantile Exchange (19 December 1986
Philadelphia Board of Trade (19 December 1986)
Chicago Board of Trade (24 April 1987)
Chicago Mercantile Exchange (24 April 1987)
Mid America Commodity Exchange (29 July 1987)
Montreal Exchange (29 July 1987)

In addition to exclusion from Schedule D, Case VI, traded options on the 'recognised' futures exchanges also have the advantage of being removed from the scope of the capital gains tax wasting asset rules. This is extremely advantageous since the wasting asset rules have the effect of disallowing a proportion of the cost over the life of the option thereby increasing the taxable profit and inflating the capital gains tax liability.

3   The new rules (that is exclusion from Schedule D, Case VI) apply only to profits or losses on futures contracts which are closed out by matching transactions or settled in cash, and to transactions in traded options on a recognized exchange. In so far as the futures transaction is carried out on an exchange not yet 'recognised' by the Inland Revenue, or the option is an over-the-counter option, then the transaction will be taxed under Schedule D, Case I if it is part of a trade or Schedule D, Case VI in most other situations.

The tax position of the various participants

The application of the tax principles laid down in the various Finance Acts will depend upon the tax position of the individual or institution engaged in the financial futures transactions.

Individuals will either be taxed at the appropriate marginal tax rate (between 27 per cent and 60 per cent for 1987) or at an effective capital gains tax of 30 per cent with a current (1987) annual exemption of £6600.

Companies, similarly, will either be taxed at the appropriate rate of corporation tax (35 per cent for 1986) under Schedule D, Case I or Case VI, or at the 35 per cent effective capital gains tax rate.

Banks, financial trading companies and insurance companies (except for their life funds) will generally have profits from financial futures and options taxed under Schedule D, Case I as part of their trading income.

Pension funds, on the other hand, are exempt from tax on income from investments and on capital gains arising from the disposal of investments. Since the Finance Act of 1984 deemed that their dealings in financial futures and traded options would be regarded as part of their investments, this has the effect of making such pension fund investments exempt from taxation. However, in so far as OTC transactions are concerned, pension funds (subject to the outcome of the Fisons Pension Fund appeal) continue to be liable to capital gains tax on their OTC options but not on their OTC financial futures.

Also local authorities, since they are exempt from income tax, corporation tax and capital gains tax, can deal in financial futures and options without having to worry about the tax implications.

The position of authorized unit and investment trusts is a little less clear. These institutions are exempt from capital gains tax so that their transactions in futures and options will also be exempt in so far as they are regarded as of a capital rather than a trading nature. What is still controversial is the tax treatment of profits from financial futures and options which were previously taxed as Case VI income. The provisions of Section 72 of the 1985 Finance Act transferred such income to treatment under the capital gains tax legislation. Such treatment would have the effect of making them exempt for unit and investment trusts. Whether Section 72 of the 1985 Finance Act applies to these institutions is still under debate with the Revenue, and the outcome remains to be seen.

In so far as Building Societies are concerned, clause 21 of the 1986 Building Societies Bill will permit the larger building societies to use financial futures for hedging purposes. It is anticipated that profits and losses arising from such transactions will be taxed as trading income under Schedule D, Case I at the appropriate reduced rate.

Changes announced in the March 1987 budget

In his budget the Chancellor proposes to extend the capital gains tax treatment in Section 72 Finance Act 1985 to certain over-the-counter financial futures and options. The main effect will be that profits on transactions in these futures and options will always be taxed as capital gains rather than income unless the transaction takes place in the course of a trade. At present they may in some circumstances be taxed as income. It is proposed therefore that Section 72 be extended to:

1   gains on commodity and financial futures (including forwards) where one of the parties to the transaction is either an 'Authorized person' or a 'Listed Institution' within the meaning of Financial Services Act 1986,
2   gains on financial options granted by or, in certain circumstances, to an authorized person or listed institution,
3   gains on options which relate to quoted shares and securities and are arranged through a Stock Exchange member.

In addition, the Chancellor also proposes to bring the capital gains treatment of over-the-counter financial options in line with that for traded options. The Chancellor therefore proposes that financial options should also benefit from two other technical changes. Unlike traded options, over-the-counter options are at present wasting assets for capital gains tax purposes. This means that their allowable cost reduces proportionately throughout the life of the asset to nil on expiry. In addition the expiry of a traded option is treated as a disposal for capital gains tax purposes which thus produces an allowable loss; this is not the case with an over-the-counter option. It is proposed in both cases to amend the rules for over-the-counter financial options to bring them into line with traded options.

Conclusion

This chapter has sought to lay down the major principles under-lying the tax position. In a continuously developing and changing tax environment, active participants in the futures markets would be well advised to seek advice on the tax implications of their dealings.

20 Currency borrowing, back-to-back loans, and currency exchange agreements

Most techniques of hedging involve taking short positions to offset long ones, or vice versa. A direct application of this approach is to hedge assets denominated in a currency by means of acquiring liabilities in that currency. An exposed position in the form of a foreign currency asset is thus hedged by borrowing in that currency. A fall in the value of the asset due to a depreciation of the currency would be matched by a reduction in the value of the liability. Likewise, a liability denominated in a foreign currency could be hedged by an asset in the same currency.

Local borrowing and investing

Management of the asset/liability position can be carried out by means of borrowing or lending in the currency concerned. Consider first the case of hedging transactions risk.

An importer anticipating a foreign currency payment on a future date could buy the foreign currency in the present and invest it with a view to meeting the payment with the principal plus interest when the investment matures. The costs involved in this operation render it equivalent to a forward purchase of the currency. This can be seen by supposing that the home currency used to buy spot foreign currency is borrowed. The net cost is represented by the excess of the interest rate on the home currency over that on the foreign currency (this cost may be negative). This interest rate differential is equal to the discount (or premium) on forward foreign exchange. Thus the costs of the two techniques would tend to be the same. Investing in foreign currency has the drawbacks of providing liquidity problems and appearing on balance sheets. Forward operations avoid these problems, but forward rates have greater bid-offer spreads than spot rates. This adds to the relative cost of forwards, and adequate forward markets are not always available.

An exporter expecting a foreign currency receipt on a future date could cover his exchange rate risk by borrowing in the foreign currency. He would thus have a foreign currency liability to offset the asset of a foreign currency receivable. The currency borrowed would be sold spot for home currency. The foreign currency borrowing plus interest would be repaid with the foreign currency payment for the exports. The net cost of such an operation could again be expressed in terms of the interest rate differential, since the home currency could be invested until the payment date. The interest rate parity relationship suggests that the cost of hedging by means of foreign currency borrowing is the same as the cost of hedging by means of a forward sale of foreign currency.

Balance sheet exposure may also be hedged by means of foreign currency lending or borrowing. If a corporation has a subsidiary in the US, the parent company has an asset valued in terms of US dollars and hence is exposed. A decline in the foreign exchange value of the dollar would reduce the balance sheet valuation of the subsidiary. This risk could be covered by borrowing in US dollars, whether to directly finance the subsidiary or to sell spot for the home currency. The effects of exchange rate movements on the balance sheet value of the asset would then be offset by the effects on the liability; reduced asset values would be offset by lower liability values.

Currency overdrafts

One specific means of hedging by means of foreign currency borrowing involves foreign currency overdrafts. This technique is particularly useful for covering transactions exposure in cases where the exposure arises from a continuous flow of foreign currency receivables rather than occasional single items.

At any moment in time the anticipated future receivables constitute assets. To the extent that these receivables are denominated in foreign currency the company has a long position in the relevant currency. This net exposure can be eliminated by taking a short position in the currency concerned. An overdraft denominated in the currency of exposure and matched in value to the receivables would achieve the purpose. Losses on the assets arising from depreciation of the currency would be offset by reductions in the home currency value of the overdraft. Figure 20.1 illustrates one possible approach to the operation of currency overdrafts.

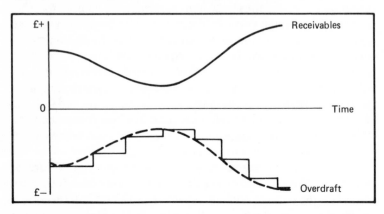

Figure 20.1   Hedging receivables with a currency overdraft

The top half of Figure 20.1 depicts the sum of anticipated receivables as it changes over time. In the bottom half, the broken line is a mirror image of the curve in the top half. The overdraft is periodically equated to the sum of anticipated receivables and then is maintained at a constant level until the next adjustment. The foreign currency receipts are not used to reduce the overdraft. The lag in adjustment of the overdraft to the receivables means that matching is imperfect.

The currency borrowed is immediately sold for the home currency. If it is used to reduce home currency debt the interest payments on the overdraft are offset by the reduced interest payments on home currency debt. If the money is used for home currency deposits the spread between deposit and overdraft rates adds to the cost of this hedging strategy.

The difference between foreign and home currency interest rates provides the basic cost of this hedging technique. If foreign currency interest rates exceed home currency rates there is a net cost. Interest rate parity suggests that under such circumstances foreign currency would be at a discount against the home currency with the rate of discount being equal to the interest rate differential. Therefore, whether foreign currency receipts are sold forward or hedged with currency overdrafts the cost of the hedging is the same.

A bank providing a currency overdraft facility might require the customer to use the currency receipts to pay down the overdraft. In such a situation there would always be a tendency for the size of the overdraft to fall below that of the sum of receivables. The sum of receivables would be continually replenished by new sales, whilst the overdraft is progressively reduced. A system for topping up the overdraft is thus needed.

For example, consider the case of a Deutschmark overdraft. The topping up system might involve adding DM200 000 to the overdraft whenever the overdraft falls to DM100 000 below the sum of receivables. The overdraft would oscillate between DM100 000 below and DM100 000 above the sum of receivables with a tendency to average out at equality with the receivables. This system involves periods during which the overdraft exceeds the sum of receivables, and this might be unacceptable to the bank providing the overdraft facility.

If such is the case, the system might be one in which the overdraft is topped up to the level of the receivables whenever it falls DM100 000 below this level. The overdraft would then, on average, tend to be DM50 000 below the sum of receivables. This average net exposure would have to be hedged by other means.

Since currencies often have stable relationships with one another it is possible to hedge risk arising from many currencies with overdrafts in just a few. Frequently, currencies form groups whose members follow the dominant currency, for example the Canadian dollar following the US dollar (although, obviously, not in a precise fashion). Other currencies have formal links, such as those participating in the exchange rate arrangements of the

European Monetary System. Receivables in several currencies of a group can be covered on an approximate basis by an overdraft in just one currency from the group. The company treasurer is faced with a trade-off between accuracy of cover and the administration costs. Use of a larger number of currencies increases the accuracy of hedging but at the cost of greater administrative complexity.

Back-to-back loans

Back-to-back loans fall into two types – parallel loans and swap loans.

Parallel loans

These loans are useful for multinationals seeking finance for overseas subsidiaries. They involve a parent company in country A making a loan to a subsidiary, whose parent company is in country B, operating in country A. Simultaneously, the country B parent company lends to the country A subsidiary operating in country B. Suppose that countries A and B are the UK and the US. Figure 20.2 illustrates the loan arrangement.

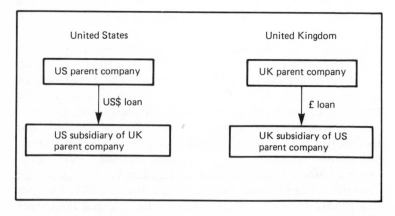

Figure 20.2   Parallel loans

This procedure avoids translation (that is, balance sheet) exposure by ensuring that foreign assets are matched by foreign currency liabilities. If the UK parent raised a sterling loan and converted the sterling into dollars for its subsidiary in the US it would have an asset valued in US dollars with no corresponding dollar liability. The company would be exposed to the risk of a depreciation of the US dollar against sterling. This operation may also help to reduce transactions exposure. The returns from the subsidiary in the US are in US dollars and the loan servicing to be financed from those returns is also in US dollars.

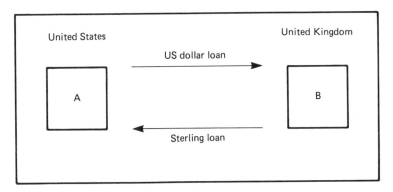

Figure 20.3 Swap loans

These exposures could also be avoided by local borrowing. The American subsidiary of the UK parent might borrow dollars in the US. This borrowing could be difficult or expensive if the subsidiary is not well known in the US. The American parent company may be able to raise a loan more cheaply, or might have surplus funds of its own to lend. Corresponding considerations apply to the American subsidiary operating in the UK.

This type of technique might be of considerable interest to institutions such as pension funds and investment trusts that wish to hedge the foreign exchange risk on their overseas assets. A British pension fund could acquire Italian assets with a loan from an Italian company and simultaneously lend to a British subsidiary of that Italian company. The pension fund's Italian assets provide an exposure that is hedged by the lire denominated debt.

Swap loans

This term has three different meanings in the field of currency risk management (see p.223). In this context, swap loans involve two companies, in different countries, simultaneously lending to each other. This is illustrated by Figure 20.3.

Company A obtains a sterling liability that might be used to hedge sterling assets, and the UK company obtains a dollar liability. The initial loans would be equal in value. The agreement may or may not stipulate future money flows, to maintain equality between the values of the two different loans, in response to exchange rate changes.

The loans could be due for repayment on a specific future date, or during a future period (with either party determining when the two loans will be repaid). The interest rates may be fixed for the full period or determined on a floating basis. Tax considerations normally preclude net interest payments on back-to-back loans. Both parties must pay interest in full.

Currency exchange agreements (CEAs)

CEAs involve companies in two different countries exchanging currencies with an agreement to exchange them in the opposite direction, at the same rate of exchange, on a future date. Using the hypothetical example of an American parent, with a subsidiary in the UK, wishing to raise a sterling loan for its subsidiary and matched with a British parent company seeking finance for its subsidiary in the US the currency swap is illustrated by Figure 20.4.

The two parent companies exchange currencies at the spot exchange rate and agree to reverse the exchange, at the same rate, at a time in the future which would typically be several years away. The UK parent lends the acquired dollars to its subsidiary operating in the US and the American parent does likewise for its subsidiary.

In the absence of a CEA the American parent might raise a loan in dollars, buy spot sterling with those dollars, and lend the sterling to its subsidiary. When the subsidiary repays the sterling loan the parent company sells the sterling for dollars at the new spot rate.

Since the spot rate cannot be accurately predicted several years into the future the parent company, at the time of buying sterling, faces uncertainty as to the eventual dollar value of the repaid sterling loan. Under the currency swap arrangement the American parent company knows how many dollars will be received, on the future repayment date, for the sterling repaid by its subsidiary.

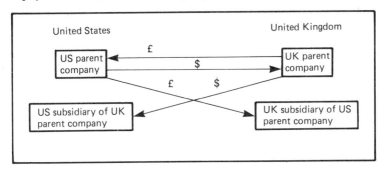

Figure 20.4   Currency Exchange Agreement

In principle, CEAs are no different to swap loans. They both involve an initial exchange of currencies with an agreement to exchange in the opposite direction at the same rate of exchange in the future. The only difference is that in one case the cash flows are called loans whereas in the other they are called currency exchanges. The difference is in name only, but this is significant. Since CEAs technically do not involve loans they do not entail interest payments. This allows the 'interest' payments to be netted out. The resultant one-way cash flow can then be regarded as a fee. The difference in name also has balance sheet implications. The loans in a swap appear on the balance sheet, raising gearing and limiting the ability to raise other finance, whereas CEA currency flows are off balance sheet.

As with back-to-back loans, institutional investors could find CEAs to be a convenient means of hedging translation risk on their foreign assets. A British pension fund could buy assets in the US with dollars obtained through a CEA. It knows that when it disposes of the assets at a future date it can sell part of the dollar receipts from that sale at an exchange rate determined prior to the acquisition of the assets.

A common feature of back-to-back loans and CEAs is that they can be used to circumvent exchange controls aimed at curtailing foreign investment. Some governments attempt to prevent, or render unduly expensive, investment by residents of their country (including companies and institutions) in other countries. Back-to-back loans provide a means of acquiring foreign assets without currency crossing national borders, thereby avoiding exchange control restrictions. Likewise, CEAs can operate without money being moved from one country to another. The money from the American parent can go straight to the British company's subsidiary without the dollars entering the UK.

21 Currency swaps

The term swap has three different, but related, meanings in the context of international finance:

1   the purchase and simultaneous forward sale of a currency;
2   simultaneous loans in two currencies;
3   an exchange of a liability in one currency for a liability in another currency.

Swaps in the third sense involve exchanging debt commitments. A company, or other body, may wish to exchange a liability in one currency for a liability in another in order to reduce currency exposure. For example, a company with easier access to the UK capital market than to the US market might seek to finance an investment in the US by raising sterling in Britain and selling it for US dollars which are invested in the US. It then has a sterling liability and a US dollar asset. It is vulnerable to a strengthening of sterling against the dollar and would have an interest in swapping its sterling liability for a dollar one.

The currency swap may be carried out by direct negotiation between the counterparties or by means of a bank acting as intermediary and effectively becoming the counterparty to each participant. Figure 21.1 illustrates the latter case. Borrower A acquired a sterling liability and sold the sterling raised for dollars in order to acquire assets in the US. Borrower B, facing easier access to the US capital market than the UK one, borrowed dollars and sold them in order to purchase assets in the UK. Both borrowers have an exchange rate exposure, having assets in one currency and liabilities in another. Borrower A would find that, in the event of a strengthening of the pound against the dollar, both the interest payments and the sum to be repaid at maturity rise in dollar value. Conversely, borrower B is vulnerable to a strengthening of the dollar.

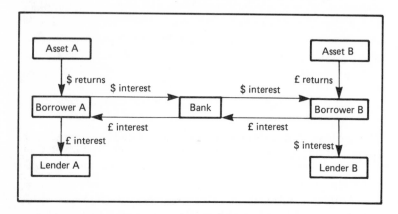

Figure 21.1   Currency swap with a bank as intermediary

They enter the swap agreements depicted by Figure 21.1. Borrower A simulates a dollar liability whilst borrower B simulates a sterling liability. This is achieved by means of borrower A undertaking to meet the interest and principal payments on borrower B's dollar liability by means of making the dollar payments to borrower B via the bank, whilst borrower B makes a similar commitment to service borrower A's sterling debt. The bank operates as counterparty to both, and borrowers A and B need not even know the other's identity. Borrower A remains the debtor of lender A, similarly for borrower and lender B. The lenders may not know of the swap.

The bank runs the risk of losses arising from default by one of the parties. If, for example, the dollar strengthens against sterling, the bank will be gaining from its transactions with borrower A but losing with B. Normally these gains and losses would cancel each other out but if A were to renege on its obligations the bank would be left with its loss-making commitments to B. The bank is committed to paying both interest and principal in the relatively strong dollar whilst receiving the same in the weakened sterling.

The risk would also be present where the bank has created a liability with a view to swapping it. In this case the bank, taking the role of borrower B, would have borrowed dollars and exchanged them for sterling which would have been lent. After A reneges, the bank is left with a liability which, owing to the dollar appreciation, has risen in value in sterling terms so that the value of the liability exceeds that of the asset.

Swaps take advantage of the relatively advantageous terms that some borrowers might obtain in particular markets. In Figure 21.1 borrower A may be able to borrow sterling more cheaply than borrower B whilst borrower B obtains a lower rate of interest than A when borrowing dollars. It is mutually advantageous for both to borrow in their more favourable market and then exchange both the currencies borrowed and the liabilities acquired. Swaps may of course arise from different motives and indeed need not involve an exchange of spot currency, there may merely be an agreement to service each other's debt.

Variations in the terms on which different borrowers can obtain funds in particular currencies can arise for a number of reasons. Exchange controls may inhibit borrowing by non-nationals, a company may be little known outside its own country and hence may have a low credit rating in foreign capital markets, or a market may be saturated with a particular borrower's debt. This latter situation is illustrated by the World Bank's borrowing of Swiss francs in the early 1980s. The Swiss franc market was so saturated with World Bank debt that the Bank was faced with increasing interest rates. It circumvented this problem by borrowing dollars and entering a swap with IBM. There were relatively few US corporates borrowing Swiss francs so such corporates could borrow them at relatively low interest rates. IBM could thus borrow Swiss francs more cheaply than the World Bank. Thus IBM borrowed Swiss francs and entered a Swiss franc/US dollar swap with the World Bank to their mutual advantage.

The second definition of a swap is equivalent to a current exchange of currencies with a commitment to a future reversal (that is, a currency exchange agreement), as is the third definition when spot currencies, as well as liabilities, are exchanged. In fact currency exchange agreements often eschew the initial exchange of currencies, leaving the parties to buy in the spot market, and this renders them indistinguishable from an exchange of liabilities.

In the case of the first definition of a swap, the forward rate will typically differ from the spot rate, whereas the rates are normally the same for the two points in time for the two other definitions. The forward premium or discount is implicit in the interest flows in these cases. Different rates of interest on the two currencies have the same effect as a forward premium/discount. For example, if the US dollar was at a premium against sterling more sterling would be forthcoming from a forward sale of dollars than were expended in the original purchase of dollars. The interest rate parity relationship entails that sterling deposits attract a higher rate of interest than dollar deposits in such a situation. Correspondingly, providers of sterling in the second type of swap would receive an interest rate which is higher than that which they pay. In the third type of swap those servicing dollar debts would pay the lower interest rate and that would tend to compensate them for paying the higher valued principal (because of the appreciation of the dollar) at maturity.

Position taking

If borrowers expect that the currency in which their liability is denominated is likely to appreciate they may swap into a currency that they expect to depreciate. If the expected exchange rate movements occur they may subsequently reverse the swap in order to lock-in the fall in the value of the liability caused by the exchange rate depreciation.

Figure 21.2 illustrates the case of a borrower with a sterling liability and Deutschmark assets. A borrows sterling which is used to buy Deutschmarks for the purpose of investment in Deutschmark denominated assets. Following a depreciation of sterling against the Deutschmark, A decides to lock-in the gain by swapping the sterling liability for a Deutschmark one. This liability is less than would have been incurred if Deutschmarks had originally been borrowed to finance the acquisition of the Deutschmark asset.

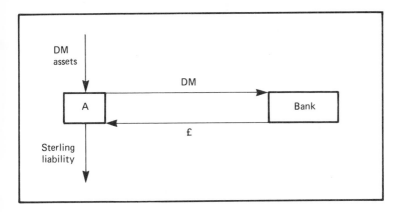

Figure 21.2   Locking in a currency gain

Case study: locking-in a currency gain

A leading British brewing group decided that there was a market for its beer in North America and built a brewery in California. To avoid currency exposure the brewery was financed by borrowing 100 million US dollars.

The sterling–dollar exchange rate had been fairly stable at about £1 = $1.50 for several months when a political crisis in the US caused the dollar to fall to £1 = $1.65. The treasurer of the parent company felt that there was no change in the underlying economic conditions to warrant a dollar depreciation and hence felt that the dollar's decline would be only temporary. He decided to lock-in the fall in the sterling value of the dollar liability by entering a currency swap. The dollar liability was swapped for a sterling liability at the exchange rate of £1 = $1.65.

About six months later the political crisis subsided and the exchange rate returned to £1 = $1.50, which was the rate suggested by the principle of purchasing power parity. The treasurer, wanting to again cover the dollar asset exposure, undertook another swap. The sterling liability was swapped for a dollar liability.

At the end of the operation the US dollar liability was about 9 per cent less than it had been at the beginning. The US $100 million debt had been swapped into a £60 606 601 liability and then the £60 606 601 debt had been swapped for a US $90 909 091 liability.

To restore the dollar liability and hence the degree of currency cover to $100 million, the company borrows a further US $9 090 909 which is the profit from the swap operations.

Asset-based swaps

Although swaps are typically exchanges of liabilities, the technique can also be used for assets. Figure 21.3 illustrates the situation in which the UK holder of a US dollar bond fears a depreciation of the US dollar against sterling and decides to swap the dollar asset into a sterling asset. The UK bond holder receives a flow of interest receipts plus the payment of principal at maturity in US dollars from the US issuer of the bond. Fearing a fall in the value of the dollar the bond holder swaps into a sterling asset agreeing to pay interest and principal in dollars in return for sterling receipts. The swap counterparty is not necessarily transacting an asset-based swap – either assets or liabilities could be being swapped.

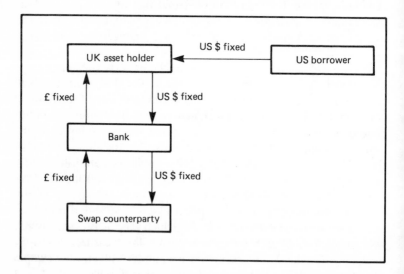

Figure 21.3   Asset based swap

22 Interest rate swaps

Liabilities denominated in the same currency can effectively be exchanged by means of swaps. This would commonly be for the purpose of changing the basis upon which interest is charged, for example from a floating rate to a fixed rate basis.

Hedging interest risk

Floating rate loans expose the debtor to the risk of increases in the interest rate. A debtor may wish to avoid this risk by taking out a fixed rate loan but finds that, owing to insufficient credit standing, he is unable to borrow at fixed rates or can only do so at a particularly high rate of interest. The borrower could attempt to swap the floating rate liability for a fixed rate liability, thereby obtaining fixed rate funds at the price of paying a premium to the other debtor who foregoes the security of being certain of the interest rate payable in the future.

The swap may be carried out directly between the two liability holders or may involve a bank as intermediary. In the latter case the bank might take the role of counterparty to both participants thereby bearing the risk of default by either party and eliminating the need for the participants to investigate the creditworthiness of the other. This has the additional advantage of allowing anonymity of the parties. It also facilitates swapping by debtors of relatively low creditworthiness.

Figure 22.1 illustrates a case in which a bank operates as intermediary. Borrower A has taken a loan from lender A at a floating rate of interest but would prefer the certainty provided by a fixed rate loan, and is willing to pay a premium for that certainty. The bank agrees that, in return for the premium, it will provide borrower A with the funds required to pay the interest on the floating rate loan and accept interest payments at a fixed rate. Lender A is unaffected, his debtor continues to be borrower A and interest payments continue to be received from that source. Lender A need never know that the swap has taken place. Meanwhile, borrower A has simulated a fixed rate liability.

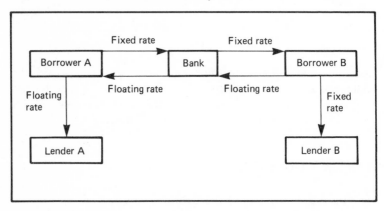

Figure 22.1   Interest rate swap with a bank as intermediary

The bank seeks to match its commitment by finding a fixed rate borrower willing to bear the uncertainty of a floating rate loan in return for a premium. By agreeing to this, borrower B simulates a floating rate loan whilst lender B retains both fixed rate receipts and the original debtor. If the bank is unable to find a borrower B that can be matched with borrower A it may take over the role itself. The bank would thus borrow at a fixed rate and swap its liability with borrower A. The bank effectively converts its debt from a fixed rate into a floating rate, whilst borrower A converts it from a floating rate into a fixed rate.

When acting as counterparty to both borrowers, whether or not it has taken the role of borrower B, the bank faces the risk that a borrower could default. This leaves the bank exposed to an interest rate risk; the remaining customer may be receiving a high rate of interest and paying a low one. The original matching allowed losses from transactions with one customer to be offset by the corresponding gains from the deal with the other customer. Once one of the two counterparties defaults, the bank is exposed to the possibility of losses, and indeed it seems that a customer from whom the bank is making gains is the one most likely to renege on its agreement. The danger is also present where the bank has taken the role of borrower since the bank could find itself paying a high fixed rate to lender B whilst receiving a low rate of return from the funds raised.

Case studies

1 A construction company embarks on a private house-building project for which it raises £2 000 000 working capital. Interest is payable on a floating rate basis. Prospective profit margins are tight and could be erased by a substantial increase in interest rates on the loan. The company anticipates that the project will take two years and takes out a two-year fixed for floating swap with a bank. The bank is prepared to act as counterparty and undertakes to meet the floating rate interest payments of the company in return for a fixed rate of 12 per cent p.a. There would be a cash flow between the company and the bank to reflect the difference between the two interest rates.

The interest rate on the floating rate debt is determined at the beginning of each quarter and paid at the end of the quarter. The resulting cash flows are shown in Table 22.1.

Interest rates on the floating rate loan rise progressively from 11 to 14 per cent p.a. The construction company initially makes payments to the bank but towards the end of the period receives cash flows from the bank. The cash flows between the company and the bank offset the fluctuations in the interest rate on the floating rate loan so as to produce a constant quarterly net payment of £57 475.

(Note that the construction company raises a loan from one bank and enters a swap agreement with another bank. A treasurer should not assume that one bank will satisfy all his requirements.)

Table 22.1
Cash flows resulting from the swap agreement
(from company to bank)

Quarter	Floating rate interest payments	Fixed rate interest payments	Cash flow from company to bank
	£	£	£
1	52 867	57 475	4 608
2	52 867	57 475	4 608
3	52 867	57 475	4 608
4	57 475	57 475	0
5	57 475	57 475	0
6	62 052	57 475	−4 577
7	66 599	57 475	−9 124
8	66 599	57 475	−9 124
			−9 001

2   A building society raises £5 000 000 by issuing a Eurobond at a fixed interest rate of 11 per cent p.a. over two years, payable six monthly, for the purpose of providing mortgages on a floating rate basis. It is exposed to the risk that interest rates might fall with the effect that interest receipts from the mortgages are inadequate to meet the interest payments on the Eurobond. The building society could eliminate its exposure by swapping its fixed rate liability for one on a floating rate basis. It finds a bank prepared to enter a floating for fixed swap on the basis of receiving LIBOR + ¾ per cent p.a. in exchange for paying 11 per cent p.a. Initially LIBOR stands at 10¼ per cent p.a. Interest payments to the bank under the swap arrangement, as shown in Table 22.2, are on a six-monthly basis.

LIBOR rises by 0.5 per cent between the first and second years with the result that the building society makes a net payment of £23 702 to the bank.

This example underlines the fact that a hedger could either gain or lose from the hedging instrument used. The essential point of hedging is that the gains/losses offset losses/gains on the positions being hedged. In this case the gain from higher mortgage receipts, arising from higher mortgage interest rates, is offset by a loss on the swap. If interest rates had fallen, thereby reducing mortgage interest receipts, there would have been an offsetting gain from the swap.

Table 22.2
Cash flows resulting from the swap agreement
(from building society to bank)

Period	Floating rate interest payments	Fixed rate interest payments	Cash flow from building society to bank
	£	£	£
1	267 827	267 827	0
2	267 827	267 827	0
3	279 678	267 827	11 851
4	279 678	267 827	11 851
			23 702

Using swaps to reduce interest costs

Investors in fixed rate instruments tend to be more sensitive to differences in creditworthiness than the banks lending on a floating rate basis. In consequence, borrowers of relatively low creditworthiness face a higher interest rate differential in the fixed rate than in the floating rate market. Such borrowers stand to gain by borrowing on a floating rate basis and then swapping into a fixed rate basis with a borrower of higher credit standing. Suppose that borrower A, with a high credit standing, and borrower B, with a lower one, face the following interest charges.

	Borrower A	Borrower B	Interest differential
Floating rate	LIBOR + ¼%	LIBOR + ½%	¼%
Fixed rate	11% p.a.	12½% p.a.	1½%

The difference in credit standing causes different interest rate differentials in the two markets. If borrower A wanted floating rate funds and borrower B needed fixed rate funds each could reduce interest costs by borrowing in the market in which it had the comparative advantage and then swapping its liability. This is illustrated by Figure 22.2 where the difference between the two interest differentials is 1¼ per cent and this is shared between the three participants in the swap transaction. Borrower A receives 11¼ per cent p.a. fixed whilst paying 11 per cent p.a. fixed to its creditor plus LIBOR to the intermediating bank. The net outcome for A is a floating rate liability at LIBOR −¼ per cent. This represents a gain of ½ per cent p.a. relative to borrowing floating rate funds at LIBOR plus ¼ per cent. Borrower B receives LIBOR whilst paying LIBOR plus ½ per cent to its creditor and 11½ per cent p.a. fixed to the bank. The net effect is equivalent to paying 12 per cent p.a. fixed, which represents a ½ per cent gain relative to the alternative of borrowing at a fixed rate of 12½ per cent p.a. The intermediary bank receives 11½ per cent p.a. fixed and pays 11¼ per cent p.a. fixed thus making a net ¼ per cent p.a. in payment for arranging the swap.

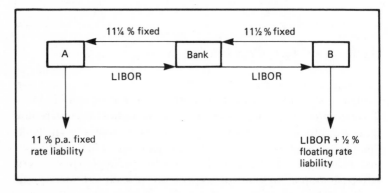

Figure 22.2   Using a swap to exploit comparative advantage

Basis swaps

A basis swap is the conversion of a floating rate liability into a floating rate liability with a different rate-setting mechanism. There are a number of alternatives upon which floating rates may be based such as LIBOR, prime, commercial paper, and treasury bill rates. Basis swaps can be used to ensure that the floating rates on assets and liabilities are determined on the same basis.

   Although these swaps may be established by means of finding

two counterparties with equal and opposite requirements they may be three-party arrangements.

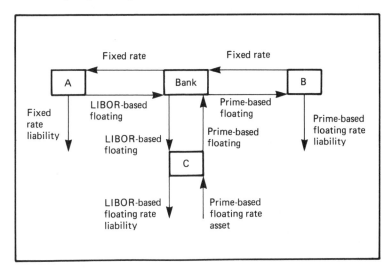

Figure 22.3   Basis swaps – a three-party transaction

Figure 22.3 illustrates such a three-party transaction. Party C transacts a basis swap with two counterparties, each of which undertakes a fixed/floating swap. Party C is able to match the interest basis of its liability to that of its asset because of a mismatch between A and B in relation to their floating rate bases. The LIBOR-based liability of party C is serviced with interest receipts from A whilst C uses receipts from its prime-based asset to service the liability of B.

Cross-currency swaps

These swaps involve changing the currency of denomination as well as the mode of funding, and may involve two, three, or more parties. Figure 22.4 illustrates a two-party transaction. Borrower A swaps a fixed rate Deutschmark liability for a floating rate US dollar liability with borrower B. There may or may not be a simultaneous exchange of currencies with A providing Deutschmarks in exchange for US dollars. Figure 22.5 illustrates a three-party swap. Borrower C undertakes a cross-currency interest rate swap whilst borrower A enters a simple currency swap and borrower B a simple interest rate swap.

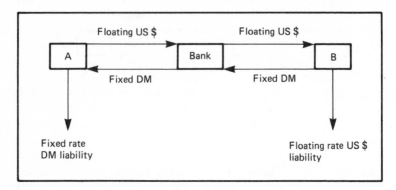

Figure 22.4   Cross-currency swaps – a two-party transaction

Zero coupon swaps

A zero coupon bond consists of an obligation by the issuer to repay the face value on a specified future date. There are no interest payments and the return to the holder is obtained through purchasing

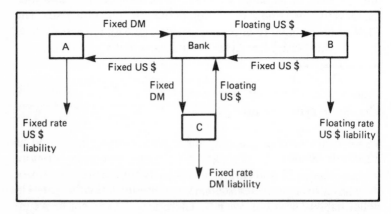

Figure 22.5   Cross-currency swaps – a three-party transaction

the bond at a discount. For example, a £50 million bond due to mature in ten years might sell at £17 million thereby implying an 11 per cent p.a. rate of return on the £17 million.

Such a zero coupon bond is equivalent to a bond with a fixed rate of return. The issuer of such a bond could swap the funding to a floating rate basis by simultaneously undertaking an interest rate swap and a reverse annuity. This is illustrated by Figure 22.6. The borrower issues a bond with a face value of £50 million, which is payable at maturity in ten years. The sum received is £17 million which implies that the £50 million has been discounted at 11 per cent p.a. The borrower enters a fixed/floating swap with a counterparty, agreeing to pay LIBOR whilst receiving a fixed 11 per cent p.a. The 11 per cent p.a. on £17 million is invested with a bank, or other financial institution, which agrees to pay 11 per cent p.a. on the sums invested. At the end of the ten-year term the money invested with the bank has accumulated to £33 million, which together with the original £17 million provides the £50 million payable at the maturity of the zero coupon bond.

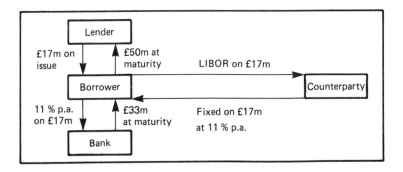

Figure 22.6   Zero coupon swap

Position taking

A swap can be entered into in an attempt to gain from an expected change in interest rates. A holder of a fixed rate liability may swap into a floating rate liability if he expects interest rates to fall. A floating rate liability would provide the opportunity to gain from a fall in interest rates. If interest rates do fall as expected, the floating rate liability might be swapped back into a fixed rate in order to lock-in the lower interest rate.

Option swaps

An option swap gives the right, but not the obligation, to enter into a swap during a specified period on terms agreed at the time of entering the option. When swapping from floating to fixed, the fixed rate agreed may be a specific percentage or may be related to the rate on a particular financial instrument. For example, the option may provide the right to swap into a fixed rate borrowing at 12 per cent p.a. or alternatively it may specify 50 basis points above Treasury 15½ per cent 1998. In the case of swaps into floating rates a particular relationship with a rate will be agreed, for example 80 basis points above LIBOR. The profile of an option swap might be the following:

Duration of option: 6 months
Notional volume: £25 000 000
Maturity from exercise: 5 years
Fixed rate: 12 per cent p.a.
Variable rate: LIBOR + ½ per cent
Option premium: £250 000

The option holder thus acquires the right to swap a £25 000 000 floating rate borrowing into a fixed rate one at 12 per cent p.a. at any time during the next six months at the cost of a premium of £250 000. If rates rise above 12 per cent p.a. the option can be profitably exercised but if rates fall so that it becomes possible to swap into a lower fixed rate then the option will not be exercised. By paying the premium the borrower is insured against having to pay more than 12 per cent p.a. when swapping a floating rate debt into a fixed rate one.

A variation on the theme is the timing option. This differs from a normal option in that the option holder is obliged to enter into the swap during the specified period. The choice relates solely to the timing of the exercise of the option.

Warehousing

Warehousing by a bank consists of doing a swap and hedging it. When a suitable swap counterparty appears the hedge is undone. One way in which the hedging might be carried out is by the use of financial futures. Figure 22.7 illustrates the case of a bank that agrees to pay fixed against receiving floating and covers the risk of a fall in interest rates by buying financial futures.

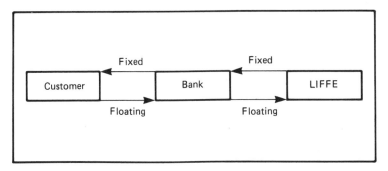

Figure 22.7 Warehousing with futures

By buying three-month interest rate futures contracts the bank can lock-in current interest rates. If interest rates fall the price of futures contracts will rise providing the bank with a gain that compensates for the interest rate fall.

The willingness to make a market in swaps has considerably increased the speed with which swaps are provided. Deals are available on demand without requiring the simultaneous availability of a matching counterparty.

Asset-based swaps

Swaps are typically exchanges of liabilities but the technique can also be used for assets. An interest rate swap could be used by a fixed rate bond holder to gain from a rise in interest rates. Figure 22.8 depicts the situation in which the holder of a bond with a coupon yield of 12 per cent p.a. feels that interest rates, now at 10 per cent p.a. for maturities matching the remaining term of the bond, are likely to rise. He swaps into a floating rate asset in order to profit from a rise in interest rates.

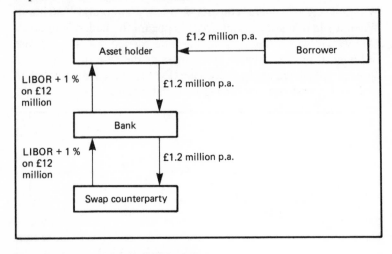

Figure 22.8   Asset-based swap

The lender originally buys an undated bond for £10 million at 12 per cent p.a. When the interest rate on undated debt falls to 10 per cent p.a. the value of the bond rises to £12 million. By swapping the fixed coupon yield of £1.2 million p.a. for LIBOR + 1 per cent on £12 million the lender obtains the opportunity to profit from a rise in interest rates. The lender could reverse the swap (by entering another swap) subsequent to a rise in interest rates so as to fix a rate on £12 million so that at the end of the operation the annual receipts are in excess of £1.2 million p.a.

23 The accounting and tax treatment of swaps

Swaps are subject to the same basic accounting principles as futures and options. The tax treatment is however complicated by the fact that swap arrangements may raise tax issues in more than one country.

The accounting issues

There are a variety of different types of swap transactions, as seen in the previous chapter, and fortunately the same basic accounting principles apply to each type. Indeed, the basic accounting principles underlying the accounting treatment of swaps are the same as those reviewed in Chapter 18 on the accounting treatment of futures and options. In particular, the accruals concept dictates that revenues and expenses should be reflected in the accounts as they are earned and incurred and not simply when they are reflected in cash flows.

The peculiar feature of swaps, as opposed to futures and options, is that it involves a company swapping one group of costs for another. This, consequently, has implications for both the profit and loss account and the balance sheet.

The profit and loss account effect

The previous chapter explained how both parties to an interest rate swap could benefit from reduced costs of borrowing without at the same time increasing their exposure to interest rate movements. The simplicity of this type of swap transaction provides an ideal example of the profit and loss account effect.

Under the terms of this type of swap agreement, each party agrees to pay the interest costs on the other party's borrowing. Thus, for each party to the agreement, the net amount charged to the profit and loss account in any one period is equal to the interest cost on the other party's borrowing. Or, to put it another way, the profit and loss account of a company is charged with the interest cost of its own loan plus or minus any amounts due from or to the party to the swap calculated on an accruals basis. Thus, if a manufacturing company's variable interest charges were £1 million, while the fixed interest charges of the financial institution which was party to the swap was £950 000, then the company's profit and loss account under the swap arrangement would show interest charges of £950 000, whereas that of the financial institution would show £1 million. In addition, of course, any arrangement fees or commissions paid by the company would also appear in the profit and loss account. Thus, the profit and loss account extract for the manufacturing company and financial institution would be as follows:

Profit and loss extract for manufacturing company

Interest on borrowings		£1 000 000
Less: Payment received from financial institution under swap	(£1 000 000)	
Plus: Payment to financial institution under swap	£ 950 000	
		£ (50 000)
Amount paid		£ 950 000

Profit and loss extract for financial institution

Interest on borrowings		£ 950 000
Less: Payment received from manufacturing company under swap	(£ 950 000)	
Plus: Payment to manufacturing company under swap	£1 000 000	
		£ 50 000
Amount paid		£1 000 000

The balance sheet effect

Whereas the profit and loss account effect is concerned with reflecting the cost of servicing the other party's loan, the balance sheet effect will reveal the company's actual loan along with a suspense account set up to deal with the effects of the swap.

To illustrate the balance sheet effect, the slightly more complicated example is used of the fixed to fixed cross-currency debt swap whereby the two parties involved not only service each other's interest payments but also their capital payments. The net effect of this, of course, is that they bear the cost of both interest and exchange rate movements on each other's loans. Consider, for example, a British company with a $3 million loan at 14 per cent entering into a fixed to fixed currency debt swap with an American company which has a £2 million loan at 12 per cent, both loans being payable in three equal annual instalments. During the year, the exchange rate changes from $1.5 = £1 to $1.25 = £1. The balance sheet entries at the end of year 1 will contain the following:

	Loan account (£)	Cash account (£)	Swap account (£)
1 Jan Loan of $3 million at $1.5 = £1	(2 000 000)	2 000 000	
31 Dec Translation effects of loan at $1.25 = £1	(400 000)		400 000
Loan repayment			
1 Paid by American company under swaps: ⅓ of $3 million at $1.25 = £1	800 000		(800 000)
2 Paid by UK company under swaps: ⅓ of £2 million		(666 666)	666 666
Balance at 31 Dec	(1 600 000)	1 333 333	266 666
	Liability	Asset	Asset

The balance sheet extract shows that at the end of year 1 the British company has a suspense asset (that is, the swap account) of £266 666 since under the swap arrangement it only has to pay £1 333 333 (that is, two-thirds of £2 million) to cover the American company's borrowing, while its own outstanding loan of £1 600 000 remains to be paid by the American company. (Note that in the event of a rising pound the swap account would become a liability. Note also that the payment of each other's annual interest cost on the loans would be reflected as usual in the profit and loss account.)

The tax issues

The tax treatment of interest rate and currency swaps is a complex and confusing area. This is particularly so in the case of industrial and commercial companies where it is not always clear that the payment and receipt of swap payments will receive symmetrical treatment for tax purposes. Moreover, this confusion is compounded by the fact that swap arrangements raise tax issues in more than one country. Thus, corporate treasurers should take great care in evaluating the after-tax implications of swap arrangements.

There are a number of important issues which companies should take account of on the tax front. Firstly, there is the need to establish the way in which the Inland Revenue regard the periodical swap payments and receipts. If it regards them as 'annual payments made not out of profits or gains brought into charge of income tax' then a 30 per cent withholding tax will be levied. This will be the approach taken by the Inland Revenue where the other party to the swap is a UK investment or trading company. However, in so far as the swap payment constitutes a normal trading receipt in the hands of the recipient, such as is the case where the partner to the swap is a UK bank, or the approved UK branch of a foreign bank, then the withholding tax may not apply and the payment may be paid gross.

Having ascertained the withholding tax position it then becomes necessary to ensure that a tax deduction will be given to the paying company. The general approach taken by the Revenue here is that a UK trading company may claim such payments as a trading expense and that a UK investment company may similarly claim them as a charge on income as laid down in the relevant sections of the 1970 Income and Corporation Taxes Act. It should be noted, however, that arrangement fees paid to banks are not regarded as a legitimate trading expense and are not tax deductible.

The position with regard to the withholding tax, of course, becomes much more complex and confusing when one of the parties to the swap is resident outside the UK. The UK company will need to establish whether or not the other party to the swap is resident in a country with which the UK has agreed a tax relief treaty, and to establish under which sections of the treaty the tax relief may apply. In particular, it will be of crucial importance to establish whether a foreign withholding tax may be offset against the UK tax liability.

The situation becomes even more complicated when currency swaps are undertaken which involve the lending and borrowing of currencies other than the domestic currencies of the companies involved in the swap. The UK company will need to establish whether the gain or loss on repayment will be regarded by the Revenue as an income gain or loss, a capital gain or loss, or a gain or loss that is neither taxable nor tax deductible. This is an extremely complicated area which companies need to take up individually with the Inland Revenue. The great danger to avoid is the lack of symmetry which may arise in tax treatment. In particular, great care should be taken where a currency swap has been undertaken to match a capital inward or outward borrowing. Since the gain or loss on such a swap will be taxable (in the case of gains) or tax deductible (in the case of losses), it is imperative that in the case of gains the match should be with a loan that is regarded for tax purposes as a chargeable asset on which losses are allowable for tax purposes.

All that can be offered by way of a conclusion to this section is the rather banal statement that the only thing certain about the tax treatment of swaps is that it is a highly complex and confusing area of study. Participants in swap transactions are strongly recommended to seek out the guidance of the Inland Revenue as to the tax implications of their transactions before they proceed.

24 Selecting a strategy

It might be useful to integrate what has gone before by proposing a method for determining the appropriate risk management strategy. Figure 24.1 shows a decision flow chart for hedging currency risk and Figure 24.2 shows a chart for interest rate risk management.

Both charts are concerned with the development of risk avoidance strategies. They are concerned with reducing risk by hedging, rather than with increasing risk for purposes of speculation. A treasury manager deciding to cover only part of the risk in the light of forecasts of favourable currency or interest rate movements might nevertheless adopt the type of decision-making process illustrated by the flow charts. The difference from a full hedge would be in terms of the value, rather than the nature, of the instruments used.

The charts are illustrative rather than prescriptive. They suggest possible decision-making stages but the processes indicated are certainly not the only possibilities.

Both charts begin with an evaluation of the nature and extent of the exposure. Economic exposure does not appear since, by its nature, it is difficult to identify and measure. Thus it would be almost impossible to specify decision processes that could lead to strategies for managing the risks involved.

The time-scale of the exposure is a crucial factor. As a rule of thumb 'short to medium term' might be regarded as referring to periods of up to five years. Swaps tend to be

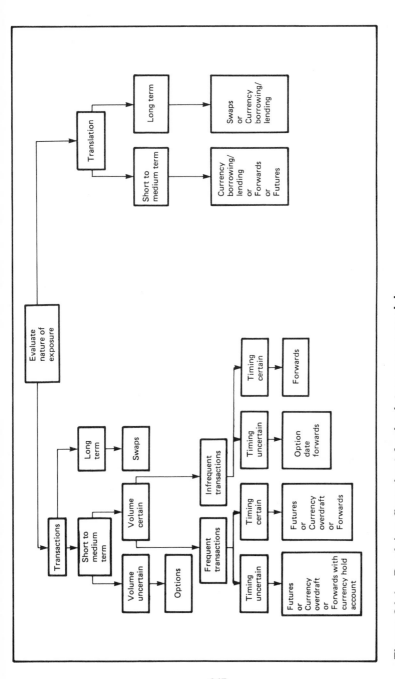

Figure 24.1 Decision flowchart for hedging currency risk

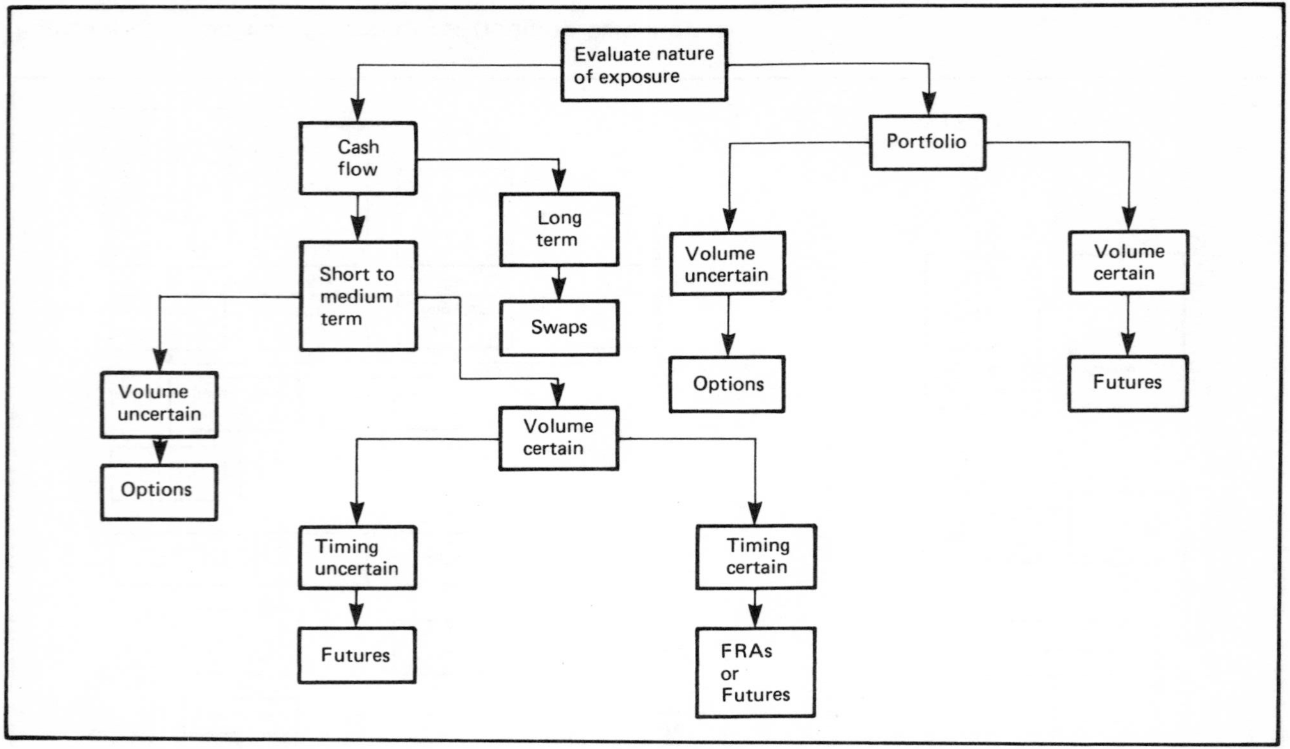

Figure 24.2 Decision flowchart for interest rate risk management

particularly useful for exposures lasting for more than five years.

Another crucial factor is whether the extent of the exposure is certain. Tendering is a case in which there is uncertainty as to whether the exposure is zero or a specific amount. Sales in a particular currency may be predicted to fall within a range but the position within that range and the ensuing level of exposure may be very uncertain. In such cases, options are particularly useful.

Uncertainty of volume might also lead to the use of options when the risk arises from potential interest rate movements. There may be uncertainty as to how much will need to be borrowed by a company, or a portfolio manager may be uncertain of the volume of cash inflow in the near future.

Even when the extent of the exposure is known for sure, its timing may not be. Uncertainty as to the dates of expected cash flows calls for risk management instruments that provide flexibility.

Index